Praise for ***Why Motor Skills Matter***

"We live in our bodies from the moment we are born. Yet, somehow, physical confidence is practically a 'missing link' in the world of child rearing literature. After dealing with thousands of kids and families, I can immediately sense children who trust their bodies—and those who feel painfully vulnerable. From first-hand experience, then, I feel strongly that *Why Motor Skills Matter,* both conceptually and concretely, is essential reading for everyone who comes into contact with children—parents, professionals, and educators alike. It's time to help children feel good about themselves from the inside out. *Why Motor Skills Matter* will do exactly that."

—Dr. Ron Taffel, contributing editor at *Parents Magazine* and author of *Nurturing Good Children Now*

"*Why Motor Skills Matter* is certain to become an integral part of the literature on child development and, more important, a staple on every parent's shelf. One of the best features of the book is the manner in which it is organized by age and developmental stage. From the time the baby is brought home from the hospital until that child goes to elementary school, *Why Motor Skills Matter* provides useful tools [illegible]. The p[illegible]oth medic[illegible] testam[illegible] of the aut[illegible]mend *Why Motor Skills Matter* to all new parents (and grandparents!), as well as to parents with concerns about their child's developmental progress."

—Susan E. Swedo, M.D., Fellow, American Academy of Pediatrics; Chief, Pediatrics and Developmental Neuropsychiatry Branch, NIMH, NIH, DHHS, and coauthor of *Is It "Just a Phase"?*

"*Why Motor Skills Matter* presents a thorough and terrifically useful synopsis of motor development in infants and young children. Parents will learn the important "whys" behind their child's motor milestones, as well as how to best stimulate children's vestibular, tactile, and proprioceptive senses to promote fluid, coordinated movement and physical self-confidence."

—Lise Eliot, Ph.D, Assistant Professor of Neuroscience, The Chicago Medical School, and author of *What's Going on in There? How the Brain and Mind Develop in the First Five Years of Life*

Why Motor Skills Matter

Improve Your Child's Physical Development to Enhance Learning and Self-Esteem

Tara Losquadro Liddle, M.P.T.
with Laura Yorke

Contemporary Books
Chicago New York San Francisco Lisbon London Madrid Mexico City Milan New Delhi San Juan Seoul Singapore Sydney Toronto

The McGraw-Hill Companies

Library of Congress Cataloging-in-Publication Data

Losquadro Liddle, Tara.
Why motor skills matter : improve your child's physical development to enhance learning and self-esteem / Tara Losquadro Liddle, with Laura Yorke.
p. cm.
Includes bibliographical references.
ISBN 0-07-140818-5 (acid-free paper)
1. Motor ability in children. 2. Cognition in children. 3. Self-esteem in children. I. Yorke, Laura. II. Title.

BF723. M6L67 2004
155.4'123—dc21 2003046108

1 2 3 4 5 6 7 8 9 0 AGM/AGM 2 1 0 9 8 7 6 5 4 3

ISBN 0-07-140818-5

This book is printed on acid-free paper.

For being the inspiration behind our work and the greatest source of our love, we dedicate this book to our children: Alexa and Harry Liddle, and Elliott and Coleman Snyder.

For tolerating us during the seemingly endless writing and publication process, we also dedicate this book to our husbands, Jeff Liddle and Dick Snyder. Thank you, gentlemen.

Contents

Foreword by John M. Driscoll, Jr., M.D. xv

Acknowledgments xvii

Introduction xix
Why Motor Skills Matter

The Importance of Monitoring Your Child's Physical Development xx

There's No Such Thing as a Lazy Child: How and Why Childhood Traits Can Be Misconstrued xxii

What This Book Will Do for You xxv

PART 1

Learning to Move and Moving to Learn 1
The Continuous Cycle of Motor Output and Sensory Input

CHAPTER 1

The System We Don't See 3
Understanding Your Child's Sensory (Nervous) System and How It Relates to Movement

The Newborn's Developing Sense of Awareness 5

Understanding Your Baby's Sensory System as It Relates to Movement 6

Automatic Movement 8

Voluntary Movement 11

How the Central Nervous System Processes Our Movement . . . 15

But What If the Sensory Systems Are Not Working in an Organized Way? Sensory Integration Concerns. . . . 17

A Window into the Nervous System . . . 19

And Always Remember . . . 19

CHAPTER 2

Your Newborn . . . 21

Birth to One Month

Your Newborn's Movement Patterns . . . 22

Ways to Encourage the Flexed Position . . . 23

Calming Your Baby . . . 28

Engaging Your Newborn . . . 29

Sensory Activities for Your New Bundle of Joy

Visual Input. . . . 30

Vestibular and Proprioceptive Input (Movement) . . . 30

Tactile Input. . . . 32

Recommended Toys for Your Newborn

Developmental Benchmarks for Your Newborn to One-Month-Old

Auditory Input. . . . 34

The Well-Balanced Checklist

Olfactory Input (Smell) . . . 36

In Conclusion . . . 36

And Always Remember . . . 36

PART 2

Faster than a Speeding Bullet . . . 37

Your Child's Development in the First Year

CHAPTER 3

Shake, Rattle, and Roll. . . . 39

Physical Development and Activities for the First Six Months

Working Through the Developmental Sequence . . . 39

The Importance of Routines . . . 40

Your One- to Three-Month-Old's Development

Recommended Toys for Your One- to Three-Month-Old

Supine (Back) Play/Skills . . . 43

Prone (Belly) Play/Skills . . . 43

Prone Propping . . . 44

Developmental Benchmarks for Your One- to Three-Month-Old

A Helping Hand: Hand Usage . . . 46

Your Four- to Six-Month-Old's Development

Supine Play/Skills . . . 46

Recommended Toys for Your Four- to Six-Month-Old

Prone Play/Skills . . . 48

Side-Lying and Rolling . . . 49

Foot Play . . . 51

Pre-Sitting . . . 51

Developmental Benchmarks for Your Four- to Six-Month-Old

Sensory Activities for Your One- to Six-Month-Old

Bath Time Activities . . . 53

Visual Input . . . 53

Vestibular and Proprioceptive Input . . . 55

Tactile Input . . . 56

Auditory Input . . . 57

The Well-Balanced Checklist

Olfactory Input . . . 58

Gustatory Input (Taste) . . . 58

Cognitive Input . . . 59

And Always Remember . . . 59

CHAPTER 4

Sit, Squat, Stand . . . 61

Physical Development and Activities for the Second Six Months

Hand and Finger Dexterity . . . 62

Your Seven- Through Nine-Month-Old's Development

Floor Play/Skills . . . 63
Sitting . . . 67
Locomotion . . . 71
Developmental Benchmarks for Your Seven- to Nine-Month-Old
Pre-Sitting, Sitting, and Kneeling Activities . . . 77

Your Ten- Through Twelve-Month-Old's Development

Sitting, Kneeling, and Standing Activities . . . 81
Developmental Benchmarks for Your Ten- to Twelve-Month-Old
Walkers, Exersaucers, and Jumpers . . . 83

Sensory Activities for Your Seven- to Twelve-Month-Old

Visual and Cognitive Input . . . 85
Vestibular and Proprioceptive Input . . . 86
Tactile Input . . . 86
Auditory Input . . . 87
Gustatory and Olfactory Input . . . 87
Recommended Toys for Your Seven- to Twelve-Month-Old
The Soles of Our Existence: Your Baby's Foot Development . . . 88
The Well-Balanced Checklist
Developmental Warning Signs in the First Year . . . 89
And Always Remember . . . 90

CHAPTER 5

From Cooing and Babbling to Sucking, Swallowing, and Chewing . . . 91
Your Baby's Oral-Motor Development in the First Year

The Foundation of Language . . . 91
Language Development Benchmarks for Your Baby's First Year
The Well-Balanced Checklist
The Foundation for Feeding Skills . . . 97
Pre-feeding and Feeding Benchmarks for Your Baby's First Year
When the Going Gets Messy: The Introduction of Semisolid Foods . . . 100

High Chairs, Cheerios, and Eating Like a Grown-Up: The Introduction of Solid Foods 102

The Well-Balanced Checklist

From Spills to Sippy Cups: The Introduction of Cup Drinking 105

How the Sensory System Affects Eating

Visual and Olfactory Input 107

Vestibular Input 107

Tactile Input 107

Warning Signs for Oral Defensiveness (Hypersensitivity) 108

And Always Remember 108

PART 3

Able to Leap Tall Buildings 109

Your Child's Development from One to Five Years Old

CHAPTER 6

Your Mobile Explorer 111

Development of and Activities for Your One- to Three-Year-Old

The Soles of Our Existence, Revisited 113

Activities and Play for Your One- to Three-Year-Old

Physical Play/Vestibular and Proprioceptive Input 115

Developmental Benchmarks for Your One- to -Three-Year-Old

Recommended Toys for Your One- to Three-Year-Old

Manipulative Play/Tactile Input 121

Water Play/Tactile Input 124

Imaginative and Symbolic Play/Auditory and Cognitive Input 125

Language Play/Auditory and Cognitive Input 125

Feeding Your One- to Three-Year-Old

Feeding Benchmarks for Your One- to Three-Year-Old

Your One- to Three-Year-Old's Language Development

Language Development Benchmarks for Your One- to Three-Year-Old

Warning Signs for Language Acquisition Impediments 129

The Well-Balanced Checklist

And Always Remember 131

CHAPTER 7

Your Walker and Talker 133

Development of and Activities for the Three- to Five-Year-Old

Taking a Fresh Look at the Developmental Continuum 134

Activities and Play for Your Three- to Five-Year-Old

Physical Play/Vestibular and Proprioceptive Input 136

Developmental Benchmarks for Your Three- to Five-Year-Old

Manipulative Play/Tactile Input 141

Recommended Toys for Your Three- to Five-Year-Old

Language Play/Auditory and Cognitive Input 143

Your Three- to Five-Year-Old's Language Development

Language Development Benchmarks for Your Three- to Five-Year-Old

Developmental Warning Signs and Solutions for Your Child 145

The Well-Balanced Checklist

And Always Remember 150

PART 4

Special Considerations 151

CHAPTER 8

There Is No Such Thing as a Lazy Child 153

How Low Muscle Tone Affects Development

Low Muscle Tone 154

Activities to Enhance Muscle Activation 156

Developmental Warning Signs for Low Muscle Tone 157

And Always Remember 158

CHAPTER 9

Appreciating Prematurity 159

The Premature Baby's Special Development

Providing Developmental Care for Your Premature Infant 161

Positioning 162

How the Sensory System Is Affected in Premature Babies

Tactile Input . . . 164
Visual Input . . . 165
Auditory Input . . . 166
Vestibular and Proprioceptive Input . . . 167
Olfactory Input . . . 168
Oral-Motor Input . . . 168
Checklist for the Premature Baby in the Neonatal Intensive Care Unit
Going Home . . . 170
Neonatal Follow-Up Programs . . . 171
And Always Remember . . . 171

CHAPTER 10
Sensory Disorders . . . 173
Manifestations and Guidelines

Vestibular and Proprioceptive Disorders . . . 173
Tactile Defensiveness . . . 177
And Always Remember . . . 178

CHAPTER 11
The Most Commonly Seen Orthopedic Conditions in Pediatrics . . . 179

Congenital Dislocation of the Hip (Hip Dysplasia) . . . 180
Knocked Knees (Genu Valgum) and Bowlegs (Genu Varum) . . . 180
Pigeon Toes (Internal Tibial Torsion) and Inward Turning of Entire Leg (Femoral Anteversion) . . . 181
Metatarsus Adductus . . . 181
Flatfoot, or Foot Pronation (Flexible Pez Planus) . . . 182
Congenital Muscular Torticollis . . . 182
Idiopathic Scoliosis . . . 183
Congenital Clubfoot (Talipes Equinovarus) . . . 184
And Always Remember . . . 184

Source Materials 185

Additional Readings 191

Helpful Organizations 195

Index 197

Foreword

Every parent has dreams and expectations for their children. Society considers children our most precious possessions, and ultimately, we will be judged by how we value them.

Over the past half century a proliferation of books exploring the development of children have attempted to provide parents with information (above and beyond that provided by their physician) about how to better monitor their child's progress. *Why Motor Skills Matter* is a wonderful, enlightening, and easy-to-read source of guidance and reassurance that should, in my opinion, be in every parent's library.

The authors have divided the book into thirteen well-organized and appropriately ordered chapters that guide parents from the time of thier child's birth through the fifth year. The book provides parents with a realistic set of guidelines and expectations for their child and clarifies the conditions under which parents should seek advice in the face of a perceived developmental lag. *Why Motor Skills Matter* offers sound advice, suggesting simple at-home techniques that parents can use to facilitate a child's normal development and providing a better understanding of the need for therapy when a child's development has deviated from the normal.

Based on my twenty years of professional experience in the neonatal follow-up clinic at our institution, I found the chapters "There Is No Such Thing as a Lazy Child" and "Appreciating Prematurity" particularly helpful to parents. It is natural for parents to compare the development of full-term children, but in the case of a premature infant, such comparisons are inappropriate and particularly unreasonable. This text gives parents of premature infants very specific milestones for their babies' development. It also provides a context for determining the appropriate level of support needed, including advice on when to seek medical assistance from a pediatrician or physical or occupational therapist to ensure normal development.

I highly recommend *Why Motor Skills Matter* for the parent of every child, and I assure those parents that they will not only enjoy each chapter but will be far more informed about the development of their children by the end of the book. The text is a remarkable addition to the current array of information available to guide parents through the first five years of their children's lives. I congratulate the authors for their significant contribution.

John M. Driscoll, Jr., M.D.
Reuben S. Carpentier Professor and Chairman
Department of Pediatrics
Columbia College of Physicians and Surgeons
Chief of Pediatric Service
Children's Hospital of New York–Presbyterian

Acknowledgments

I would first like to thank Francine Stern, P.T., my mentor in the field of pediatric physical therapy. She was my inspiration to specialize in this field. I would also like to thank all the clinicians I studied with and who helped my specialization process. Their lectures and knowledge have been valuable tools that I have used over the years to improve my treatment approach. A huge debt of gratitude goes out to the following people for their help with this book:

- Laura Yorke, my friend and coauthor. Without her interest in child development and her expertise in the editing field this book would not have been completed. She has taken potentially dry and humorless material and helped to make it a fun and enjoyable read for all. She also needed to light a fire under me more than once to keep us on track. I am extremely thankful to her.
- Marjory Becker-Lewin, O.T.R., my colleague who taught me the importance of sensory integration. Marjory read and reread several chapters of the manuscript, and her input was invaluable. Marjory is in private practice in New York City.
- Lori Nitzberg Rothman, O.T.R., my dear friend and colleague who read through many versions of this text and who answered many "emergency" calls without hesitation. I will not forget how helpful she has been throughout this project. Lori has always believed in me as a friend and as a professional. She is also in private practice in New York City.
- David M. Kaufman, M.D., F.A.A.P., a pediatric neurologist in New York City. He has read the original manuscript and has always believed in me.
- Anna Greco, M.D., a pediatrician in charge of the neonatal follow-up program at Lenox Hill Hospital and Carrie Strauch, O.T. R., who is also affiliated with the program. Both have been wonderful colleagues to work with and have read and edited various sections of the manuscript.
- Julie Madonia Kopka, M.A., C.C.C.-SLP, is a speech pathologist at the Hospital for Special Surgery in New York and also maintains a private practice. Julie specializes in feeding and swallowing and motor speech disorders in children. Julie has provided invaluable information and has referred me to the necessary sources needed to complete the sections on feeding and language.

- Debra K. Hagen, M.A., C.C.C.-SLP, is the director at Pediatric Associates for Language and Speech in New York City. Debra also read and edited the sections on feeding and language.
- Michael Fox, P.T., S.C.S., M.T.C., and his partner own Sports Therapy and Rehabilitation, a private practice in New York City. Michael is a friend and longtime colleague who read and edited the section on body mechanics.
- Lawrence Deutsch, M.D., is the pediatric orthopedist associated with University and Neuro-surgical Specialists in Haddonfield, New Jersey. He was kind enough to read and edit the chapter on common orthopedic conditions.
- Jeffrey Garland, M.D., is a neonatologist at St. Joseph Regional Medical Center in Milwaukee, Wisconsin. Dr. Garland read and edited the chapter on appreciating prematurity. His notes and comments were very helpful.
- Pamela Gallan, M.D., F.A.C.S., F.A.A.P., is a pediatric ophthalmologist at Columbia Presbyterian Hospital in New York. Pamela was kind enough to provide valuable information regarding visual development. Dr. Gallan is also the author of *The Savvy Mom's Guide to Medical Care*.

Thanks to my dad who lets me know that he is always proud of me, and to my mom who passed away just as this project was about to begin. Memories of her kept me going whenever things became difficult to handle.

—and most of all—

Thanks to my little patients who inspired this project, and to their parents who encouraged me to put it down on paper.

—T. L-L

Tara and I met in Lenox Hill Hospital, where my son, Coleman, was born. As a preemie, he spent the first month of his life in the N.I.C.U. He was diagnosed with low muscle tone and referred to Tara through the hospital's excellent neonatal follow-up program.

Tara's engagement with Cole was immediate and palpable. He was besotted with her at the end of their first visit and, because of his affection for her, worked very diligently to please her. During the course of that year, Tara and I became good friends, as well. At one point she asked me if I knew anything about publishing, since she wanted to write a book. I told Tara that I would help her find a writer, an agent, and a publisher—but she wanted me to write the book. That thought had not occurred to me. Two people convinced me that I could—and should—write the book: my friend, agent, and business partner, Carol Mann, and my dearest friend, Kim Witherspoon. Thank you both for scoffing at my insecurities, helping me have a sense of humor, and supporting me in getting this done. And thank you, Tara, for asking me (repeatedly) to do it. Coleman and I are both forever grateful to you, and we will always have this book as a testament of what you have done for him.

I would also like to thank our editor at Contemporary Books, Matthew Carnicelli, for being so easy to work with, so supportive of the project, and so smart in his editorial insights. I doubt it's easy for one editor to edit another, and Matthew did it with skill and grace. Thanks also to editorial assistant, Mandy Huber, for handling all the myriad details promptly, efficiently, and courteously, and to Katherine Dennis, who managed the production of the book. A final thanks to our illustrator, Gary Torrisi, for his clear (and prompt!) line art.

—L Y

Introduction

Why Motor Skills Matter

"Every time I put my two-month-old on her stomach, she cries. Am I hurting her?"

"Why won't my 10-month-old stand or have his feet touch the ground? I thought he'd be standing by now."

"My nine-month-old just wants to sit all day. She's very happy, but shouldn't she be moving around more?"

"I don't have a baby-sitter during the days when I work out of my home. I keep my baby in her stroller or the car seat by my desk when I have to work, and in an exersaucer when I'm in the kitchen. Is that bad for her?"

"My two-year-old loves the playground but absolutely refuses to go down the slide. Is it normal for him to be so scared?"

"My three-year-old is constantly tripping and bumping into furniture. He slides off his chair at mealtime. Is he just clumsy?"

"Our son's preschool teacher feels that he is disruptive in class because he likes to lie down during story time. Why should that be an issue?"

"We're such energized people, and we're surprised by how sedate our daughter is. I know "girls will be girls," but I just have this feeling . . . am I overreacting?"

"When I try to finger paint, bake, or play in the sandbox with my daughter she won't participate. She doesn't like to get her hands dirty. What should I do?"

Have you ever had a nagging thought about some aspect of your child's development, only to brush it aside, thinking you're being "neurotic"? Or maybe your spouse thinks you need to stop being so hypervigilant. Do you wonder about your child's activity level, or behavior, only to second-guess yourself? Perhaps you tell yourself that whatever traits you pick up on that just "don't feel right" to you are really minor issues that will fade with time. If so, you're not alone. Many parents experience nagging concerns, but rarely voice them. As a pediatric physical therapist with almost 20 years of experience as well as a longtime consultant to the neonatal unit at Lenox Hill hospital in New York City, I find it frustrating to hear how many parents have questions about their child's development but don't seek out professional advice to get correct answers and explanations. The result, unfortunately, can be well-meaning but misguided parenting. For example, the mother whose child cries when placed on his stomach may be told that she should pick her baby up. In fact, that's not a good idea—and other solutions are available. Or, parents might feel compelled to encourage their baby to crawl even when he or she isn't ready to because of the myriad child development books' "developmental milestones" timetables that say he or she should be crawling. So when should you push your child to do more? When should you just let him be? When should you start to worry about the levels of fear and frustration your child experiences? They seem extreme to you, but are they? And who makes up those developmental milestones anyway? Does it really matter if your child reaches them "on time"?

As a parent, how can you determine where your child fits on a developmental continuum? How can you know if observed traits and behaviors ("shyness," "laziness," etc.) are ingrained in your child's temperament, or are attitudes merely attributed to her in an attempt to explain subtle (and sometimes not so subtle) physical delays or limitations? Interestingly, while all good resources for parents (including all the best books on child development) will tell you what your child's physical milestones are, they don't tell you how to determine where your child lies on a normal continuum for physical development. Nor do they tell you how to ensure that your child reaches the proper milestones, what to do if he or she misses them, what the repercussions could be, or how and where to get additional support if it is called for. *Why Motor Skills Matter* will guide you through these critical issues, and more. Throughout this book, I explore the many ways in which we can enhance our babies' and toddlers' physical development to benefit them for the rest of their lives.

The Importance of Monitoring Your Child's Physical Development

Nothing is more important to parents of young children than ensuring their proper growth. We cook fresh foods for our infants to give them the best nutrition. We play Mozart with the hope that it will enhance their IQ. We send our toddlers off to countless playgroups to stimulate their creativity and activate their social development. Yet surprisingly, we take for granted our children's most obvious growth concern—their physical development. When we get down on the floor to play with our kids—something we do spontaneously—we don't think about the simple ways in which we can bolster their motor skills, strength, and coordination. In fact, we don't think about the significance of such play at all. We simply assume that our kids will develop physically along the "normal continuum" measured by those milestones we read about. Consequently, we don't pay enough attention to our child's *actual* ability at play. We should.

All the play we do with our babies contributes to their development. The most obvious benefits of play are that it builds physical strength and stamina. But equally important is how it contributes to the bonding process between us and our children, and how it teaches them basic social skills like sharing, cooperation, and healthy competition. Play also enhances our children's perceptual-motor skills, language skills, attention span, and emotional development. It improves circulation, helps maintain muscle tone and thus postural control, and can help in fighting obesity. Perhaps most important in a child's early years, play allows for repetition, and repetition is one of the keys to healthy development.

A critical component of play is exercise. As adults, we are aware of the merits of exercise. Many of us rack up endless hours either in the gym embracing the latest fitness craze, or participating in some kind of sport. Yet exercise is as important for babies and toddlers as it is for adults. Exercise establishes core physical strength and the biomechanical patterns that will last a lifetime—patterns that in large part will determine how a child approaches and reacts to the world. Indeed, physical movement, affect (emotions), and cognition are critically linked in a continuous cycle of sensory input and motor output. Sensory input (for example, Mom strokes her baby on the cheek) causes motor output (the baby automatically turns his head to find the instigator of the touch). More input begets more output. More output allows a child's worldview to expand so she receives more input. Consequently, when physical development (and thus motor output) is limited, sensory input is limited as well. If a child cannot crawl to the toy he sees from across the room, he tends to forget about it. If he forgets about it, he can't explore its shape, color, texture, and taste. In short, if he can't physically explore something, then he is not engaging his mind to learn about it.

Recently, a couple came to see me with their 11-month-old son. John wasn't crawling and could not get himself into a sitting position. Yet when he was propped up, he would sit happily all day. John's pediatrician told his parents that he was fine. He would eventually "outgrow" this stage. A psychologist who was a friend of the family told the mother not to worry—"We're the type A people," he said. "Your son is different. He is happy *being*, not *doing*. Let him just be and take in all the information around him."

The problem with this advice is that the child can't take in all the information around him because his body is not allowing him to experience his environment. In order to absorb that information, he needs to hear, look at, move toward, touch, and feel all the various stimuli. Without these abilities, he will not be able to develop into a well-balanced child—unless he receives proper intervention from parents and possibly even professionals that will provide him with the necessary sensory experiences.

For John, the help needed could have been as simple as structured floor play at home, if his muscle-tone issues had been dealt with early enough. But as the case with John also illustrates, many "experts" will say that infants with normal nervous systems don't need specific handling and play; they will adapt and grow properly with the basic cuddling, cooing, and peek-aboo games parents engage them with. I strongly disagree. When parents provide an environment full of possibilities and understand the basic principles of physical development, they can enhance their child's gross and fine motor skills and his speech development, among other things. In turn, these enhancements benefit the child's emotional well-being and the development of higher self-esteem. With higher self-esteem comes a greater ability to take charge of situations, and to thus feel more secure. It is also important to recognize that each infant and child is unique: Each will have his own way of communicating likes and dislikes, stress factors, and natural abilities. Each will develop at different rates, within a continuum.

Unfortunately, parents and doctors of children like John can wait too long to take action, opting for the "wait and see" approach. Often a referral to a specialist isn't made until something obvious like a speech delay or an inability to physically keep up with other kids is detected—perhaps at around two to three years of age. By then, many of these children with minor unresolved developmental issues have compensatory movement patterns and postural instability, and demonstrate signs of insecurity and shyness. Ironically, then, by following the "laissez-faire" traditional wisdom, parents can be setting up their children to be typecast by either their peers, teachers, or professionals in a number of ways. And once children are labeled, self-fulfilling prophecies often occur.

There's No Such Thing as a Lazy Child: How and Why Childhood Traits Can Be Misconstrued

"She's extremely shy."
"He's a loner."
"She's afraid of everything."
"He's just lazy."

These are phrases used to describe children every day. Yet they are often misleading—and detrimental to a young child's growing sense of self. In truth, the shy child could become the class clown, the loner could become an eager participant, or the lazy child could become full of exuberance. So why should such kids appear to be so different than their true personalities? One answer is that these children might be slow to warm up—that's their genetic make-up. But another possibility is that they have physical inadequacies and related sensory issues that their parents aren't aware of.

These issues often manifest themselves in a child's first year—even though their signs can be easily misinterpreted. The infant who is always crying may not be colicky but may need fewer stimuli in her environment in order to feel calm. And the four- to five-month-old who won't roll over isn't lazy or stubborn; she may be afraid to move. Later on, the child who can't master the monkey bars seems like a loner because he opts not to try. In reality, he might not have the strength or balance to keep up with his peers. The girl who won't participate in dance "parties" that her friends enjoy seems shy, when in fact her coordination is a bit delayed. She is embarrassed at the thought of bumping into people by accident. The second grader who only likes to play goalie on his soccer team isn't lazy—he feels bombarded by stimuli when he attempts to jump into the fray and go after the ball.

As parents, we need to realize that there is no such thing as a "lazy" child. Such an adjective is only *our perception* of a child, rationalizing behavior that is actually an outgrowth of a more basic issue—the child's physical and sensory development. We need to be more aware of what our children's physical abilities are and less of what we would like them to be. We need to be aware that children develop at different rates, and sometimes need bolstering for a period of time. Indeed, not all infants and children can achieve their physical milestones without some additional input, sometimes in the form of professional intervention. The children I am referring to are perfectly *healthy*, but might have some developmental lags that can be hard to diagnose initially. On the continuum, these are children who might have started out like John, but who continue to show increasing delays or subtle deficiencies over time in the form of their movement, balance, and sensory reactions.

Sadly, many pediatricians are not willing to discuss subtle limitations or to bring in some extra help for children who show even minor weaknesses. Their reluctance is partially due to those parents who become skittish at the suggestion that extra attention be paid to their child's development. Instead of viewing their role and/or that of a specialist as supplemental to their child's proper growth, these parents can feel that the additional focus will contribute to the creation of a stigma for their perfectly healthy child. More often, they are sure that their child will just outgrow whatever issues exist.

Several years ago, a 10-month-old girl was referred to me by her pediatrician. He was a forthright and intuitive doctor, and saw potential delays in the child's physical development. He opted to act on what he observed. Diana had no problems prenatally or at birth, and there was no explanation as to why she had slightly low muscle tone. What was clear was that she was not crawling or able to get into a sitting position by herself. She was a little girl who wanted to be upright and walking, but who had weak stomach muscles, postural instability, and immature balance reactions. I knew she could possibly become "the funny-looking kid" at school, the child who is last to be picked for teams in sports.

Diana's parents did not see their child in the same light and were skeptical about seeing a pediatric physical therapist. When they placed their daughter in a sitting position she was able to play for long periods of time and was happy. To them, this indicated that there were no real issues. Dad insisted that her developmental lags were something that she would outgrow. He even went on to say how as a child he was not athletic and refused to participate in sports. As he got older he was determined to work harder at sports and excelled in certain activities. He even became captain of his crew team at the university he attended.

Despite their reluctance, both parents agreed to give physical therapy a try. In the process, they learned a great deal about movement and physical development. They were also reassured that there was nothing "wrong" with their daughter—she simply needed additional bolstering, and they were on target for helping her. In a short time they saw progress—and unfortunately decided there was no longer a need to continue therapy. Again, they felt she would outgrow what lags remained. I left them with a home exercise program to follow. Children with mild developmental lags can thrive on a home program if their parents are diligent in using it. But if parents are predisposed to deny that their child has any physical issues, a home program will simply fall by the wayside.

I did not hear from Diana's parents for several years. When she turned five and was about to enter kindergarten, they called. I was not surprised to hear what they told me. Diana was a child who cried when it was time to go to dance class. She never wanted to go to the park. Her parents felt that she was becoming increasingly quiet and withdrawn—characteristics that didn't mesh at all with the little girl they knew and loved. They wanted me to see Diana again, because they were aware that while she wanted to run, tumble, and climb with her friends, she could not keep up. When I saw her, I noticed that she continued to have the weaknesses that I had observed earlier. Yet I was impressed with her ability to compensate and her determination. In therapy, she enjoyed the activities we worked on and she also saw the progress it made, as did her parents. I noticed that Diana's self-esteem and her self-confidence rose in direct proportion to the improvements in her physical abilities, muscle strength, and balance. Within six months, Diana felt comfortable playing with her friends. She stopped her physical therapy with me, but continued a rigorous home program. Her parents kept in touch with me and expressed their delight in Diana's growing competence—and happiness.

The good news is that as a general population, parents are moving away from the notion that developmental lags or inconsistencies will stigmatize their children. Culturally we are becoming more open to proactive and preventive therapies, and are less fearful in asking for help. More and more often couples come in to see me with very mild concerns about their babies. Often they have a nagging concern—they "just have a feeling that something isn't quite right." Or, they simply have many questions regarding proper development and ways to purposefully "play" with their infant.

Recently, a very pleasant family, the Jamisons, came to see me. They were referred to me by their pediatrician because of their concern over the fact that their son was not achieving all of his developmental milestones within the expected time frames. Mrs. Jamison was an attorney and Mr. Jamison had a doctoral degree. They were smart enough to realize they didn't know the basics and craved any and all information I had to share with them. They truly wanted to understand the importance of the developmental sequence (the necessary progression of graduating from one physical stage to the next) and the neurological basis behind it. Yet this educated couple lacked the basic knowledge of how to play effectively with their child. They assiduously wrote down everything I could tell them that would assist in enhancing their son's development. Their worries were allayed, and their son thrived with the greater input from his parents. Hearing the concerns of similar parents many times has made me realize the need for this book.

What This Book Will Do for You

I have written this book to provide answers to all of the above issues as well as give parents like the Jamisons activities to get their kids on track physically and to keep them there. My intent is to provide an understanding of the importance of touch, movement, and play in your child's life, and to illustrate the effect that these things have on the neurodevelopment of your child from birth through three years. I am not attempting to provide you with ways of improving your infant's IQ level, but rather to assist you in raising an emotionally well-balanced, more coordinated, and happier child who is able to easily integrate the environment around him. I hope to help children be regarded for who they are and to help them reach their potential. It might be surprising that mild deficiencies in physical development could have a major impact on self-esteem and well-being—but unfortunately, it's true.

Through my experience both as a pediatric physical therapist working with children with special needs and as a mother of two children, I have found that the principles I use professionally are beneficial to *all* infants and children. I tend to play with my own two children in different ways due to the differences in their body types. My nine-year-old daughter has always had a better quality to her movement patterns. She rolled over early, sat up early, crawled early, and walked early. My six-year-old son, on the other hand, was slower to move. The quality of his movements was not as stable; he sank into gravity and had a round back posture when he sat on the floor, preferring to sit with his legs behind him (we call this "W" sitting). Until this past summer, he looked awkward when he ran because his legs dangled in all directions. Although it sounds as if my daughter would be a better athlete, she has her limitations as well. What she has in strength she lacks in flexibility, and what my son lacks in stability he has gained in flexibility. So for my daughter, play positions and sports that focus more on stretching her muscles are best, while activities that focus on my son's trunk muscles and overall strength are advantageous for him. Both children are also encouraged to participate in activities that they love, or have a strong interest in—even if they are not the best in the group.

Applying the principles of this book to each of my children has helped them tremendously—not only in enhancing their posture, balance, coordination, and strength but also in enhancing their self-image and self-esteem from an early age. Though they (like most of us) have areas in which they struggle, they are both extremely confident children. However, they have not self-selected themselves out of various activities because of their body types. They have the confidence to try new skills.

This book is based on the following principles:

- Achieving the developmental sequence is critical for the well-balanced child.
- Effective play will set the foundation for more challenging activities to come.
- Allowing a child to explore leads to more creative thinking.

- Achieving proper alignment and postural control early on can help prevent many postural and orthopedic problems that often crop up later on.
- An environment enhanced by different sensory experiences will promote physical movement and development. These functions will in turn facilitate new learning experiences. The net result of this constantly developing and expanding sensory input/motor output cycle is that your child can have a greater sense of confidence in the world.
- Having good proximal stability and trunk control supports the emergence of fine motor skills (including handwriting), which are important aids to a child's ability to learn.

Part 1 of this book provides a basic understanding of the sensory system: how it works and how it relates to your child's activity and emotional state. I also detail newborn development. Part 2 details development throughout your child's first year. Given that much of the foundation of a child's development is set during the first year, you will find that there is a greater amount of information regarding the formation of your child's motor skills and her sensory systems in this section of the book. Activities for this period are accompanied by explanations of their usefulness in enhancing gross and fine motor skills. Separate sections detail activities to enhance sensory input for your baby. This format holds true throughout the book. Additionally, each chapter provides "Developmental Benchmarks" that will enable you to assess your child's relative place on the developmental continuum. I also offer a "Well-Balanced Checklist"—a summary of what you can do to bolster your child's development at each stage of growth. Lists of recommended toys (to buy or fabricate) that are developmentally advantageous to your child are also included.

Part 3 (ages one to five) discusses your child's continued mastery of fine and gross motor skills, as well as language development. Activities to bolster your child's development are presented, as are sensory activities. Through these activities and the discussions that accompany them, you will be able to determine what your child's strengths and weaknesses are and which exercises would be the most beneficial to him. Sections on "Developmental Warning Signs" highlight the subtle ways in which your child might be having difficulties. "Well-Balanced Checklists" highlight activities you can do to ensure that your child stays on track, developmentally. In addition, there are lists of recommended, age-appropriate toys to engage your child's motor output and sensory input. "Common Concerns" throughout the book present the most frequently asked questions by parents—from whether it's OK to use a walker, to dealing with a child who has difficulty excelling in the sport he loves—and my answers to them.

Please keep in mind that although this book provides ways to enhance your child's development from newborn to age five, it is important not to become overly zealous and jump-start your baby's development. Activities targeted for an 18-month-old or a two-year-old should not be given to a nine- or twelve-month-old. Remember that babies need to go through the developmental sequence. Babies need to be babies. They grow up fast enough without having us add to their pressures of learning and performing.

Part 4 focuses on special considerations: children with low muscle tone, premature babies, sensory integration disorders, and the most commonly seen orthopedic conditions in pediatrics. Since most of my work was initially with children who have low tone, and since they still comprise a large and critical part of my practice, I feel strongly about addressing low-tone children specifically. In addition, I provide lists of resources for parents who need further assistance, as well as a list of recommended readings.

Finally, this book is based on a set of goals. I would like to:

- Provide you with ways to build a firm foundation for good biomechanics and better postural control for your child.
- Teach you how to use repetition as a way of practicing and building skills.
- Show you ways to enhance the balance reactions of your child.
- Help you understand the importance of proximal (shoulder and hip) strength and abdominal strength.
- Help you realize that infants and children are *not* lazy—if they seem so, there may be an underlying sensory-motor cause or problem.
- Help you understand that if we achieve all of these goals, our children will have fewer physical limitations and will have a greater sense of self throughout their lives.
- Help you recognize that healthy premature babies have their own specific set of developmental criteria to achieve.

It is my hope that the activities in this book will be able to assist you as positively as they have the children in my practice—as well as those children in my own home.

PART 1

Learning to Move and Moving to Learn

The Continuous Cycle of Motor Output and Sensory Input

CHAPTER

The System We Don't See

Understanding Your Child's Sensory (Nervous) System and How It Relates to Movement

Though we may not see or understand it, the sensory system is important. Understanding the importance of the digestive, cardiovascular, and respiratory systems is easy—without them we could not survive. But without our sensory system, which is composed of a network of interrelated systems, we could not function. If we think of our brain as a computer, then our sensory system—our eyes, ears, skin, and nerves—serves as its conductors and wiring, responsible for transmitting all incoming data. In the same vein, all the information we receive about our world is transmitted by our sensory system and subsequently processed by our brain. How well this network of systems functions has a direct effect on our behavior, emotions, and our quality of movement.

It's easy to understand how the basic sensory system helps us: our senses of vision, hearing, touch, taste, and smell all protect us in our environment. They allow us to learn about positive and dangerous input, or stimuli: a child knows not to put his hand on a stove top because it will get burned; we know not to walk out into the street if we see a speeding car or hear one honking at us; we smell smoke and think "danger" well before we locate the cause.

However, two critical parts of the sensory system are not as easy to understand: the *vestibular* system (our sense of movement) and the *proprioceptive* system (our sense of body position). Our vestibular sense orients our body position in relation to the surface, or ground. It is responsible for our balance and automatically coordinates our eye, head, and body movements as they relate to gravity and space. Vestibular sense enables a child to stand on one leg or run up and down an incline (such as a slide) without falling.

Through our tendons, joints, and ligaments, our proprioceptive sense tells us where—and how—our body is oriented in space. It lets us guide our limbs without having to watch where we are putting them. For instance, the proprioceptive sense lets us know how much to bend a knee when we're climbing a step and how to keep our body upright when we trip. It enables a pianist to read sheet music while playing, because he doesn't have to focus on locating the notes for his fingers; with enough practice his fingers "know" where to find the keys.

If asked what the most important senses are, most people would answer "vision and hearing," since the uses of these senses are the most obvious. Yet the senses of touch, movement, and body position are crucial for us to function on a daily basis. In fact, the *tactile* (touch), vestibular, and proprioceptive systems begin to function in an interrelated manner as soon as we are born. In order for us to accurately interpret our surroundings and form appropriate responses to them, *all* of our sensory systems need to be functioning properly and in conjunction with one another. Our ability to utilize our senses in this manner—to absorb information, sort it out, and then respond to it—is what we call *sensory integration*.

When the sensory systems are working properly and the environment is being interpreted appropriately, a child is able to function in an organized manner. He has good motor skills and good play skills that contribute to his feelings of competence and self-assuredness. He is able to enjoy his dance classes, partake in kick ball at recess, jump rope. In short, his physical abilities facilitate his socializing, which bolsters his confidence (this isn't to say that there aren't children who are extremely agile who lack strong social skills). As we mature, an efficient sensory system does even more—it allows us to concentrate on and complete an activity without being distracted by extraneous noises or activities. It allows babies to focus on reaching an object, and enables children to sit quietly and do their homework (even with background noise); it allows a mother to pay bills while keeping an ear out for her kids in the next room. But if a child's central nervous system cannot fully process or organize the information it receives from its senses, then the child won't be able to function properly. If his experience of the world is distorted, it follows that his cognition, movement, and behavior will be distorted as well: he might not be able to concentrate, or put puzzles together with relative ease, or tolerate any appropriate frustration when trying a new activity.

To parents it may appear that the amount of information small children need to integrate is modest. If we think of all the multitasking we do on a daily basis, then an activity such as taking a bath seems like a welcome relief—not a major accomplishment. We need to put ourselves back in our babies' booties in order to empathize, for a moment, with their reactions to the "great unknowns" of their emerging universe. Any new place, person, or situation can be challenging. Needless to say, as we get older our task of integration increases exponentially. I believe that how well we manage this task has a direct impact on our emotional and physical development from birth through adulthood.

The Newborn's Developing Sense of Awareness

Prior to birth we are cozy in our mother's womb. But the moment we begin our journey through the birth canal, we begin to sense many changes—the bumpy ride, getting stuck, being pulled out. Then, *kaboom!* Lights, camera, action! We don't have a second to adjust to all these new sensory inputs—the noise, the lights, the movement. From this moment on, parents need to be aware of babies' responses to all this input. We need to learn to read our baby's signals, or warning signs, that will tell us if he is happy, tired, or stressed.

A healthy newborn receives and responds to many sensory experiences. From birth, we parents provide tactile input when we hold our babies, visual input when our babies see us, and auditory input when we speak to them. Vestibular input is provided when we rock, move, or carry our infants. The senses of taste and smell are activated when we feed them (interestingly, a newborn can identify its mother by the smell of her breast milk). We also improve our babies' awareness of their body parts (proprioceptive sense) by touching and kissing their torso, hands, arms, legs, and feet. Think of your newborn in his bassinet: If he hears a sound he will turn his eyes and head toward it. If you stroke the soles of his feet, he will wiggle his toes. Touch his forehead and he will blink. Move a toy in front of him and his eyes will try to track it.

As our infants get older, we activate their sensory system in order to teach them new motor skills. For example, when we are helping our babies to master holding their heads up by themselves (practicing head control), we have them look directly at us, or at a rattle that we hold up for them to see. As we visually attract our babies' attention, we also use our voice for auditory input.

Babies learn sensory awareness of their individual body parts early on. They begin by looking at their hands and progress to reaching through space with their arms in order to grasp objects. When babies rub their feet together or bang their legs and feet on the floor, they are learning about their limbs as well as how (and to what extent) they can move them. Mouthing, manipulating, and playing with various objects further develops their sensory awareness. By allowing babies to explore their environment we are helping them not only develop an awareness of their bodies and the world around them, but also develop spatial perception as well as their proprioceptive, vestibular, and tactile senses.

Babies need to be able to do more than just explore their environment. They need to be able to react to that environment in order to learn the nature of "cause and effect." We, then, must be aware of our actions and remain vigilant to our babies' responses to them. It is important, therefore, to know your baby's temperament. Learn what he likes and dislikes. In particular, pay attention to how he reacts to sounds, movement, light, and touch. Treat your baby's sensitivity to stimuli as you would your own—then take into account his individual nature. His responses may be more exaggerated than yours owing to his age. For example, while you might routinely conk out with the lights on and the TV blaring, bright lights and loud noises might create "sensory overload" for your baby. Or, your baby might be comfortable sleeping with background noises such as the drone of the TV in the library—but unexpected ones, such as the vacuum cleaner revving outside of his room, might startle and upset him. In general, if your baby is crying or fussy, turning his head away, fidgeting, or even spitting up a lot, he is most likely telling you to change the way in which you are handling him (and thus change the stimulus) at that moment.

Babies give many such cues to help you understand their comfort level. Paying attention to these cues and responding to them is the key to making your little one feel secure in her world. We can also make our babies feel safe by holding them, talking to them, and gently moving them. From this constant and loving world that we provide, our babies will want to explore their environment. Movement, of course, is what enables their explorations.

Understanding Your Baby's Sensory System as It Relates to Movement

If we were to make a diagram to illustrate the relationship between movement and the sensory system, it would look like this:

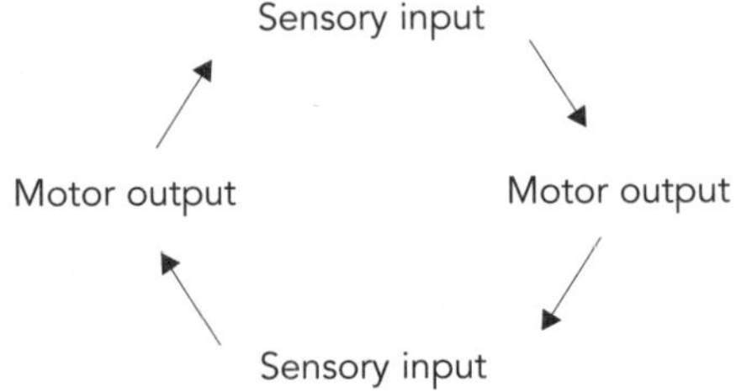

More input always leads to more output, and vice versa. The outcome is increased sensory awareness. This cycle is the foundation of how we learn to explore and make sense of our environment, the very cornerstone of our physical development and our emotional security. In order for this cycle to continue, our central nervous system needs to process the sensory input and respond to it through our movements. In order for us to move, various mechanisms need to be in place.

Most people have no idea how many components make up our movements. A basic act, such as a baby rolling over, is a combination of automatic and voluntary movements and uses most of the senses. It requires a point of stability (a surface from which to move) and adequate muscle tone. Movement generally occurs as a response to some form of visual, tactile, or auditory stimulation. For instance, a baby might roll over because he hears his mother clapping but can't see her. Or, perhaps he wants to grab the Wiggleworm but can't reach it without moving toward it (via rolling over). As he rolls, the baby needs perceptual awareness to know which limb is moving. His proprioceptive sense tells him how—and where—his limbs are moving through space, while his vestibular sense makes him feel secure in rolling over. Finally, the speed of his motions and the amount of effort he must expend also play a large part in how successfully the baby rolls over.

As children get older, the job of moving does not get any easier. For a toddler to simply catch a ball, she needs to have a stabilized stance, requiring postural control. To ensure that she can balance and simultaneously use both hands, she needs her vestibular system to function properly. Her proprioceptive sense tells her where to place her hands in order to catch the ball. She uses her vision to follow the ball's direction. Finally, she uses her perception to determine the rate at which the ball is coming toward her.

Exhausting, isn't it? Is it surprising, then, that the "simple" act of rolling over, or later on of catching a ball, can be difficult for some children? Some babies don't know where to put their arms to assist them in rolling over. Others might not like the way it feels to be lying on their stomachs (feeling a sense of imbalance or insecurity), so they won't initiate movement. Some toddlers can't seem to sense when to put their hands out, or how close or far apart their hands should be, in order to catch a ball. Imagine the feeling a child has when he can't engage in such an "easy" age-appropriate activity. His friends tease him, he looks clumsy, and after a while he just gives up. Unfortunately, this sense of defeat doesn't apply just to a game of catch. What if your child were an awkward runner, or couldn't swing a baseball bat or tennis racket, or properly pump himself on a swing? In contrast, when a child *can* participate in such activities, he will have a sense of accomplishment in performing them. Of equal importance in terms of his learning and development, he will be experiencing moving his body against gravity and through space as well as planning (problem solving) the motor activities involved in the task at hand.

For adults, the mere task of putting on a pair of pants requires all of the same components as catching a ball. We need our motor abilities along with our vestibular and proprioceptive senses in order to shift our weight, lift one leg up, and balance on the other. Additionally, our proprioceptive sense lets us pull on our pants without having to visually determine where our legs, arms, and torso are in relation to each other. Our fine motor skills allow us to pull up the pants zipper and fasten the waist button. Finally, our tactile and proprioceptive senses enable us to do these tasks without looking. Think about all of that the next time you get dressed, and you will understand both how amazing—and daunting—the sensory system is.

All of our movements comprise both automatic and voluntary responses to stimuli. To fully understand how we move, we need to take a closer look at all of the components of both kinds of responses. Then we can see how they are processed by the central nervous system.

Automatic Movement

Some movements are preprogrammed into our central nervous system. These movements are automatic, requiring no conscious thought. Automatic movements usually occur as a response to a stimulus from the visual, tactile, or vestibular systems. They include our righting reactions (automatic reactions that occur so we remain upright) and equilibrium reactions (automatic balance reactions). For instance, if we are standing on a moving surface, like the deck of a boat, or are knocked off balance by someone bumping into us, we automatically adjust our position in order not to fall.

FIGURE 1.1 Rooting Reflex

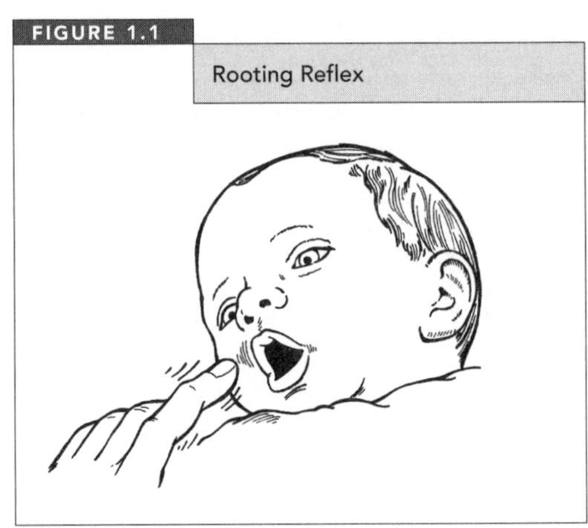

FIGURE 1.2 Moro, or Startle, Reflex

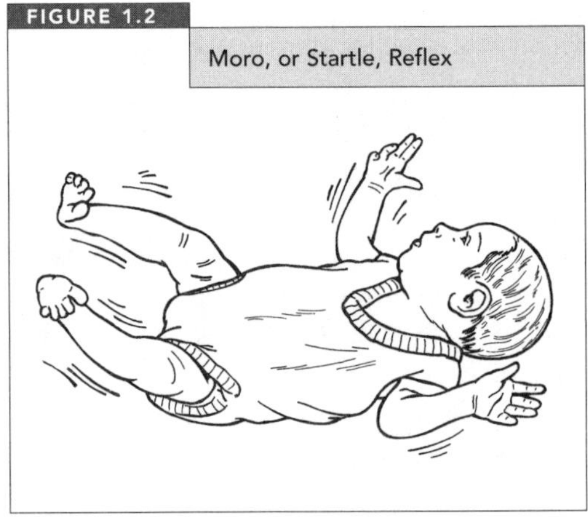

Primitive Reflexes

We shout with excitement at seeing our baby take her first steps way ahead of schedule—until we realize what we are witnessing are really her reflexes in action. In fact, many of the movements and responses we associate with newborns are due to primitive reflexes. These are automatic reactions that we are born with.

The following is a partial list of the primitive reflexes your baby will exhibit.

The Rooting Reflex One of the most familiar primitive reflexes is the *rooting reflex* (see Figure 1.1). When you stroke the side of your baby's mouth he will turn his head to suck. This instinctive reflex is preprogrammed into his nervous system so that he will search for his mother's nipple (he will also search for the nipple of a bottle if it is touched to the side of his mouth).

The Moro—or Startle—Reflex Another primitive reflex is the *Moro*—or startle—*reflex* that occurs when an infant is moved too quickly or dropped backward. Loud noises can also trigger this response. The baby's arms shoot out from her sides and her fingers splay out as she cries or shudders (see Figure 1.2). Parents are often frightened when they first see their babies startle in this way—it's a surprise to everyone! This reflex is perfectly normal, however, and usually disappears by three to four months of age. It's not surprising that babies shudder like this (or even more often) when you consider how often they encounter unexpected sounds, touches, or flashbulbs. But you can reduce the effect by remembering

FIGURE 1.3

Asymmetrical Tonic Neck (Fencing) Reflex

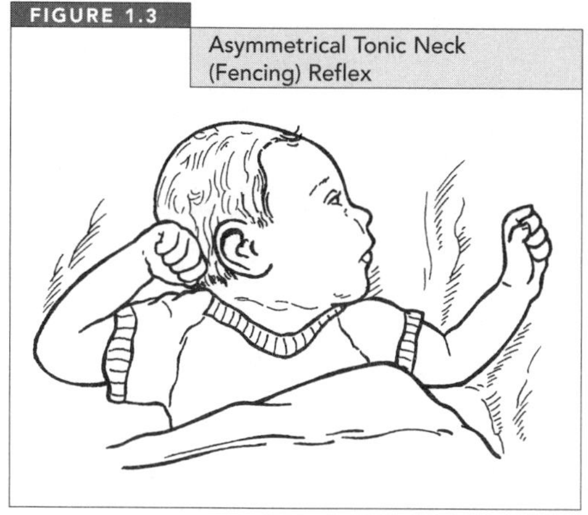

FIGURE 1.4

Palmar Reflex

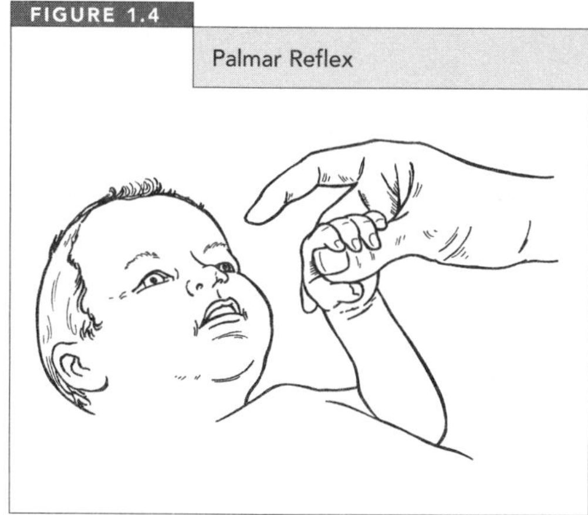

to be gentle when you move your baby. Rest assured, the Moro reflex is far more unnerving to you than it is to her!

The Asymmetrical Tonic Neck Reflex (or "Fencing Reflex") When your infant turns his head to look at a face or an object that piques his interest, the arm on his face side will move straight out from his side, in a *fencing* posture (see Figure 1.3). While it might appear as if he is actually trying to reach for an object from this position, he isn't yet. That will come in time.

The Palmar Reflex When your infant strongly grasps your finger, she is exhibiting the *palmar reflex* (see Figure. 1.4). Parents are often shocked at how strong their newborn's grasp is. Remember, her strength is just a reflex at this point and usually diminishes by three months of age. At that point, your baby will start to actively move around and purposefully grasp objects, thus gaining muscle strength.

Reflex Progression

At birth, our movements are uncontrolled. We cannot move against gravity, and our primitive reflexes are dominant. As an example, think of what happens when you place a newborn on his stomach. He will try to move on the floor by randomly waving his limbs, but gravity is pulling him down. Consequently, while his stomach, arm, and leg muscles are working, the baby cannot yet lift his head, neck, or trunk off the ground. When you place him on his back, he is again fighting gravity. Trying to move up and off the floor, he might arch his back and again randomly wave his limbs, but he will have no success in lifting his head.

Our more advanced automatic movements—righting and balance reactions, along with ensuing volitional movements—will not emerge until our primitive reflexes fade (or become integrated into the nervous system) at between four and six months of age. If primitive reflexes persist past this point, they can—and often do—hinder the development of subsequent movements. For instance, if a baby didn't "outgrow" the asymmetrical tonic neck reflex, she wouldn't be able to bring her hands to her mouth. Her wiring would tell her to keep extending her arm away from her face, instead of letting her desire to put her hand to her mouth take over. It's not hard to imagine how such an inability could stunt a baby's development. She would miss out on a major part of her early sensory explorations—mouthing objects—which, of course, is one of the most crucial ways a baby learns about her world. In such instances when primitive reflexes don't fade or integrate, a dysfunction in the central nervous system is usually the cause, requiring the attention of a pediatric neurologist.

FIGURE 1.5

Neck Righting Reaction

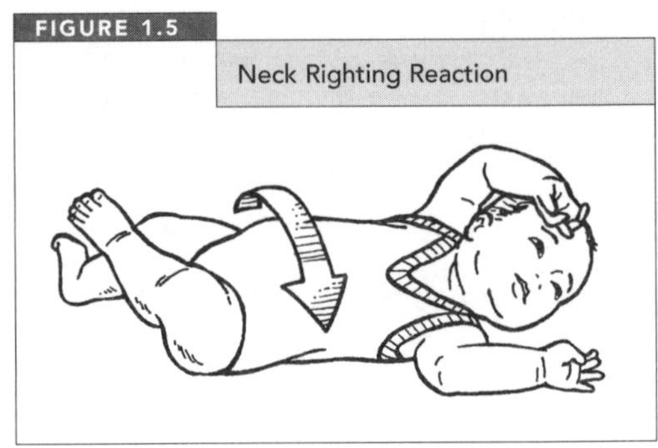

FIGURE 1.6

Labyrinth Righting Reaction

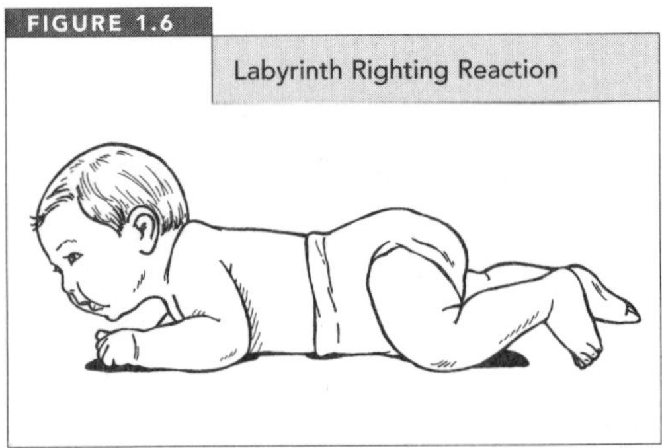

Postural Reactions

Postural reactions are automatic reactions that enable us to adjust ourselves against gravity or readjust ourselves when we are shifted off center. They include our righting and equilibrium reactions. As infants we develop our postural reactions by adjusting ourselves when we are held, picked up, or washed. Think, for example, of what happens when you lift your baby into the air, horizontally. He will arch his head and neck upward as he splays his limbs. In doing so, he is righting the position of his head so that he can properly perceive his surroundings. This response is known as the *Landau reaction*. There are a number of postural reactions, and they are all extremely important because they allow babies to shift their bodies into different positions. Babies will need these weight-shifting and balancing abilities to engage in purposeful, or voluntary, movement. The following is a partial list of the postural reactions your baby will exhibit.

The Neck Righting Reaction From birth to five or six months, you'll notice that when you turn your baby's head to one side, her entire body will follow. This motion is known as "log rolling" because your baby's limbs, torso, and head cannot yet move separately (see Figure 1.5).

The Labyrinth Righting Reaction This reaction allows your baby to lift his head up when he is lying on his stomach and, eventually, when he is lying on his back (see Figure 1.6). Most babies can accomplish the former by two months of age. The labyrinth righting reaction is also partly responsible for a two-week-old's ability to briefly lift his head and turn it when he is lying on his stomach.

The Body-on-Body Righting Reaction This reaction is an outgrowth of the neck righting reaction, appearing at seven to twelve

FIGURE 1.7

Body-on-Body Righting Reaction

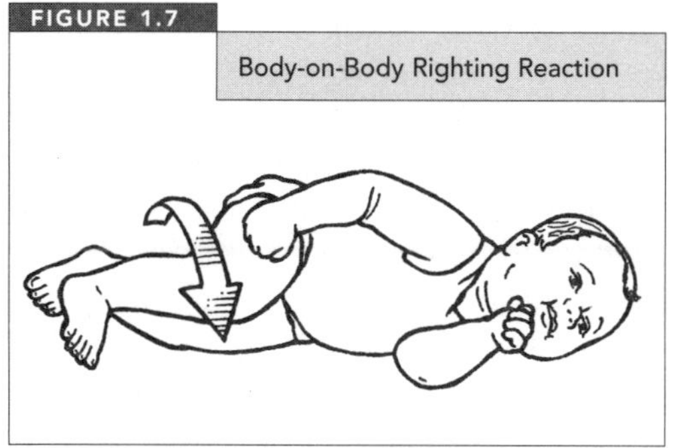

months. When your baby is lying on her back, if you bring her leg up over her body and to the side, the rest of her body will follow (see Figure 1.7). She needs this reaction to make the transition from log rolling to segmented rolling (when her torso, limbs, and head and neck can roll independently of one another). Later she will use it to sit and stand.

Postural Progression

Postural reactions also include our ability to properly align our limbs. Usually we find ourselves in better alignment when we are in an alert state—when we are poised for action—because we need to be more efficient. When we are relaxing, or at rest, we tend to have poor alignment, which leads to muscular aches and pains along with skeletal imbalances. Just think of how we tend to scrunch up our neck and shoulders when we talk on the phone, slouch in our seats when we watch a movie, or stand in a slump when we're waiting in line. The same holds true for children. They are slumping in front of their computers, doing homework, or playing games, and these habits only get worse with time (as do our ailments!). So, let's teach our kids good posture and biomechanics early on.

Voluntary Movement

Voluntary, or volitional, movements are purposeful movements that have to be learned. You can't develop voluntary movements without automatic ones. For example, think of how a baby usually begins to roll over: he sees an object and wants to reach for it. In the process, he turns his head and/or brings his feet up and then "falls" over. The motion is unintentional. But if the movement feels good to him, he'll "practice" it time and again until it becomes voluntary, or purposeful. His automatic reactions are what allow him to perfect rolling because they enable him to right his head and trunk as he rolls. In order for the transition from unintentional to voluntary movement to occur, all of his sensory systems need to work together.

In general, volitional movement shows up at about four months, when we notice our babies beginning to reach, grasp, and roll over. It emerges alongside our babies' cognitive and perceptual development (an awareness of our body parts and where they are located in space). Volitional movement also develops in conjunction with motor planning (the ability to organize thoughts and plan movements to complete an activity). For instance, when your baby rolls under a chair to grab a shiny rattle, she is exhibiting a coordinated effort of voluntary movement and cognition, as well as her developing perceptual awareness and motor planning abilities. To obtain efficient volitional movements we also need good muscle tone; a base of support; stability around the joints; speed, effort, and compensatory movements; and bilateral integration.

The Importance of Muscle Tone

Muscle *tone* is the amount of resistance we have to passive movement. It is also the elasticity of the muscle (when we push in on a muscle, it should spring back). We need enough tone to hold us up against gravity and to maintain good posture and alignment, but not so much as to make us stiff, or rigid. When you think about muscle tone, think of it in terms of the firmness of the muscle and its ability to react when being lengthened. When a limb is being passively moved, its muscles need to respond with a certain amount of firmness and extensibility—or resistance—to the movement (or stretch). Normal muscle tone responds to being moved or stretched with a slight increase in muscle tension and a slight resistance. In essence, the muscle responds to accommodate our actions, tensing and relaxing as needed. For instance, our muscles tense to run and relax to stretch.

Low muscle tone—too little tone—responds to passive movement with diminished muscle tension and less resistance than normal. On the other hand, if you have too much muscle tone (high tone), your muscles will be too tight to stretch, resulting in a shortening of the muscles. Think of a runner who does not believe in stretching. His leg muscles are firm; however, they have also tightened (or shortened) over time. This could lead to muscular imbalances, aches, pains, and possible injury.

Good muscle tone isn't easy to define—it takes experience to understand what "normal" tone feels like. In addition, there's a range of normal muscle tone. Some people have lower tone (less firmness and resistance in response to passive movement) while others have higher tone. Furthermore, the amount of muscle tone we have changes from infancy to adulthood. As newborns we have more tone *distally*, meaning in our hands, which are fisted. Our shoulders are weak. As we develop, our tone increases *proximally*—at the shoulders and hips—freeing the use of our hands for manipulation and fine motor skills.

Your pediatrician is testing your baby's muscle tone when he has your infant grasp his finger. He then gently pulls on your little one's arm to see if he can still keep his grasp. Pediatricians also check tone by assessing a baby's passive range of motion. While it's not uncommon for babies to have low muscle tone, if it is severe enough, your pediatrician might suggest some additional, professional help. Chapter 8 discusses more symptoms of low muscle tone.

Muscle Strength and Connection

"The shoulder bone's connected to the . . . " We all know the old folk song that sort of teaches us how our bones connect. The most important sequence to learn initially, however, is not about our bones, but about the strength of our muscles and how *they* are connected. If we don't develop strength in our shoulders and trunk first, then we won't be able to strengthen our fine motor skills through the use of our hands. This lack of development results in big setbacks in our ability to absorb information and learn from it. Fortunately, most babies' strength develops in the appropriate sequence and within appropriate time frames.

Why the Fuss over Floor Play?

You might be wondering how a child can "skip" floor or belly play, which happens quite often. Parents don't always realize the benefits of such play. If they see their child fussing when he is put on his belly, they might immediately pick him up instead of helping him work through his frustration so that he can explore new stimuli from his unique vantage point. One couple recently told me they didn't keep their baby on the floor—but in an exersaucer, instead—because she "seemed bored" on the floor. She didn't move much when prone. Well, for one thing, there is no such thing as a bored baby. (Understimulated babies might *appear* bored and/or fussy . . . but it's our job to keep them engaged and stimulated.) Second, of course this little girl won't have the experience of moving around a lot if she is placed in an exersaucer or "jolly jumper" for extended periods of time. That being said, babies do become frustrated and tired after periods of floor and belly play. It's a lot of work—the equivalent of doing a lot of push-ups for us. Furthermore, the amount of time an individual baby can tolerate lying and playing on her stomach varies. If you notice that your baby is getting increasingly frustrated, try rolling her out of this position onto her side or back before picking her up. This movement alone may be enough to change her demeanor. Chapter 2 will discuss ways to minimize your baby's frustration while keeping her motivated and engaged during floor play.

For example, watch your baby when he is playing on his belly. At a certain point in time (usually around three months) he will prop himself onto his elbows. This indicates that his shoulder strength is developing. From being prone on his elbows, your infant will begin to prop onto extended arms, further developing shoulder and arm strength as well as trunk control. Once he has enough strength, he can begin to lift one arm up to reach for an object. One arm then becomes the stabilizer while the other arm is able to manipulate toys. He will then be strong enough to prop himself up to grasp a desired object and explore it in one hand while he balances himself with the other shoulder, arm, and hand. This progression perfectly exemplifies the diagram on page 6 of sensory input and motor output: increased motor development enables greater sensory input and awareness, because your baby is able to reach, touch, and manipulate an object in a manner he couldn't previously.

Just as alignment improves when we are poised for action, muscle tone also increases if we are in a state of readiness/arousal. The novelty of experience is a good catalyst. For instance, a baby who is propped up on his elbows will arch his trunk and head higher and higher to engage with a new toy put in his line of sight but out of reach. In the process, he is strengthening his back, shoulder, and neck muscles.

Development of trunk control is important for refined, coordinated, and controlled movement. If the neck and trunk muscles are weak, a child will have difficulty maintaining body positions and progressing through the developmental sequence. If a child skips this early phase of floor play, she could have weakness in the shoulders and arms, which could lead to difficulty with hand-eye coordination, fine motor skills, and gross motor skills. Consequently, playing might frustrate her and thus be less effective in helping her develop properly.

Our Base of Support

For voluntary movement to occur, we need a stable base in the form of a surface, such as a floor. We call this our *base of support*. Our body needs to be aligned over the base of support, and part of our body needs to be in contact with it. A child who is sitting on the floor with her legs extended will have a better base of support than a child sitting in a "ring" position with her legs off the floor and just her ankles touching it. The child in this wide "ring" position can only maintain her balance by rounding her spine and sinking backward. On the other hand, the child with her legs extended or in a "half ring" position (one leg straight and one bent) can press her legs into the floor. This helps her keep her spine erect and activate her stomach muscles, giving her additional support to help her balance.

Stability Around the Joints

We need our muscles to tighten, or contract, around our joints for stability. This tightening occurs when the *flexor* (front-side) and *extensor* (back-side) muscles work at the same time, contracting around our joints. Babies initially develop the ability to contract their neck and shoulder muscles when they are lying prone, propped on their elbows. Later, this contracting of the neck muscles enables babies to keep their heads erect and helps in the development of their visual perception, feeding, and speech. Without stability around the joints, our movements would be uncontrolled, appearing exaggerated and jerky. For instance, a child who is just learning to stand will actually plop into a sitting position as opposed to lowering himself into one. He hasn't practiced the movement enough for the contracting required of his muscles. Consequently, the actual motion of lowering himself into a sitting position is uncontrolled.

Speed, Effort, and Compensatory Movement

Just as we need appropriate muscle tone and stability around the joints, we need to move at an appropriate pace. Slow movements require greater concentration and control. Walking through the park I marvel when seeing people perform tai chi. Their movements are slow (but not too slow), coordinated, and balanced as well as centered—a beautiful image. If our movements are too fast, we cannot call upon our balance reactions. For instance, a gymnast in the midst of a tumbling pass has exceptional coordination and athletic ability—but, ironically, her fast "chain reaction" of moves actually shows her to be in a continuous state of loss-of-balance. Think what would happen if you shouted at her to "freeze" mid-pass.

In general, the greater the effort needed to complete a movement, the more stability we need and the more compensatory movements we will use. Notice the manner in which an infant walks after she first learns to stand up. Compensatory balancing movements abound: her arms are poised way up in the air, her shoulders are hiked up to her ears and her feet are placed so far apart that she actually waddles by us. Or, look at an adult learning how to play tennis or golf: his back is stiff, his shoulders are raised, he overhits (or underswings). He needs a lot of practice to get the stroke and his posture just right.

Amount of Effort *Effort* is a combination of our comfort level in accomplishing a movement, the complexity of the task, the strength needed to perform the activity, and the type of support surface involved (e.g., a paved road versus a rocky path). But how should we apply this definition to our children? How much effort is too much effort?

As parents we want to find a good balance between our children's level of effort and their level of frustration. For instance, if you place a toy out of your baby's reach, she will begin to either roll toward it or inch toward it on her tummy. Be patient and don't try to rush her—reaching that toy requires a big effort on her part. She'll start to grimace, then grunt, and then . . . the telltale sign of cries. All babies have different degrees of strength and abilities—and different personalities that go along with varying degrees of tolerance. See how long your baby maintains her interest before she starts to cry—and then get the toy for her. Remember, we want to encourage new movements, but not to the point where they become negative experiences for our children.

Bilateral Integration

Not all volitional movements depend on bilateral integration, but most advanced movements do, so it's worthwhile to explain the concept. *Bilateral integration* refers to the coordinated use of the two sides of the body. Information from the two sides of the brain is integrated, enabling each side of the body to be aware of—and cooperate with—the other side. The result is efficient and coordinated movement. A baby first coordinates the use of the two sides of his body symmetrically—for instance, when he reaches for an object with both hands, claps, holds his bottle, or rolls over. A baby then learns to coordinate both sides of his body by alternating their use—for instance, when he starts to crawl, climb up a ladder, or eventually skip. Bilateral integration ultimately leads to the awareness of one side of the body as dominant, as well as a person's sense of right-left direction. It also affects the timing, sequence, and rhythm of movement.

How the Central Nervous System Processes Our Movement

As we've seen, movement is a sensory-based phenomenon. It relies on an intricate series of processes that are organized through the central nervous system. The central nervous system receives sensory input from our exteroceptive receptors (receptors for vision, hearing, smell, touch, taste, pain, and temperature). It also receives input from our proprioceptors (receptors in our muscles, tendons, ligaments, joints, and fascia—the lining around our bones), as well as from our vestibular system (information received through our inner ears about balance, movement, and gravity).

The vestibular, proprioceptive, and tactile systems are particularly important in giving babies information, not only about how their bodies move, but also about how their movements can be used to impact their environment. Making sense of how their actions affect things in their world is, of course, one of the primary ways that babies learn. Let's take a closer look at each of these important systems.

How the Vestibular and Proprioceptive Systems Function

The vestibular system is located in the inner ears and is activated by both head movement and gravity. It helps us know if *we* are moving or if *the things around us* are moving. The displacement of fluids in the inner ear tells our brain *how* we are moving—horizontally, vertically, or rotationally. The vestibular system communicates positional changes to the *ocular* (eye) muscles and to other parts of the brain that control movement. It also recognizes the speed and duration of our movement. It allows us to stand upright and to develop postural security against gravity. It also regulates our balance, or equilibrium, along with our posture, muscle tone, and eye-motor control (for quick locking in on—or localization of—an object). Because it orients us in space, the vestibular system lets us feel secure as children when our parents carry us or rock us to sleep, or when we jump on beds, climb over furniture, twirl on swings, or hang from a tree.

The proprioceptive sense is activated by movement that stimulates special receptors in our muscles, joints, and skin. As we've seen, the proprioceptive system tells us where our head, torso, and limbs are located in space without our having to see them (i.e., develop a body scheme). It enables us to know that our legs are crossed under a chair, to copy something down without having to watch ourselves write, or to reach out in the dark to turn on a lamp or open a door. It also tells us how much force our muscles are using, and how much (and how fast) our muscles are stretching. In conjunction with an efficient vestibular system and good stability around the joints, our proprioceptive sense helps us move in a coordinated and controlled manner—not too quickly or awkwardly. Consequently, it gives toddlers the ability to use their fine motor skills for tasks like eating with a spoon and fork.

Having the vestibular and proprioceptive senses working in tandem also helps with motor planning. *Motor planning* (or *praxis*) is the ability to plan, organize, and carry out new actions. It is what allows a baby or toddler to crawl under a table without banging his head, or crawl through a play tunnel without losing his sense of direction, or climb onto a chair and seat himself without falling off. When the vestibular and proprioceptive senses are not working correctly, a toddler has great difficulty motor planning. His vision—along with tactile and auditory cues—helps him figure out what to do, but learning new tasks becomes extremely frustrating, to say the least.

How the Tactile System Functions

Babies learn about their environment largely through touch because it is the most developed of the sensory systems during the first few months of life. We can divide the

Common Concern

I don't like to be hugged and touched a lot. Does this mean that my baby won't like hugs and snuggles?

On the contrary, your baby might love to be touched, stroked, and massaged. Sensory issues such as sensitivity to touch are not necessarily hereditary. The important thing for you to focus on is your baby's unique responses to stimuli—and how you then respond to your baby.

---

tactile system into the protective system and the discriminatory system. Our *protective system* alerts us to painful or dangerous input. For example, it alerts us to and prevents us from touching something hot. The *discriminatory system* tells us about the nature, quality, and quantity of the stimuli. In other words, it lets us know where we are being touched and with what kind of intensity (a light versus a heavy touch). Consequently, our tactile system teaches us the difference between a welcoming hug or pat on the back, and a sharp pinch or prod. When we're babies, the tactile sense teaches us about shapes, textures, and size through the mouthing of objects and later by manipulating those objects with our hands. As we mature our tactile sense enables us to orient objects in our hands without having to see them: we know whether we are feeling our keys or loose change in our pockets.

But What If the Sensory Systems Are Not Working in an Organized Way? Sensory Integration Concerns

It's clear how critical our sensory system is to our ability to move, feel, and process information. Through sensory integration (SI), all the parts of our nervous system work together so that we can experience and interact effectively with our environment. What are often unclear are the subtle shifts in behavior and ability that can occur when one part of the system isn't functioning properly. Sensory integration dysfunction can manifest itself in a number of ways: it can present itself as a motor, learning, social/emotional, speech/language, or attention disorder. Of course, the greater the dysfunction, the more obvious subsequent problems will be.

A baby with sensory integration disorders might not be able to roll or get into and out of a sitting position. Such a baby might be incapable of weight-shifting to move toward or to grasp an object slightly out of reach. Children with sensory integration disorders can be disorganized and incapable of readily performing new tasks. They might also have difficulties later on relating and learning at school. Such a child might be the one that runs under the desk during music class, keeping away from the other children. Perhaps she is the "clumsy" one in dance class. In art class he might not want to touch the "icky, slimy" paints. Or, he might relate well and do well in school, but it requires a lot of effort for him to stay focused and in control of a given situation.

This intense effort can result in an emotional meltdown with little or no obvious provocation. Such a child might resist changes in her routine or be unwilling to participate in new activities without the support of a teacher (or parent) nearby. She relies on the structure, or routine, of her daily life to keep herself feeling in control. While children are generally adaptable, a child with a sensory integration disorder may not be able to adapt to a stressful situation.

In social situations, children with a sensory integration disorder might shy away from participation. These children can nevertheless appear to be hyperactive, constantly moving and crashing into things. Their parents often make excuses for them, creating a predictable environment that they feel is a safe and happy one for their children at that particular moment. For example, play dates might always have to be at their house. Or at a birthday party (with an abundance of stimulation), the parents often remain on edge, making sure their children do not overreact in anger or tears to a situation. In general, parents aren't fully aware that they compensate for their children in these ways. They may make excuses for their child ("he's too tired," "she didn't eat right," "he's getting sick").

It often seems as if these children have behavioral problems—and sensory integration disorders can lead to behavioral issues—but parents and educators need to understand that the root causes of a child's obstinacy, passivity, or irritability might be physiological and/or neurological. Sadly, children with SI disorders are often misdiagnosed and injuriously labeled. It's difficult to diagnose a disorder initially because no one person will necessarily catch all of the child's symptomatic behavior—much less group it together in any comprehensive or conclusive manner. The child who can't tie his shoes might be the same child who can't ride his bike and who has difficulties with handwriting in class. Separately, these symptoms wouldn't add up to much, but taken together they tell a different story. Furthermore, while pediatricians are beginning to refer an increasing number of babies and toddlers with sensory integration disorders to specialized therapists (such as myself), we generally don't see these children until they are in preschool. There, their teachers might notice a problem such as a short attention span, a language delay, or an inability to keep up with peers at choice time.

Parents can become overwhelmingly frustrated in trying to decipher their child's behavior and help modify it. Yet a parent's exasperation is nothing compared with how compromised these children can feel. For this reason it's important that we assess any weaknesses, likes, or dislikes that our children may have. Granted, we all have our aversions and limitations. But when these aversions far outnumber what we like to do and what we are capable of—when they interfere with our everyday activities—then a sensory problem might be the cause. If a child continuously exhibits symptomatic behavior, some form of professional intervention might be called for.

If you suspect that your child has a sensory integration disorder, evaluations can be made—and subsequent therapy introduced—by an occupational therapist trained in sensory integration; a physical therapist for balance, coordination, or muscle tone; and a speech therapist for possible language, speech, and feeding issues. Parents, doctors, and educators should keep in mind that the earlier that intervention is applied, the better a child will respond to therapy. The younger the child, the more malleable the nervous system. The appendixes in this book offer additional information on sensory disorders as well as resources for finding appropriate therapy.

A Window into the Nervous System

The intent of this chapter has been to help you appreciate the stunning complexity of our sensory system. At the least, now you can look at your baby or toddler with a genuine sense of awe when you see him attempt a new activity. Given the myriad individual systems (as well as their collective input) required for our children to properly develop, it's not hard to see how problems might occur that can create long-lasting difficulties of one sort or another. Consequently, the rest of this book is devoted to teaching you activities and play you can engage in with your child to assist his continued, proper growth. It is also geared to alerting you to the potential, subtler developmental delays that can occur.

Every child goes through normal developmental stages that include aggressiveness, pickiness, apparent hyperactivity, and even awkwardness. Consequently, it's important that we don't scrutinize every aspect of our children's behavior. At the same time, if we notice ongoing, telltale-warning signs that interfere with a child's daily life, we might need to intervene. The key, then, in helping your child reach her potential is to be vigilant but not overreactive to her behavior—whether she is a newborn or toddler. How she reacts to stimuli will speak volumes about her ability to process and integrate new information. Your child's behavior is the window into her nervous system. Remember that there's no such thing as a lazy child. If your son or daughter is chronically out of sorts or showing disruptive behavior, chances are there's a reason. The activities presented in this book will give you occasion to see a confident glow on your child's face and a purposeful volition to his or her movements.

And Always Remember . . .

- *A secure and happy child is a well-balanced child, in every sense of the word.*

CHAPTER

2

Your Newborn

Birth to One Month

We start bonding with our babies long before birth. We talk and sing to them in the womb (sometimes even playing music for them). We rub mothers' bellies as a means of tactile contact with them. Upon learning that they are pregnant, mothers immediately change their diets, activity levels, and sleep patterns to accommodate the babies growing inside.

From the moment our babies are born, our love and nurturing provide them with continuous sensory input. Instinctively, we make funny faces and coo to them. We bring them to breasts to nurse, lift them over our shoulders to burp, and rock them to sleep. These basic activities give our newborns enormous visual, auditory, tactile, proprioceptive, and vestibular stimulation. In the days and weeks to come, our babies' level of sensory input increases exponentially. While we want them to develop an active curiosity for their ever-expanding world, we also want them to feel secure in the process. When our babies are calm and self-regulated, they tend to be relaxed and content—an optimal state to receive stimulation. We might have the best of intentions, but if we engage in play that is too advanced for our infants, we can make them feel physically uncomfortable, frustrated, or emotionally insecure. Consequently, we need to understand how our babies are developing mechanically in order to stimulate them with appropriate activities.

FIGURE 2.1

Physiological Flexion

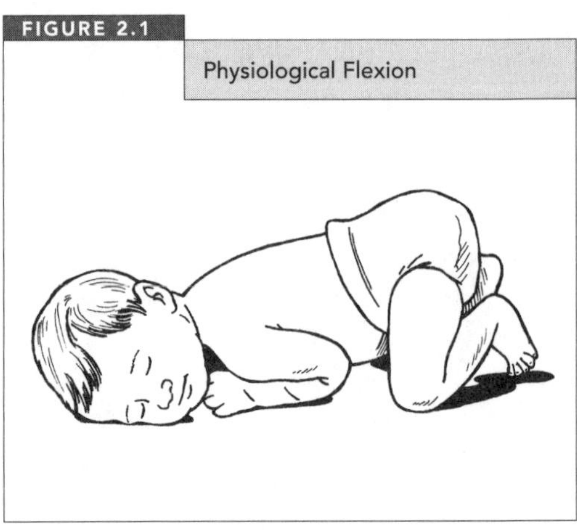

Your Newborn's Movement Patterns

A full-term baby is born curled up. We call this curled-up position *physiological flexion* (see Figure 2.1). This flexion is due mainly to the position of the growing fetus in the womb. The space is limited and the baby accommodates by curling up. Because of this flexion, when we first hold our newborns and try to straighten their elbows, hips, knees, or ankles, these joints "snap" back into the position that feels comfortable to them . . . the one they have been in for the past several months. A newborn will instinctively curl herself into this flexed position. She faces down with her head turned to one side. Her legs are tucked up under her hips, her little bottom pushed up into the air. Her hands are fisted and her arms are curled up under her chest. Because her shoulders are so weak at this point, her weight is shifted forward onto her face.

The newborn's strength develops from head to toe. Her shoulder strength develops before her hand strength, and her hip strength develops before her ankle/foot strength. In general, her movements progress from gross (large) movements to fine (refined) movements. It's important to keep this sequence in mind as we try new activities with our babies.

When you look at your baby lying on her back (supine) you will see that her head is turned to one side. She cannot maintain her head in midline because her neck muscles haven't developed yet. (Midline refers to the centerline of the body—up to down, back to front, right to left). As described, when you place your baby on her stomach (prone), the flexion in her hips tends to shift her weight to the head and neck area. This makes it even harder for your baby to lift her head. However, by one month of age, most full-term newborns are able to momentarily lift their heads up high enough to clear the surface they are lying on and turn their heads to the opposite side. This ability is largely due to the labyrinth righting reaction that is activated within a baby's first month and that enables a baby to lift her head against gravity. You may notice your baby getting stuck in the middle of this motion, with her face pressing down. After a moment, most babies will continue to turn their heads to the side. If your baby doesn't, please turn it for her.

If you try to roll your newborn, you'll notice that she moves as a unit: when you move her head or a leg to one side, the rest of her body automatically follows, as described on page 10 (the neck righting reaction). We call this motion "log rolling" because babies lack the spinal mobility needed for segmented rolling (body parts moving independently).

Movements of the newborn's arms and legs are random and asymmetrical (one side may be flexed while the other is extended). If you place your infant in a sitting position it's clear that her trunk muscles aren't developed yet, either. She needs you to fully support her head, neck, and torso to maintain any upright position. But to your amazement, when you attempt to stand your baby she automatically bears weight on her feet and may appear to be walking. This is only a reflex (the *automatic walking reflex*, also known as *spontaneous walking*) and will soon disappear. There is no need to encourage this posture and response. It has no bearing on how strong your baby will be or when she will walk.

Encouraging the flexed position is important for several reasons (and is especially important for premature babies; see Chapter 9). For one thing, it helps babies conserve body heat and energy, which helps them gain weight and grow. Flexion also makes it easier for babies to get their hands to their face and their fingers in their mouths for sucking. We call sucking on thumbs, hands, toys, and pacifiers nonnutritive sucking. This type of sucking is very important in that it helps babies develop their facial (or oral-motor) muscles for feedings and later for speech. It is also used as a self-comforting tool. Finger sucking increases salivation and simulates the natural way in which nutrients are ingested, consequently improving digestion. Studies with premature babies have shown that nonnutritive sucking assists in weight gain primarily because it calms a baby and decreases irritable crying, thus allowing the baby to conserve calories and use energy more efficiently. Therefore, it's important to encourage your baby to bring her hands to her mouth as well as to put her fingers and safe toys into it.

The flexed position helps bring a baby's shoulders, arms, and hands down in front of her face so she can see, hold, and manipulate objects. Flexion also serves as a helpful tool for frazzled parents. A common tendency in babies is to arch or extend backward when they are upset or unhappy. Flexing your baby during these times can help decrease her irritability.

Ways to Encourage the Flexed Position

There are a number of ways you can help your infant comfortably maintain flexion. While you might not know it, many of these positions and motions are already a regular part of your baby's routine. Once you become aware of them, you can foster their occurrence more frequently.

Supine Flexion

When playing with your baby on her back, place a rolled towel (the size of a facial towel) under her knees and try to get her to bring her hands to her mouth. You can also make a "bird's nest" for your baby to lie in by taking a somewhat larger rolled towel and placing it around her. Make sure you place the roll under her shoulders. This helps bring her arms forward to midline and makes it easier for your baby to get her hands into her mouth.

Side-Lying Flexion

When playing with your baby, position her on her side with her arms in front and hands up toward her mouth. Since they are not yet in control of their movements, some babies may feel lost in space in the side-lying position (feeling that they may fall forward or back). You can help your baby feel more secure and supported in this position by placing a rolled-up towel behind her back. It is important when you're making a roll out of a baby blanket or towel that the fabric edge is placed on the roll's underside (abutting the mattress or floor). This way, the roll won't come undone. Additionally, baby stores usually carry special wedges to help keep babies on their side. One of the reasons newborns like physical boundaries is the association with all those months spent in the womb. You can provide this reassurance by placing your hand on your baby's rib cage (using gentle but firm pressure). Your baby will let you know how long she needs the pressure of your hand to comfort her and help her feel safe.

Prone Flexion

Laying your newborn on her stomach automatically encourages flexion. You can help her into the flexed position by tucking her arms and legs underneath her torso. Her hands might automatically go into her mouth. Do not leave your baby unattended on her stomach at this age. As I mentioned earlier, some babies are not strong enough to lift up and turn their head fully in order to clear the surface to breathe. While some infants can only tolerate the prone position for 10 seconds, others can tolerate it for a minute. Some babies resist being put on the floor altogether. If your baby is one of them, try lying down on your back and placing your baby—on her stomach—on your chest. Many babies find being prone on their parents' chests and stomachs more comforting, initially, than being prone on the floor. Regardless of how long they can tolerate it, being on their stomachs is an extremely important position for babies to experience. We will be returning to its significance time and again as our babies develop.

Common Concern

My pediatrician says my baby should be on his stomach 15 minutes each day. Does it matter if I place him in this position for one 15-minute period, versus a total of 15 minutes throughout the day?

Yes! Very few babies will be able to tolerate being on their stomachs for 15 minutes at a stretch. They are likely to become frustrated, irritable, and fussy. They will benefit from being placed in this position numerous times—whether for a few seconds or a few minutes—throughout the day.

Use of a Bassinet

A bassinet is a wonderful place for your baby to sleep in. It is small and therefore provides more boundaries for your newborn (just as the uterine walls provided boundaries in the womb). Personally, I do not feel that a bassinet or crib area should be used as a playpen. Sleep spaces are for sleep . . . play spaces are for play. That being said, some objects around the bassinet or crib are useful for quiet sensory input upon waking or before sleep. You might consider placing the following items in your baby's sleep area: a baby-proof mirror (babies love to look at themselves and other babies), a mobile over the head, or a tape player with a recording of your voice or calming music.

FIGURE 2.2

Towel Roll Around Baby's Head

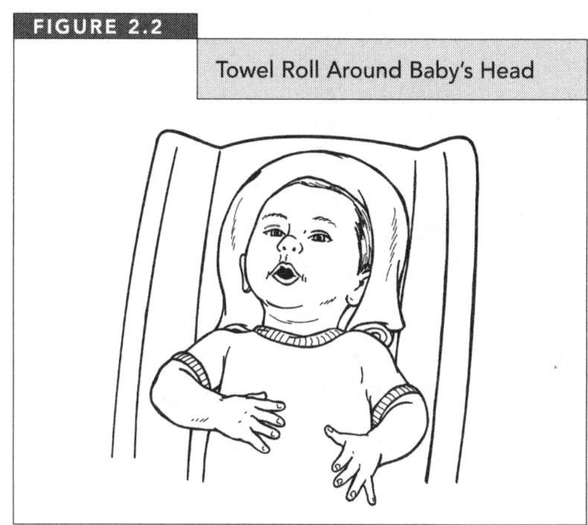

Positioning in the Infant Seat, Car Seat, Baby Bouncer, and Swing

In addition to their obvious uses, both the infant seat and the car seat are wonderful supports that keep your baby in a flexed position. The baby bouncer seat is also a terrific device that I highly recommend. Several companies make them and no one seat is necessarily better than the others. I do recommend that you buy one with a bar across it, either with toys attached or to which you can attach your own toys. The toys will help with visual fixation and will also encourage your baby to bring her hands forward to later play with the toys. The bouncer seat not only facilitates flexion and the ability to bring hands to midline but also provides gentle movement when the baby shifts or when you press down on it. Some of the bouncers have a vibratory device as well. Some infants find its sensation extremely soothing while others find it irritating. (Please be aware of your infant's response. Remember, her behavior is telling you how she feels.) To further facilitate getting your baby's head position to the midline in an infant, car, or bouncer seat, you can place a towel roll in the shape of an upside-down *U* around your baby's neck and shoulders (see Figure 2.2). The roll helps center the head and bring the shoulders slightly forward. Again, this makes it easier for your baby to bring her hands forward and to her mouth.

The infant swing is another nice place in which to put your baby. You can use a towel roll or head support to keep your infant's head in midline while she swings. Some babies find the swing a wonderful place to nap, since the rhythmic movement can be extremely soothing. However, some experts recommend stopping the swing once the baby is asleep so she doesn't become dependent on constant movement. Swings with attached trays can also entertain your baby. Place toys on the tray (suction cup toys are the best because they won't fall to the floor). Just like the bar toys on the baby bouncer, the tray toys enable your baby to bring her hands and eyes to midline while reaching out.

Carrying Your Baby

You can encourage flexion when carrying your baby as well. Keep her head in the crook of one elbow while bending her knees over your other arm. Both of her arms should be in front of you (see Figure 2.3).

FIGURE 2.3 Carrying Your Baby

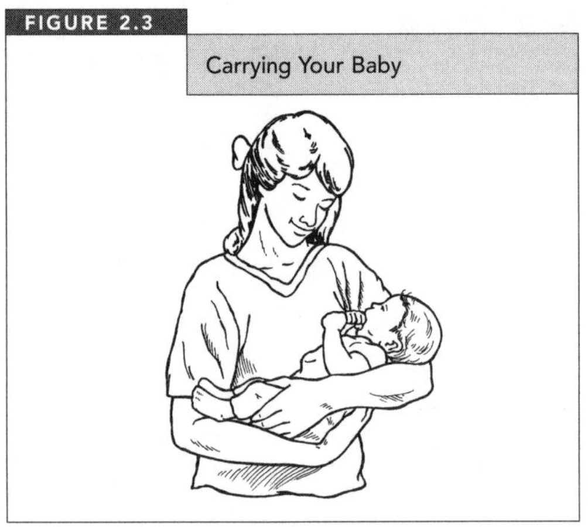

FIGURE 2.4 Carrying Positions (Sideways)

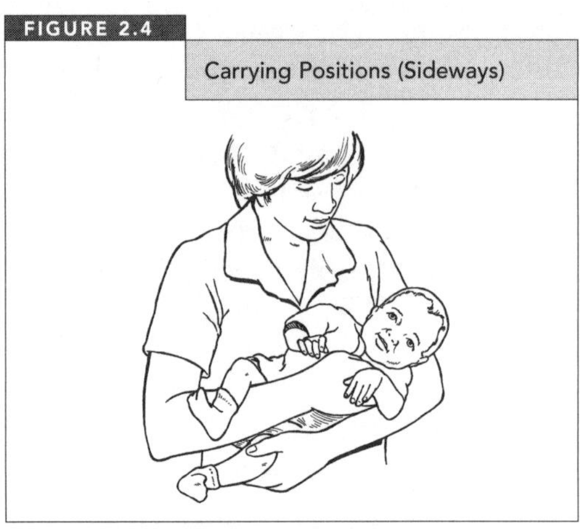

FIGURE 2.5 Carrying Positions (Outward)

FIGURE 2.6 Carrying Positions (Stomach)

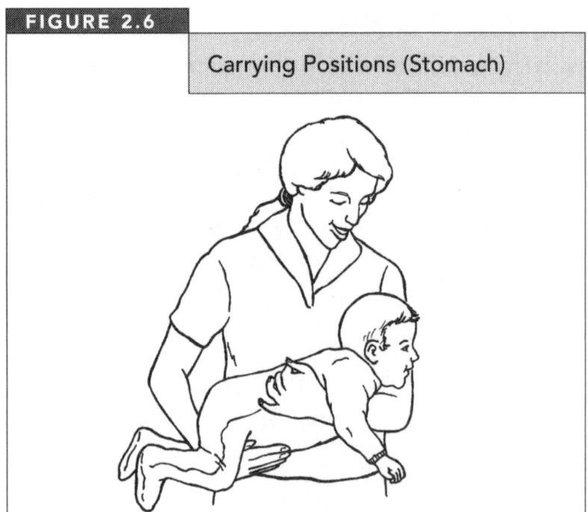

However, you don't have to sit your baby up in your arms for her to be flexed. She can still be flexed with her knees bent while lying flat.

Other carrying positions that promote flexion include:

- Laying your baby sideways in your arms, facing out; bend her top leg up while you are holding her (see Figure 2.4).
- Sitting your baby facing outward in your arms (see Figure 2.5).
- Laying your baby on her stomach in your arms. Make sure to support her under her armpits and belly, so that her throat is not resting on your arms. Rocking in this position—but with your baby moved away from your body—is often very soothing to a fussy infant (see Figure 2.6).
- Holding your baby upright with her head over your shoulder (as if you were going to burp her). Scoop her legs up under her a bit, so she is not totally straight (see Figure 2.7).

FIGURE 2.7

Carrying Positions (Upright)

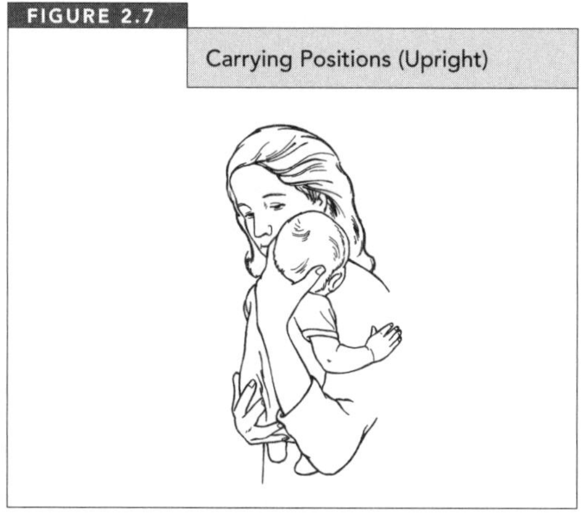

FIGURE 2.8

Feeding Your Baby

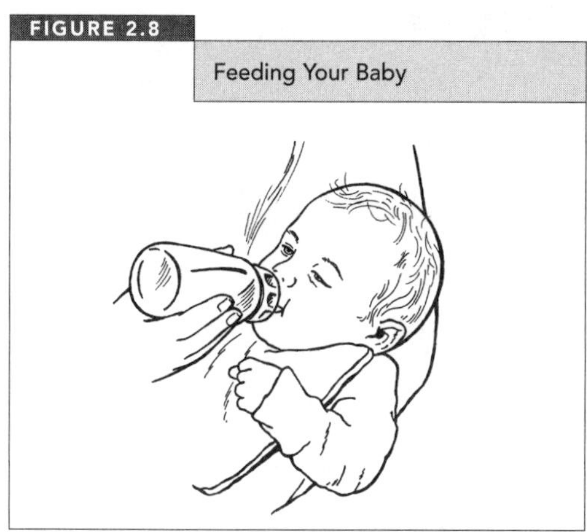

Feeding Your Baby

As a rule of thumb, your baby's head and neck are in optimum position for feeding when her ears are on the same plane as her shoulders (see Figure 2.8). If her ears are behind her shoulders there is too much extension and your baby needs to work harder to suck and swallow. If her ears are in front of her shoulders there may be too much flexion, which could cause closing of her airway. Try it for yourself: tilt your head back. Your tongue automatically goes back and it is harder to close your mouth. Now place your head so your ears are in line with your shoulders, and you will find it easier to swallow.

During feedings, try to place the nipple near her bottom lip, in the middle. Once the nipple is in her mouth, apply pressure downward. This encourages head movement and flexion. If you are bottle-feeding, the nipples that best resemble a breast nipple are the NUK and Playtex nursers (the Playtex nipple also helps decrease the amount of air getting into your baby's tummy and that means less gas). The Advent bottle and nipple and "angled" bottles are also good.

Swaddling Your Baby

In addition to helping your newborn baby feel safe and comfortable, swaddling promotes flexion. Swaddling refers to wrapping your baby so that her limbs are in contact with her body (see Figure 2.9).

To swaddle your baby, follow the steps presented here.

- Open up a baby blanket.
- Place it in a diamond pattern in front of you.
- Turn the top corner down.
- Place your baby on the blanket with her head on the folded corner.
- Fold the left or right side of the blanket over your baby and tuck it under her on the opposite side (your baby's arms can fold across her chest).
- Bring the bottom corner upward and fold the other side over the top and around.

As you lift your baby, the swaddling now forms a little cocoon and provides warmth and comfort for your baby.

FIGURE 2.9

Swaddling

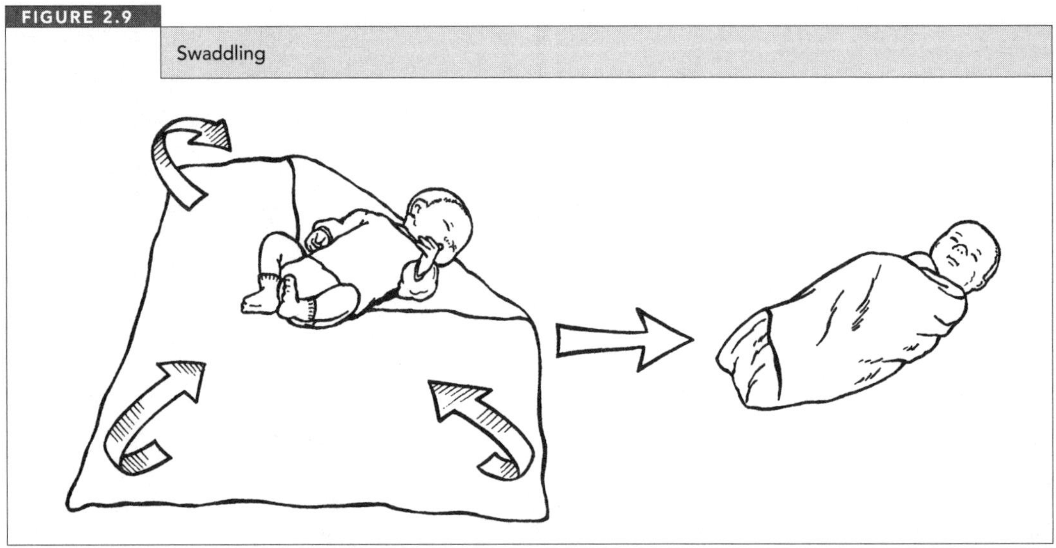

The swaddled position is useful when you are trying to encourage visual tracking because your baby isn't focusing on the movement of her limbs. Consequently, she can better attend to the actual activity being presented, such as visually fixating on you or a toy. Swaddling is helpful during feedings for this reason. It can also help calm your infant, particularly when she is fussy—arms and legs flailing about—and it can be especially calming when accompanied by gentle rocking. Some infants prefer to be swaddled when sleeping because it provides the security of boundaries (like the uterine walls in the womb). For this reason, swaddling is commonly used with premature infants.

Calming Your Baby

Crying and fussing is your baby's way of communicating to you that she is hungry, tired, uncomfortable, or wet. When responding to your baby's cry you are developing a bond of trust and are fostering further communication. On the other hand, if communication is ignored, your baby may develop a sense of helplessness. There are a number of ways to soothe your baby, swaddling being one of them. The following are some others.

Your baby derives a sense of security by being close to you. If your baby is lying down, try to rub her belly and talk to her calmly, or sing to her. Try to hold and rock her. Take her for a walk in the carriage, or place her in the infant swing or infant carrier and *gently* rock or bounce her. This kind of subtle, constant movement generally calms little ones. Do not shake or forcefully bounce your baby. Such extreme motions can cause head trauma.

Hold your infant close to your chest. Listening to and feeling your heartbeat can also soothe her. You can also try changing the noise level around her. For instance, the noise from the stereo, the TV, or the vacuum may cause sensory overload for your baby at certain times. On the other hand, some babies actually prefer background noise to absolute quiet. For these infants, you can play lullabies at bedtime or even put a heartbeat device in their cribs. This device, available at most baby stores, simulates the sounds heard in the womb, which many infants find comforting. One good brand is "Mommy Bear" by Dex. It is a cuddly bear with the sound device concealed inside. You can also find CDs and cassettes that simulate the sounds of the womb.

Engaging Your Newborn

If you were to ask your mother what she did to stimulate you as an infant, she would probably give you a blank stare. "*Stimulate* you?" she might ask. "I just put you in your playpen and you played." Well, times have changed. Floor play begins with your newborn. I tell parents to put a quilt on the floor and get down and play! Of course, that's easy for me to say, but engaging in such play activities with a new baby can be daunting (even scary) for a lot of us—particularly when we bear in mind that total development not only involves physical well-being but mental and emotional well-being as well. Therefore, getting to know your baby's likes and dislikes is extremely important. While infants share many common behaviors, every baby is unique. Take a mental note of the things you find that excite, alert, and calm your baby. Also be aware that she communicates with you and the world through body language. She will tell you the best time for you to provide sensory input in the form of floor play, bath time, feedings, and sleep periods.

There are several ways to tell whether or not your baby is ready for interaction:

- She may have a soft, relaxed facial expression.
- She may either fixate on you or talk back to you when you babble at her.
- When she is happy, calm, and fed, it is a perfect time for you to begin your playtime.

On the other hand, you will want to avoid more playtime if she seems overstimulated:

- An overstimulated baby will avoid looking at you directly.
- Her posture may change—she may pull, turn, or arch away from you.
- She may begin to hiccup or spit up, and she may have a "worried" or unhappy facial expression.

These are all signs that your baby needs some time for just relaxing.

Our babies are able to tell us when their nervous system is ready to handle input of any kind. By observing and learning to read your baby's body language you will be able to determine what causes her stress and will then be able to modify your behavior to meet her needs.

Sensory Activities for Your New Bundle of Joy

Of course, we all love snuggling with our babies in our beds. It's a delightful way to spend time with them. But it is not the same type of "work" for your baby as floor play. She is using her muscles in a different way when she is on the floor than when she is on the bed. Just think of how much easier it is for you to get out of a hard chair rather than a soft one—your muscles work more efficiently. Consequently, a hard surface provides the best base of support from which your baby can activate. A tabletop is also suitable. You can sit in a chair supporting your back while your baby gets the input she needs. (Needless to say, do not leave your baby unattended on a table!)

The best time to play with your baby is when she is fed, dry, and rested. Begin all of your play activities by positioning your baby in the flexed positions explained earlier in the chapter. Play with your baby in all three positions—back, stomach, and side-lying—on the floor. In each position encourage your baby to look at you and to track your movements as well as any objects that you move for her. During back play, move her limbs to encourage flexion.

Visual Input

In general, babies get plenty of visual input through the normal course of development. But we can actively help them along the way. Visual stimulation helps improve tracking, hand-eye coordination, spatial awareness, discrimination of objects, and memory. You can encourage visual tracking by moving objects side to side and up and down in front of your baby. Side-to-side tracking will encourage head turning. Later, your baby will want to track and then reach for these objects.

When your newborn is on her back, her head is usually turned to one side because she can't maintain her head in midline. Consequently, when you are trying to get your baby to look at a toy (like "Red Rings"), strive to place the object in your baby's line of vision (*not* in midline, as she will not be able to see it there). When you move the object to midline your baby will be able to follow it briefly and then will turn her head back to the side.

Try not to place objects above or behind your baby's head. This promotes extension and arching, which we do not want to encourage at this time (especially in premature babies who have a predominance of extensor activity). For this reason, you should hang mobiles in front of your baby and not over her head. Hang the mobile 8 to 10 inches away from your baby and raise it once your baby begins to reach out for it. This way, she won't pull it down in the middle of the night. Mobiles—in fact, all infant toys—are preferable when made of contrasting or primary colors (not pastels) because newborns respond better to greater contrasts in color (our brains are programmed to respond to contrasts).

Smile and talk to your baby a lot. Looking at your face above and in front of her will help your infant learn to keep her head in midline. Also, watching your facial expressions change as you speak to her teaches your baby visual cues that are the building blocks of socialization.

Vestibular and Proprioceptive Input (Movement)

Carrying, rocking, and swinging all provide vestibular input to your newborn baby. This type of input not only is soothing but also improves coordination, balance, muscle tone, and visual alertness. It is important that we provide this stimulation daily, and as your baby grows you will have many other ways to increasingly provide vestibular (as well as proprioceptive) input. At this point, babies are receiving proprioceptive input—learning about how their bodies move through space—through their random movements. This sense comes more into focus in the months ahead, when babies have increased motor control.

When you move your baby in your arms, try moving her in both vertical and horizontal positions (up and down and sideways). See which way is more calming to your baby and which way is more arousing. I have found that holding a fussy baby prone in my arms and rocking her from side to side is quite effective. Let your baby experience different movements by moving her through the air or bouncing her on your lap (or on a pillow on your lap). Try dancing with your baby in your arms. Take walks on rough and smooth surfaces with your baby in the carriage. Be alert to your infant's responses (e.g., is she overstimulated? feeling insecure?) and adjust your input accordingly.

FIGURE 2.10

Incorrectly Picking Up Your Baby

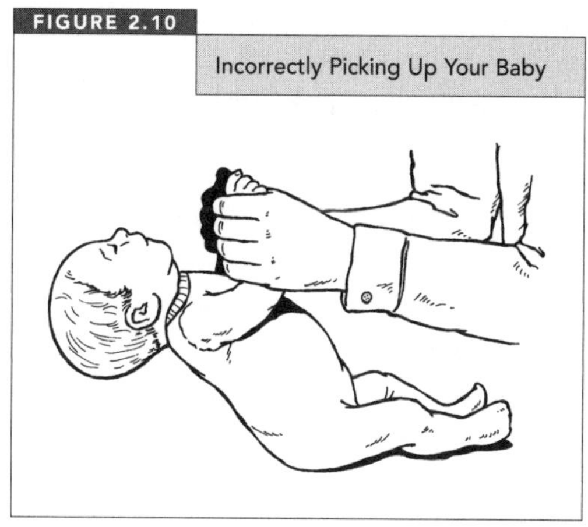

Picking Up Your Newborn

It is never too early to develop good habits. A common "bad" habit of parents and caregivers is pulling when picking up a baby from the floor or changing table. We tend to lift our babies by scooping them under the arms and pulling them straight up to either a sitting or standing position. As our babies gain greater motor control we tend to change our hand placement and actually pull them up by their hands (see Figure 2.10). There is nothing advantageous about pulling up a baby in this manner. Some parents believe they are "stretching" their baby's arms or helping the baby develop abdominal muscles by doing so, but this isn't true. In actuality, this motion can cause additional stress on a baby's neck, shoulders, and arms. In particular, pulling up premature babies in this way can place strains on their neck and back muscles, especially if they have head control lags or delays. Babies with low muscle tone shouldn't be picked up by the hands because it could overstretch the already loose ligaments in their shoulders, elbows, and wrists, possibly leading to either subluxation (the joint moves out of alignment but has not completely slipped out of place) or dislocation.

I believe we first learn this way of picking up our babies in the doctor's office. This is the manner in which doctors pick up babies—however, when they do it they are looking for developmental benchmarks such as head and trunk control. The same is true when doctors stand a baby. They are looking for reflexes and automatic reactions.

There is a way of picking your baby up that is beneficial to her development and that also allows her to do more "work" on her own. It requires one more step. Turn your baby to the side—with your hands around her body (under her arms)—before you lift her up. This one simple step has many positive outcomes. It helps your baby work on head righting (rather than leading to head and trunk extension). It later helps with trunk rotation and lateral protection (a reaction where we put our arms out to the side), which babies develop in order to protect themselves from falling. This lateral protection also allows weight bearing through the arm and shoulder, which aids in improved shoulder stability.

Think of how many times a day you pick up your baby. Just by adding this one step to your motions, you can help strengthen your infant and improve her stabilization by leaps and bounds.

Tactile Input

Tactile input improves perceptual awareness and problem-solving abilities. Studies have shown that it also improves weight gain and gastrointestinal function in premature babies. Tactile input can also be used to arouse or to calm an infant.

Touch

Spend time rubbing your baby. Discover what parts of her body she likes having touched and which parts she doesn't. Think of the kinds of touch you find soothing—too much pressure is uncomfortable, and tickling is arousing (if not irritating) to most of us. The same holds true for your newborn: light touch (like tickling) is generally not as calming as a firmer touch.

Stroking various objects in the palms of your baby's hands helps her discover shapes, sizes, and textures. Try placing a rattle in her hand by touching it to her fingers. Once she gets a grip on it you will need to pry open her hand to get the rattle back.

Something that many babies find soothing is being placed on lamb's wool during play. The wool provides warmth and comfort. In addition, the wool fibers move along the surface of your baby's skin, providing wonderful tactile input. Many families have used lamb's wool in the carriage or stroller. Try using the lamb's wool when your baby is naked, or in a diaper. This allows for greater freedom of movement and greater sensory input.

Massage

Massage is a wonderful way for you to bond and communicate with your baby. Most babies love skin-to-skin touch. A nice 10-minute massage is not only soothing but also provides tactile input that helps overly sensitive babies become less sensitive. It is important to massage your baby daily (even twice daily if possible).

Bath Time

First baths are generally sponge baths until your newborn's umbilical cord falls off. This is of course a perfect bonding opportunity for the two of you. You are providing not only tactile input but visual and auditory input as well. Once the umbilical cord falls off in the first few weeks after birth, your baby is ready for the infant tub. Initially, she might not enjoy the bath. Both parent and baby are new at it and it may be stressful for everyone. So don't feel compelled to bathe your infant at a prescribed time—before bed or upon her waking.

Recommended Toys for Your Newborn

- "Red Rings" (aids in visual tracking and is a good teether) by Early Start.
- "Track-n-Tube" (aids in visual tracking and wrist movements) by Early Start.
- Age-appropriate stuffed animals (for tactile input).
- Lamb's wool (for sensory input); mostly sold through catalogs.
- Baby-proof mirror (for visual input) by Battat and Wimmer Ferguson. They make a great line of toys of contrasting color, as well.
- Toys that display colored lights on the ceiling and walls and play soft music as they move around by Battat, Disney, and Fisher-Price. There are also lamps with cutout shades that provide lovely images but do not produce sound. Carasel Lamps makes a nice one.
- Activity mats by Battat and Manhattan Group, and "Gymini" by Tiny Love. "Kick'n Crawl" by Fisher-Price converts into a small crawl-through barn for later use. Similarly, "Kooka-zoo" by Play to Learn Toys converts into a colorful tunnel for kids to explore.
- Many companies offer textured, brightly colored, and occasionally sound-producing toys. I recommend those made by Lamaze, Brio, Chicco, Fisher-Price, Infantino, Sassy, and Talo.
- The infant bouncer seat.
- Infant carriers by Baby Bjorn (highly recommended) and Snugli.
- Catalogs for toys:
  - Constructive Play Things: (800) 832-0572, www.constplay.com
  - Toys to Grow On: (800) 542-8338, www.ttgo.com
  - One Step Ahead: (800) 274-8440, www.onestepahead.com
  - The Right Start: (800) 548-8531, www.rightstart.com
  - Back to Basics Toys: (800) 356-5360

Choose a time that works best for you and your baby, and then stick to it. When you feel calm and secure it helps your baby feel the same way.

Infant baths are wonderful. Most babies love them. Keep in mind that babies' skin is very sensitive, so be sure to check that the water temperature is right (it should feel neutral to the touch when you splash it on your wrist). Spend time exploring your baby in the tub. Rub the washcloth all over her body. Massage her scalp and wiggle her fingers and toes. Don't forget the neck area. Many babies are particularly sensitive to touch in the neck region.

Feeding

Whether you are using the breast or a bottle, touch your baby during feeding. Let her hold your finger, grasp your breast for comfort, and so forth. Some babies prefer to be swaddled during feeding (for security) while others may fall asleep when

Developmental Benchmarks for Your Newborn to One-Month-Old

Your baby can/will:

- Focus on faces, in particular, as well as objects from 8 to 14 inches away and can visually follow an object in a 90-degree range.
- Imitate some simple facial expressions (like sticking out her tongue).
- Turn her head to the sound of your voice and turn her head away from perceived danger (such as a sudden motion in her range of vision).
- Startle when hearing a loud noise.
- Comfort herself by getting hands to her mouth.
- Be easily comforted and mold into you when being held.
- Turn her head to the nipple when the nipple touches her lip.
- Lift her head briefly off the surface to turn it to the side.
- Grasp onto your finger or a toy.
- Easily move her arms and legs randomly.

swaddled (they need freedom to move their arms and legs when feeding). Also, many babies like it when you talk to them as they suck, while others tend to stop sucking when they listen to you. Decide what works for your baby.

Common Concern

My two-month-old seems to be hungry every 45 minutes to one hour, while my sister's baby eats every two to three hours. Am I doing something wrong?

You are not doing anything wrong. Each baby takes in what he or she needs to feel sated. This amount varies depending on a baby's weight, size, and comfort level. If your baby needs to be fed every 45 minutes, let her enjoy it. Before long, as your baby grows, he or she will be taking in more food per feedings. It's important to check with your pediatrician to make sure your infant is receiving the appropriate nutrients and calories.

Auditory Input

Auditory stimulation encourages curiosity and enhances socialization. Your baby acknowledges sounds by blinking or turning her head to the sound. In general, a baby prefers being introduced to auditory stimulation gradually (such as softly calling her name as you approach the crib) rather than being exposed to a sudden onset (such as slamming the door and speaking loudly as you enter her room).

The Well-Balanced Checklist

What You Can Do: Birth to One Month

- Shower your baby with love and attention. It is important to realize that *you can never spoil your baby!* Babies need attention and love to be happy and secure.
- Get to know your baby's likes and dislikes regarding all of her senses.
- Encourage your baby to focus on you or other objects.
- Massage your baby.
- Avoid bright lights and fast movements (both tend to startle a baby).
- Place your baby in different positions throughout the day—supine/side-lying/prone.
- Keep talking to your baby and be as silly as you want. By the end of the first month she will be smiling at your interactions.
- Encourage your baby to place her hands or fingers in her mouth (this can be used as a self-comforting mechanism). You can also give a "special friend" (one soft toy or a baby blanket that is woven with holes for air) to your baby at playtime. She will derive tactile stimulation from it and it can become a comforting object later on.

Common Concern

I recently bought a toy for my newborn that lights up and makes noises when he kicks it. I thought he would be delighted by this, but it seems to upset him. Why?

A toy that has this much stimulation may be overwhelming to your baby—especially if it is placed in his crib. Seeing a response to their actions gratifies babies, but if they receive this kind of stimulus, particularly when they are resting, it can overload their senses. Just banging their feet on a surface or having you rub their feet with your hands is satisfying—don't overdo the stimulation in an effort to give your baby "the best of everything."

Talk, talk, and talk to your baby. Use plenty of exaggerated facial expressions and feel free to act like a child. Change the range in your voice. Most babies prefer a higher-pitched voice ("baby talk") to a deeper one. However, if your baby tends to become upset or fussy with high-pitched sounds, try lowering your voice and speaking calmly and softly. Overall, use a simplified vocabulary, short sentences, and exaggerated intonations. Again, every baby (and adult) has a preference for what he or she likes. Your baby will enjoy you better and absorb more if she is happy and calm. Read your baby's cues.

Rattles and bells also produce pleasing sounds that engage infants. Also, classical music is often calming at sleep time.

Olfactory Input (Smell)

Smells help an infant identify her mother and also help her digest her milk or formula. It's no surprise, then, that babies like to smell breast milk, sweet smells, and cooking smells in general. They find polluted odors like cleaning detergents and cigarette smoke to be noxious.

Aromatherapy is very popular today for adults as a means of healing and calming. Combinations of herbs, spices, and oils are used in treatment. While an in-depth discussion of aromatherapy is beyond the scope of this book, it's interesting to note that it has made inroads as a treatment for babies as well. Studies are also being conducted to determine the physiological effects of various odors on hyperactive children as well as premature babies in the neonatal unit.

In Conclusion

As parents, it is up to us to provide an environment that is rich and rewarding for our babies. We can—and should—provide them with information through all the senses. If we give our infants a solid foundation to build on, we help them have optimal movement patterns, biomechanics, posture, and overall motor control. Their future body awareness—built on the foundation we provide for them—not only assists in preventing physical injuries, but also helps prevent social, emotional, and learning deficiencies down the road. In essence, then, what we hope to give our children, from infancy, is an early start to a lifelong commitment to good health and self-awareness.

And Always Remember . . .

- *You can't spoil your baby:
  if she is fussing, pick her up.
  She is communicating with you.*
- *You can never give your baby too much love.*

PART 2

Faster than a Speeding Bullet

Your Child's Development in the First Year

CHAPTER

3

Shake, Rattle, and Roll

Physical Development and Activities for the First Six Months

For new parents, the first six months of a baby's life are thrilling to watch. Changes occur daily. Whether our infants are holding a rattle, holding their heads in midline, beginning to roll, or even babbling at us, they are showing us how their innate and random movements are now becoming purposeful, functional, and more coordinated. We also notice distinctive personalities emerging, as we learn to understand our babies' rhythms and routines. Facial expressions that were arbitrary now take on significance as our little ones strive to make their wants and needs known. Instead of frequently startling at sounds, our babies are creating sounds of their own.

Working Through the Developmental Sequence

Most of the parents reading this book have children who will progress through the developmental sequence—from supine and prone play, to side-lying and rolling, to sitting, to creeping and crawling, to pulling up and standing, to cruising. (Children with sensory disorders, low tone, or neurological disadvantages might not follow this sequence.) But what we need to keep in mind is the *quality* of that progression—not the timing of it. I cannot stress enough that children develop at their own pace. Every child is different. As long as your child develops within the general continuum presented in each chapter, please don't worry about specific parameters or time lines. Do take notice of how movements are occurring: Is your baby weight-shifting to both sides? Does he have good head control? Is he using both hands to grasp objects? Does he sit and creep? It's also important to keep in mind that movement strengthens muscles. Consequently, all infants and children need motor activities. The driving force to this movement is the environment we provide for babies. The more appropriate stimuli you present to them, the more you'll be enhancing that critical cycle of sensory input–motor output–sensory input outlined in Chapter 1.

The Importance of Routines

Routines are important to establish at this stage. Studies show that routines help a child feel secure and in charge of his environment and himself. During the first six months, there are three areas where I believe routines are extremely helpful: naps and bedtime, baths, and feedings.

Naps

One of the most important things to remember in setting a nap schedule is to stick to it! Later, between one and two years, you may even be lucky enough to say "naptime" to your toddler and have him march to his room, ready to rest. Schedule outings and activities around the nap schedule—and be aware of your baby's limitations and ability to make the transition from one situation to another. Exposing him to too much activity before, or directly after, a nap is generally not a good idea: either your baby will be too tired and fussy to focus on the activity beforehand or he won't be alert enough to participate directly after. In fact, helping your baby make the transition back to daytime activities after naps is often more of a task than getting your baby to nap in the first place. Be patient.

Baths

Personally, I like an evening bath routine (although many new parents tend to bathe an infant in the morning—only to have to change the routine as their newborn grows). The bath-bottle-book-bed routine works well to calm and settle your baby, even through the toddler years and beyond. Remember, good habits start early.

Feeding

It is important (as well as helpful) to establish a feeding schedule. Most newborns are fed on demand, but they still manage to adhere to a schedule. Generally, they feed every two to three hours—or every three to four hours if they are "big eaters." As your baby grows he will feed every four hours, and you might even have an infant who can

Appearances Can Be Deceiving

A good friend of mine has a five-year-old son whose teacher recently told the parents that he has difficulty holding crayons, tearing paper, and cutting. She suggested to the parents that he might benefit from an occupational therapist's evaluation. The mother became quickly concerned and decided to confide in me. She told me that she was surprised at her son's apparent delays, since he went through all the developmental stages. Yet once I started to inquire how he moved, she realized that her son never really crawled on his hands and knees. He went from commando crawling (what most of us erroneously think of as creeping—it's actually the army crawl where you move along on your belly) directly to pulling up to standing. He also spent about two hours per day in an exersaucer.

What I learned in this brief exchange was that this young boy really did *not* completely progress through the developmental sequence. He cheated a bit. He actually compensated for some innate weakness or sensitivity (or both) and fooled everyone. Perhaps he had undetected trunk or shoulder weaknesses. Perhaps he suffered from tactile defensiveness or vestibular and proprioceptive issues. At any rate, now in kindergarten it is harder to fool people. The challenges are becoming too great. This is a prime example of how an incomplete sequence of development may lead to difficulties later on.

end the day sleeping five to six hours between feeds. Try not to establish sporadic feeding—neither you nor your infant will feel calm or rested if that is the case (and he might be perpetually hungry).

Bedtime

As part of the bath-bottle-book-bed routine, you may want to rub your baby's back and sing a song to him in the crib. Slowly dim the lights and say your good-nights before you sing. For many years I sang the same song to each of my children at bedtime. If I forgot, my baby would remind me with a grunt or a cry, and later on, he or she would tell me. These bedtime rituals provide loving memories for years to come. If, during the night, you need to change your baby's diaper, keep the lights dimmed so that you don't interrupt the sleep-wake cycle.

Your One- to Three-Month-Old's Development

In the first three months, the physiological flexion that we discussed in Chapter 2 is diminishing. Gravity and increased movement are helping to extend your baby—to literally uncurl him from his in utero position. This lengthening of your baby's muscles prepares them for functional use.

Recommended Toys for Your One- to Three-Month Old

While the following toys are particularly appropriate for your infant, they can also be used throughout the first years of his life.

- Baby mirror: Put one in the crib. Babies learn to entertain themselves and receive tremendous cognitive and visual input from looking at themselves.
- Mobiles: From one to three months, place mobiles eight to fourteen inches away from your baby. Once he can reach it with his arms extended, move the mobile out of reach. Also, move the mobile to different sides and try not to have it hanging behind your baby's head. Hanging the mobile in front of your baby's head encourages the desired flexion, while hanging it behind causes extension.
- Small rattles that are easy to grasp: "The Red Ring" by Johnson & Johnson is a good choice.
- Gund snake: It has great texture and sound and is easy to grasp. The colors are also appealing.
- Toys on suction cups: These are nice to have on the tray in front of your baby swing or stroller and, later on, the high chair. They allow your baby to swat and swipe at a toy without having it constantly land on the floor (or get lost on the street).
- Play gyms with overhead toys: These are great visual aids and encourage reaching, swatting, and crossing midline. They are also excellent to help develop shoulder girdle stability and to teach cause and effect (e.g., the baby reaches for a toy, then hears a sound when he actually swats it). There are many terrific play gyms on the market.
- Soft toys: They are easy to grasp and feel good. When you build a tower out of soft blocks, your baby won't get hurt when he knocks them all down.
- Plush toys: All those stuffed animals you received as baby gifts are great for tactile input, hugs, and holding.
- Stacking cups and blocks: These visually attractive toys help establish causal relations and object permanence later on. Plus, babies just have fun swatting at them once you stack them. Later, they'll enjoy stacking them themselves before knocking them down.
- Toys for belly play such as "See-n-Spin" and "Whale of a Tale" by Battat: The "See-n-Spin" is excellent for teaching your baby cause and effect. Babies as young as three months can gently swipe at the clear yet colorful toys while they prop on their bellies. The "Whale of a Tale" is a water-filled play mat that helps babies to weight-shift as they move while playing.

Muscles need to be at an optimum length to work efficiently. Consequently, a shortened muscle is at a physiological disadvantage. Think of your bicep. You do not strengthen this muscle with your arm bent all the way. You strengthen it from a lengthened position, with your arm straight.

Each time you see your baby moving on a surface, his tendons and muscles have to lengthen in some areas and shorten (or contract) in others in order to accommodate the pressure changes that occur on his body parts when he shifts his weight. In addition, these soft tissues must have the proper amount of elasticity for such accommodation to occur. Clearly, then, we must give our babies plenty of opportunities to move, so that they can lengthen their muscles and work on their balance reactions when weight-shifting. These skills won't happen if we hold our babies all day long!

Supine (Back) Play/Skills

When playing with your baby on his back, you'll notice that he can't keep his head centered yet. Consequently, his side vision tends to develop more quickly and he'll be able to focus most easily on toys placed by his side. In fact, even a two-month-old will try to swipe at toys placed at his side. Generally, by three months your baby is able to keep his head in midline and bring his hands to his chest or together. By this time his hands are open and free to grasp objects. Don't be surprised, though, if your baby doesn't automatically let go of something he grasps. Think, for instance, of how tightly he can grip your finger—and how surprised you are when he won't let go! He isn't actually trying to keep hold of you. The truth is, his ability to voluntarily release objects develops after his ability to voluntarily grasp them.

To work on head centering, place your baby on his back. Talk to your baby and use visual aids (toys, rattles) to encourage him to hold his head in midline. Remember, your baby may feel more secure with your hand gently resting on his chest.

Prone (Belly) Play/Skills

Belly play might not seem like a necessary or important activity to new parents—particularly when their babies don't tolerate it for very long. But in truth, belly play is crucial to your baby's core (torso) development. This "little" activity provides the preparation for a lifetime of physical activity. In fact, if there's one dictum about physical development that you take away from this book, it should be "Don't give belly play short shrift!" For the sake of our babies' well-being in adulthood—from their posture to their athleticism to preventing aches and pains—don't take belly play for granted.

When your baby first learns to play on his belly and turn his head to look at something, he will tend to shift or move his weight to the side he is looking at (known as the *face side*). Due to the increased weight on that side, the arm naturally rolls (or turns) outward and the palm faces up, while the other arm rolls inward (with the palm facing down). This outward movement is called *supination* and the inward movement is called *pronation*. This response is an important preparation for many activities your baby will be engaged in later on. Think of all the activities we do, whether as babies or adults, that require supination of the arm—feeding, exploring and manipulating objects, and even dressing.

Try feeding yourself or putting on a shirt without turning your arm.

When playing with your one-month-old on his belly you will notice that his "tushie" has come down and that there is less space between the ground and his hips and thighs. This is part of the body lengthening that occurs as physiological flexion decreases and the pull of gravity takes over. Consequently, weight is shifted from your baby's neck, allowing him to lift his head up a little more, as well as turn it more easily. This, in turn, helps increase mobility in his neck and upper spine. By the time your baby is two months old he can actually turn his head all the way to the side when he is on his belly. This head turning helps improve spinal rotation, which is necessary for later rolling, sitting, playing, creeping, and walking.

Common Concern

My baby doesn't like to play on his tummy. What should I do?

Remember, belly play isn't about doing an exercise once or twice a day for 10 minutes. It's about routine throughout the day—even if that routine is 30 seconds, or one minute, many times throughout the day. By engaging your baby in these frequent, brief periods of belly play, you will help him strengthen and develop. If your baby truly hates being on his stomach, try some of the activities in Chapter 2. Perseverance is the key to getting an easily frustrated baby used to prone playing.

Prone Propping

True prone propping begins at around two months, when your baby is able to tolerate weight bearing through his shoulders and hands. Between one and two months, when your baby props, his elbows are located behind his shoulders. By two to three months, his elbows are in front of his shoulders. Your baby's ability to push up on his elbows when they are in front of or under his shoulders happens once his shoulder and upper back muscles are working more and can support more weight. This weight bearing in a prone position helps extend your baby's wrists, which helps stretch the wrist flexors that have been shortened in utero. In turn, the stretching of the wrist flexors helps open your baby's hands.

Babies need good neck development (head control) for good shoulder development. If a baby can't hold his head up, he won't be able to prop up on his forearms (and later on extended arms). Consequently, shoulder development as well as development of the trunk musculature will be affected. To encourage head control, hold your baby upright and over your shoulder. You'll notice that his head bobs up and down in this position because he is working his head and neck muscles. Soon he'll gain more muscle strength and control, and the bobbing will stop. Your baby will enjoy holding his head up high and taking in the view.

During this period your baby is beginning to have pelvic play. When he plays on his back and lifts his legs, he is using his abdominal muscles, and consequently, the pelvis tilts back. When he plays on his belly the pelvis tilts forward. Try it—you will experience the same thing (and perhaps

Developmental Benchmarks for Your One- to Three-Month-Old

- Smiles.
- Regards face.
- Visually tracks to midline.
- Is beginning to react when you move outside of his field of vision; is beginning to understand object permanence.
- Lifts head and turns it when in prone position; is able to lift head to 45 degrees by two months; 90 degrees by three months.
- Vocalizes *ah, uh, eh, ooo.*
- Bicycle kicks (reciprocal kicking) when lying on his back.
- Brings hand to mouth; sucks on fingers.
- Expresses likes and dislikes; cries when uncomfortable.
- Rolls to side-lying.
- Starts playing with his feet.

Elvis will come to mind . . .). We need this pelvic motion to enable smooth, controlled muscle movements. We also need pelvic movement for our balance reactions to occur properly. When playing with your baby on his belly, you can place your hand on his buttocks and apply gentle pressure downward (toward the floor) and back (toward the feet). This helps your baby use his pelvis as a base of support and also helps take weight off of his face, thus making head turning and lifting easier. Most often, just the weight of your arm is enough pressure to help him out.

Common Concern

When my three-month-old is playing on her belly she tends to push all the way up with her arms straight. Does this mean she is stronger than most babies her age? Is she ready for different activities?

At this age you really don't want to see your baby mostly propping with straight arms. Generally, this means that the baby is cheating by locking her joints. It may appear like superfunctioning, but it really isn't. It creates the same illusion of strength as standing your three- or four-month-old. You might think she has great control, when she is just locking her joints. The reason some babies prop in this manner is lack of shoulder stability—it is actually easier for a baby to lock her joints than it is to prop using her shoulder, chest, and upper back muscles all at the same time. Other babies maneuver in this way because they don't like the sensation of having their bellies on the ground, and they push with all their might to get their bellies off of it.

By three months your baby is actively extending his head, neck, and upper back muscles when he is propping. His legs may be opening more, or abducting. This motion provides a lengthening to the inner thigh muscles (the adductors). Again, the lengthening of a muscle helps prepare it for later use. Your baby will need his inner and outer thigh muscles for rolling, crawling, and, eventually, walking.

When your baby is propping at three or four months, you may also notice that the shoulder blades (scapula) stick out. This is known as *scapular winging* and usually goes away once the surrounding muscles work more. Both belly crawling and pivoting in a circle while prone help develop these muscles and will be discussed in the second half of this chapter. Prolonged scapular winging can also be a sign of low muscle tone.

When your baby is propping on his belly or playing on his back, his feet will rub together. From a tactile perspective, this helps prepare the feet for standing later on. Foot-on-foot play is also important for a baby's proprioceptive development, since it helps him understand where his feet are in relation to the rest of his body.

A Helping Hand: Hand Usage

Little babies' hands are like small ferns—they start out tightly fisted and then, relaxing, open up and spread. Weight bearing in a prone position helps extend a baby's wrists, which in turn helps open his hands. But you can give your baby some additional help. Massage his palms and fingers and rub different textured toys into his palms. The tactile experience often helps relax the hand in addition to providing sensory input as to what it feels like to have the hands open. (Remember, if it feels good, your baby will repeat an activity or motion more and more often.) If your baby's hands remain fisted by four to five months and your baby is not able to grasp objects, you may want to consult with your pediatrician.

Your Four- to Six-Month-Old's Development

During the next three months your baby will continue developing important motor skills. Some of these will be refinements on the skills he learned in the first three months. Others will be completely new accomplishments.

Supine Play/Skills

At four to six months, when your baby is playing on his back you'll be able to see a lot more reaching up with extended arms to grasp at toys or your face. However, your baby may not be able to reach across his body yet—this takes greater control of the oblique abdominal (flexor) and rotary muscles. While on his back, you'll also notice your baby reaching for his knees. This motion helps strengthen his grasp, improve his hand-eye control, and increase his body awareness (especially of the lower extremities), as well as improve his sense of touch.

When you want to work on reaching, place your baby on his back in a semi-reclined position (as in the infant seat).

Recommended Toys for Your Four- to Six-Month-Old

- Activity center: There are many terrific ones on the market.
- Textured books/pop-up books: Lamaze has wonderful first baby books, mirrors, and soft toys (all in great colors).
- "Gertie Ball" by Battat: This ball comes in a small box and you blow it up with an enclosed straw. It has great texture, is easy to grasp with one hand, and is the perfect size.
- Cause-and-effect toys: Chicco, Battat, Manhattan Baby, Early Years, and Tiny Love make great ones.
- Toys that attach to stroller handles: "Stroller-Mates" by Summer are charming. Babies love to mouth them. Taf Toys also has a good "Stroll 'n Roll Bar." Tiny Love has a "Take-Along Arch" for the stroller, which I also recommend.
- Soft toys: Brio makes great ones, as does Manhattan Baby ("The Whoozit").
- Textured teether toys (for oral-motor input and eye-hand coordination): Manhattan Baby and Early Years make good ones. A great little secret in the "therapy" world is using dog toys sold in pet shops. These are fabulous chewy and textured rubber toys—wonderful for a teething baby. (Make sure to buy unpainted ones.)
- Stacking rings (to chew on for now).
- Picture books made out of cloth, cardboard, and plastic: Find books with pictures that your baby is familiar with—these toys will help your baby identify objects, animals, and people that he sees on a regular basis. You can consider making your own laminated photo book using pictures of Mom, Dad, siblings, extended family, pets, and everyday objects.

Your baby is then working on muscle control from different angles. Encourage reaching with both arms (try not to favor one side over the other). Don't forget to work on reaching across the body and to the sides in addition to upward and forward. Don't place objects too high or too far out of your baby's reach—you don't want to promote neck hyperextension.

Whether your baby is in a semireclined or supported sitting position, you'll notice more purposeful reaching with both hands occurring. Your baby will likely be shaking most objects in his hands. He is also able to view objects from different angles by purposely turning his arm up and down (supination and pronation). You'll recall from the first part of this chapter that this movement was passive just a few months ago: when your baby played on his belly and turned his head to the side, one arm turned up while the other arm turned down, or reached up, for an object. Now this movement is also voluntary—your baby has conscious control over his movement.

When your baby is on his back you may also notice a lot of "bridging" going on. Believe it or not, babies can actually get into the bridge position (arching their bellies up to the ceiling with their weight on their hands, arms, upper back, and feet). For anyone who practices yoga, this is a strenuous pose. It's *incredible* that our babies have the arm, leg, and trunk strength to achieve this posture! Not surprisingly, this exercise has the same muscular effects for a baby as it does for us. It works and isolates the hip extensor muscles, which we use for sitting and walking.

FIGURE 3.1

Prone Play/Skills

Prone Play/Skills

When your baby is playing on his stomach you'll begin to see that he keeps his legs pressed down on the surface more often, with better pelvic (hip) control and weight-bearing ability. This is important because if his hips and legs did not come down on the surface, your baby's weight would remain anterior—or forward—and he would have to hyperextend his head and scrunch up his shoulders to look up and prop. In such a position, a well-developed balance between the flexor (front) and extensor (back) leg, stomach, and neck muscles could not occur. Moreover, shoulder stability could not occur, resulting in shoulder weaknesses and compensatory postural patterns. In contrast, your baby's new ability to keep his legs down establishes a more stable postural stance, which allows his trunk and arms to work more efficiently (see Figure 3.1).

A nice activity to work on with your baby during belly play is reaching. Hold a toy low, high, and to both sides. Holding toys to the side helps encourage belly pivoting (prone pivoting). While this sort of pivoting—or moving in a circle—may not truly occur until seven or eight months, you can begin to encourage it. Prone pivoting is important because it works on your baby's ability to weight-shift from one limb to another, strengthens his lateral trunk muscles, and encourages activation of his flexors and extensors (especially in the head and neck area). It is also a prerequisite for crawling.

During belly play you'll begin to notice that your baby can prop to his forearms with good shoulder control and use of the head/neck and chest muscles. He is also likely propping up on straight arms, with good wrist and finger extension. (Now that he has had several months of propping on his forearms, he has gained enough shoulder stability to push up on extended arms.) There is also a much better balance between the upper trunk extensor (back) muscles and the flexor (abdominal) muscles, which accounts for the good posture we see at this stage. That being said, your baby may still lose his balance and fall to the side when turning his head to look at something. Use the fall to his advantage—once he is on his side, you can continue to work on reaching from this position. Try not to appear nervous when your baby falls. Falling at this stage is quite common, and since you're probably playing on a rug or soft blanket, the fall won't harm your baby. Babies tend to become more frightened when they see that their parents are upset.

Common Concern

When my baby rolls to her belly, her arm gets stuck under her. What should I do?

This predicament usually happens when a baby has difficulty weight-shifting and moving her body away from her arm. You can help by placing your hand on your baby's tush and slowly moving her body away from her arm. For example, if the right arm is stuck, shift her weight to the left side. The arm should then be able to move freely into the correct position for propping. Continuing to practice rolling will help. Remember to roll your baby to both sides. Do not favor one side over the other.

You'll notice that, while in prone propping, when your baby is reaching for an object with one hand he can manage to keep the other arm extended. The shoulder doesn't "collapse" as easily. (Try maintaining this position yourself, and see how long you last!) This tells us that the shoulder muscles are stronger, tolerating greater amounts of weight. Indeed, the more your baby turns his head to look at objects (or reach for them), the more the shoulder muscles get to work and become stronger. As your baby's ability to make greater weight shifts grows, so do his balance reactions, which will continue to improve during prone play. Consequently, your baby may prefer to play more on his belly than his back at this time. By about five months, during belly play, your baby is also able to keep his legs down on the surface more effectively. This enables him to push back on his belly when he tries to reach for a toy, which results in his moving backward. For some babies, this is the first indication of independent mobility (other than rolling over)—and some babies become quite proficient at it.

Side-Lying and Rolling

You may be noticing a lot of side rolling going on these days. At this point your baby probably appears to be "falling" over onto his side and then rolling, which is a more controlled motion for him. But as I mentioned in Chapter 1, if a movement feels right to a baby, he will do it again and again. Consequently, the more he practices, the more control he has over initiating the move to his side. In this way, purposeful rolling to the side begins.

Common Concern

My baby is not propping, rolling, or crawling when the developmental books say she should be. Why? She looks good otherwise. Should I worry?

It's important to know that, while the progression of development is generally the same for all babies, the rate

FIGURE 3.2

Side-Lying and Rolling

FIGURE 3.3

Foot Play

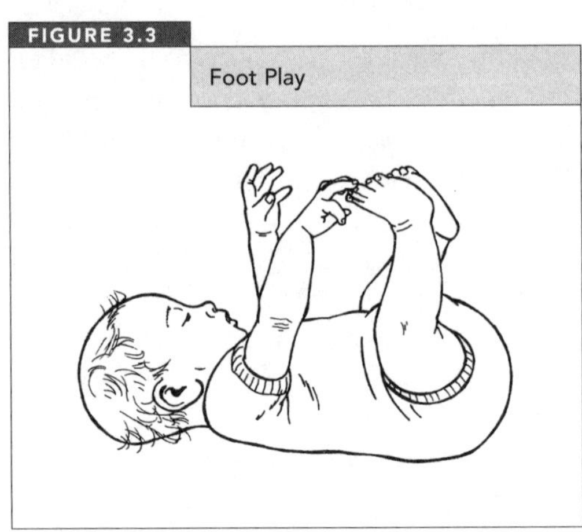

varies from one to another. For example, all babies sit before they walk, but the age at which they learn to sit and walk varies. Some babies also don't like certain phases of the developmental sequence (such as floor play) and, if given the opportunity, will minimize the time they spend in it. If your baby is not sitting by 10 months but loves to stand, then she might be short-shrifting part of the developmental sequence. In such an event, it's important to consult with your pediatrician.

Studies show that infants sleeping on their backs have delays in the gross motor milestones of rolling and crawling (these delays are not permanent—babies do catch up). Nevertheless, it's very important to have your baby sleep on her back because studies also show that back sleeping decreases the risk of SIDS (sudden infant death syndrome). What these studies really tell us is that our babies need to spend as much time as possible awake on their bellies to play—not that we should change their sleep patterns. It's far better to keep your baby safe than to worry about potential minor developmental delays, particularly when increased belly play can be compensatory.

If your baby is not propping by four to five months and her head control is still poor at five months—or if your baby is not crawling by 10 months—you should consult with your pediatrician.

To help your baby with lateral head righting and control, roll him into a side-lying position. As you roll him into this position he will lift his head up to the side. Once in side-lying, his head will remain on the surface at this age. Eventually, he will be able to pick it up from this position (see Figure 3.2).

When lying on his side, your baby needs good alignment and must really use his flexor and extensor muscles. Consequently, the more time a baby spends playing in this position, the better control and balance he will develop between his front and back (flexor and extensor) muscles. In side-lying, the pelvis needs to be in a neutral position—not too far forward or back. To facilitate this posture, you can place your hands on your baby's pelvis. When you slowly move the pelvis back, the flexor (abdominal) muscles will work harder, and when you slowly move the pelvis forward, the extensor (back) muscles will work more.

Common Concern

I work at home and can't always be with my four-month-old. I thought a playpen would keep him safe and occupied. But is he too young to be put in a playpen alone?

If you think you may be interested in putting your baby in a playpen later on, it's actually best to start now. If you wait until your baby is moving around, he might feel as if he is being held back. However, if the playpen is a place he is comfortable in, he might actually enjoy his own private space. In any event, don't keep your baby in the playpen for long stretches—infants do not like to be unattended for long periods of time. Being picked up by parents or caregivers helps provide emotional security. And of equal importance, while playpens are great for providing boundaries, they limit a baby's curiosity—and thus his sensory input.

Foot Play

At around five months, you'll also notice that, while lying on his back, your baby is beginning to play with his feet a lot more (see Figure 3.3). As I mentioned earlier, this foot play is great for desensitizing the feet for later standing and walking. It is also working the critical abdominal muscles. We need our stomach muscles for everything: rolling, side-lying, sitting, and walking. They are what connect our body together, keeping our backs straight and our balance reactions in check.

Pre-Sitting

At between four and six months some babies are on their way to sitting alone, while others are stabilizing themselves by propping up to sitting using one or two hands. Don't be alarmed if your baby can't support himself in sitting yet. Remember that babies develop at different rates. Also keep in mind that you need good abdominal, back, and hip muscles for sitting. These muscles are working hard long before actual sitting takes place. If your baby continues to use his arms for support in sitting, you might consider playing more in the prone and side-propped positions to strengthen the trunk muscles. When you do sit your baby to play, you might need to give him support at the hips, which will help him sit upright and free his hands for explorations and manipulation of toys.

You might have noticed that while your baby has good head control when placed on his belly and when supported while sitting, his head still tends to slump forward if he's

Developmental Benchmarks for Your Four- to Six-Month-Old

- Turns to your voice; recognizes mother and father.
- Recognizes the difference between happy and sad faces.
- Is attentive—listens to you when you are speaking to him.
- Reaches for objects with extended arms.
- Has good head control.
- Visually tracks objects past midline.
- Regards his own hand.
- Grasps objects with each hand (your baby should not have a hand preference at this time).
- Has a growing sense of object permanence and causal relationships. (For instance, he looks for a bell/rattle when he hears it, instead of merely startling at the sound.)
- Plays with feet more frequently.
- Rolls from back to front—may also be rolling front to back.
- Can hold his head up to 90 degrees in belly play.
- Can sit with support or while propping on his own hands.

sitting without total support. This is because the spinal extensor muscles are not yet strong enough to support the head and neck. You can improve your baby's muscle strength by fully supporting him in sitting on your lap—or sitting behind him while supporting his head and trunk—and then decreasing the support (by lowering the placement of your hands on his torso) a little bit at a time. Don't let his head snap forward. By six months, your baby should be in total control of his head movements—meaning that his head doesn't drop forward, snap backward, or fall to the sides.

By five months, you might also see a lot of "swimming" motions (arms and legs moving in the air) during belly play. This is due to the tremendous amount of extensor play going on at this age. Your baby may also like to stand a lot. In fact, each time you try to sit him, he probably wants to stand. This new and exciting activity provides new vestibular and proprioceptive input to him. Although your little explorer loves to stand, *please* do not focus on this activity. It is not yet real standing; it is extensor activation. Your baby actually loves the sensation of pushing into the surface, which activates his muscles to work more. You can provide the same sensation when pushing or leaning on your baby's feet while he is in the back-lying position. In addition, your baby still has yet to learn many important "lower-level" developmental skills.

Finally, many people believe that this is a good age to put your baby in an exersaucer. The common myth is that it helps with independence, balance, and spatial exploration and strengthens leg muscles. I will discuss exersaucers and walkers in greater length in Chapter 4. It's enough to say here that exersaucers are *not* beneficial for your baby. There are far more enticing and developmentally advantageous activities to engage in at this stage.

Sensory Activities for Your One- to Six-Month-Old

The best time to engage in one-on-one play with your baby is when he is alert and happy—for instance, once fully awake after a nap or after a feeding (unless your baby is one who drops off to sleep after eating). Remember to look for your baby's cues that tell you when he is focused versus when he's had enough. When your baby has had enough sensory input, he will close his eyes, turn his head away, cry, wiggle, or even hiccup. Follow your baby's cues and don't overload him! Instead of helping him learn to focus and track, you will only frustrate him, turning a positive experience into a negative one. Your baby will always let you know when he is ready for more stimulation.

Bath Time Activities

At around five or six months when your baby's back muscles are becoming mature, you may want to consider bathing your baby in a real tub. Some sitting control is needed for this activity, so use your judgment as to whether your baby is ready. (You don't want him to slip down into the water—a frightening experience for both of you.) For additional support, use a bath ring. (Safety First makes one that swivels, making bathing easier for you.) Some babies don't like water on their faces, in which case, you might want to use a visor in the tub.

An entirely new sensory phenomenon occurs in the tub. It's a fabulous experience for both of you. You don't need an entire bathtub of toys, however; a rubber ducky and a sponge are great. Your baby will remain occupied with them until the bath water becomes too cold to keep him in any longer—trust me! You may want to buy bubbles and blow some around the tub. Trying to catch them is a great visual-motor activity, and popping them is great fun also. (Babies with sensory issues, such as tactile defensiveness, might not enjoy bath time. Certain products, such as foam baby soap, and some activities, like blowing bubbles, might be too much for them to tolerate. Refer to Chapter 10 for more information.)

Visual Input

At this age, keeping note of your baby's visual development is very important because a young baby's movement is based on motivation, and the primary source of his motivation is visual input. In addition to helping develop his motor skills, visual input elicits communication between you and your baby. For the first couple of months the greatest visual stimulus you can offer your baby is yourself! Babies *love* to watch faces—especially their mothers' and fathers'—as well as to watch your movements. By four to six weeks your baby will smile when you speak to him or show him pictures of faces. By three months, a baby is usually having a great time looking at his own hand movements as well. It's wonderful to watch babies entertaining themselves. Self-entertainment or play is an important self-calming skill that babies need to learn, and it is also great for autonomy. It's also nice to include auditory input with visual input. For example, use rattles. Your baby will see the rattle, and reach to touch it when a sound is produced.

When working on visual input, try not to have a lot of activities going on around your baby, as they will needlessly distract him, and focusing is hard for such a little guy. Remember, pay attention to your baby's cues. You'll know if he has had enough visual input if he closes his eyes, turns his head away, cries, wiggles, or hiccups.

A great position for your baby to be in while working on visual input is a reclined sitting position such as in a car seat or bouncer. It is easier for an infant to pay attention in this position because the seat provides support, allowing the infant to focus on what he sees instead of where he is in space and how he is moving about. You can also engage in visual activities when your infant is on his back. If you choose this position, put your hand on his chest. This gentle, firm pressure helps ground your baby, giving him a sense of security on the surface, so that he doesn't feel lost in space. It also helps keep his head in midline. As your baby's proprioceptive sense develops and his body feels more organized, he'll need less comforting from you.

When you are not directly working on visual activities, it's a good idea to change your baby's position in the crib. This gives him a chance to look at you as well as what's going on around him from different angles and, thus, different perspectives.

Back Play

When your baby is on his back, lean over him, your face over his face. You can use your hands to gently place his head in midline. Then move your head to each side of his face and encourage him to follow your face with his eyes (or whole head) from side to side. Make funny faces. You can also hold up brightly colored or light-reflecting toys—such as silver rattles or plastic prisms—for maximum input. Move them from one side to another.

By two months of age your baby can see the ceiling. To help him focus on images that are farther away, try toys that reflect lights onto the ceiling to stimulate your baby when he is on his back. Overhead toys, like the play gyms, are wonderful visual aids, and encourage reaching as well.

Belly Play

When your baby is playing on his belly, use toys as visual cues—for head righting, propping, and later for reaching. By three months of age you can begin to use "cause-and-effect" toys (see toy lists).

Mirror Play

Place a mirror on the floor in front of your baby when he is on his stomach. Seeing himself will encourage him to lift his head up and to prop. Holding your baby upright over your shoulder while he looks at a parent, a sibling, or himself in the mirror is also a nice way to work on head control using visual input.

Having your baby mirror you is also a great activity. Smile at your baby. By two months, he will smile back at you. Between four and six months, babies love to reach for toys beyond their grasp. Place your baby on his back, belly, and side and guide his hands toward toys from all of these positions. (However, don't actually pull his hand—it will generate a reflex that will cause his arm to pull back.)

Vestibular and Proprioceptive Input

We want to foster development of all body systems, and that includes the sensory system. The vestibular system helps us influence muscle tone and develops our sense of balance and equilibrium. The proprioceptive sense lets us know where our limbs are in relation to each other and in the context of our surroundings. It tells us what our muscles are doing at any given moment. Both of these senses, as we've seen, are developed as we learn to move through space, which is why babies are instinctively driven to move against gravity. Consequently, we want to keep them moving!

For Vestibular Input

Rock your baby when holding him and when in a rocking chair. Also, move your baby vertically (up and down). Also, roll your baby. We are unaware of it, but as parents we place our infants in different positions rather than roll them into different positions. But actual rolling is much more beneficial. When you place your baby on his back or stomach, you are doing all the work for him. When you roll your infant, you are helping him weight-shift, right his head, and work on activating his front and back muscles.

To roll your baby from his back to his stomach, take one leg (this will become the upper leg) and move it across the body—the body will follow. The more slowly you move your baby out of the side position, the more muscle control it will require. To maintain side-lying, he needs both the front and the back muscles to be working. By rolling your baby you will also be helping him perfect lateral head righting (head righting to the sides). Practice rolling to both sides, and don't favor the "easier" side if your baby exhibits one.

Take your baby for strolls in the baby carriage or stroller. The movement and bouncing in the stroller provides vestibular input. Push the stroller both slowly and quickly. And once your baby has good head control, use the bucket swing in your yard or local park. Place your baby in the swing and put his arms over the front of the swing (most babies prefer leaning forward as opposed to leaning backward). I like to bring a burping cloth with me and use it over the front of the bucket swing because many babies try to bite down on the seat and drool. Sit down on the ground and talk and sing to your baby as you gently push him.

By four to six months your baby will have developed good head control and improved motor control. Consequently, you might consider playing with him on a gymnastic ball (the medium, green, 26-inch size works best). Place your baby on the ball, on his stomach, hold his trunk, and slowly roll the ball to the sides, forward, and back. Take your time: some babies can tolerate and enjoy moving more quickly than others. Your baby may also enjoy sitting on your lap for added support, while you sit on the ball and gently bounce and shift your weight. As an added benefit, if you have a colicky baby, bouncing on the ball might soothe him. Playing on the ball is also a wonderful way to activate the muscles of babies with low muscle tone. Continue rocking, roughhousing, and "airplane" rides. All of these games place your baby in different positions to move against (or challenge) gravity.

For Proprioceptive Input

Encourage your baby to bring his hands to his feet. Play finger and toe games like "here is thumbkin" and "this little piggy" or "I'm going to get your . . . knee/foot/belly" and so forth. Clap his hands together. Raise his arms over his head to play "how big?" Try playing "patty-cake." These games will become favorites for years to come.

Tactile Input

In Chapter 1 we discussed the importance of tactile input. How your baby's body responds to various textures and pressure during different movements corresponds to how well he integrates sensory information and forms a concept of his body and world, among other things.

Massage your baby and stroke him. While it's nice to set aside special time for a baby massage, you can give your little one this sort of tactile input at any time of the day. While you are holding or carrying your baby, rub his legs, his arms, and the soles of his feet. Or, just hold his feet.

Place different textured objects in your baby's hands. In so doing you are not only providing tactile input, but also providing information about shapes, sizes, and firmness. This is also a nice way to encourage hand-to-mouth play, and it can help desensitize the mouth as well.

Continue to help your baby experience different textures on his body. Rub cotton, terry cloth, and plush toys over your baby's skin. Continue to place your baby on lamb's wool—now that he is moving around a bit more, he will most likely enjoy how it feels. (My five-year-old still plays with his lamb's wool and lies on it to read.)

If your baby appears sensitive to different textures, let him experience them slowly, on his own terms. This is his way of mastering his own fears. In my office I have a particular toy (a rubber porcupine dog toy) that I use for tactile stimulation or sensitization. While some babies go right over to it—squeezing and mouthing it—others will look at it, attempt to touch it lightly, and then back away from it. They will approach it again, touching it with one finger—and then slowly they'll take hold of it. Your baby might exhibit a similar response to mushy textures (such as yogurt or pasta) or grass and sand (especially when he begins to walk later on). Let him get comfortable at his own pace and don't force him to experience something he clearly backs away from. Try to slowly reintroduce the textures he is not comfortable with. If he has difficulty with them at one period, try again in a week or so. You can also demonstrate on your skin first, to see if that helps encourage him.

Keep in mind that massage and deep pressure also help babies and children tolerate different sensations and textures.

Between four and six months, we can increase our babies' oral-tactile experiences by the various foods we introduce and by increasing the number of different textures of toys and teethers that enter their mouths. Babies (closer to six months of age) love to crumple paper. Let them do so, but be nearby, as they will want to eat it. Your baby will also love to knock over towers at this age. Let him experiment with manipulating different kinds and shapes of blocks that you build into towers for him. Also let him play with blocks and shapes with different levels of firmness (foam rubber and plastic, for example).

Auditory Input

Remember, every baby responds to noises differently. Some do not mind sirens and vacuums while others become very upset when they hear loud, unexpected noises. Consequently, it's important to provide auditory input using different frequencies and pitches. We want our babies to become familiar with many different sounds. Localizing to sounds and having the ability to identify cause-and-effect relationships through sound (if he moves his arm, the rattle will make noise) are very important.

It's also important to recognize your baby's responses to sound—such as eye shifting, smiling, or excessive blinking. (Head turning is a more advanced response to sound.) Since babies move in response to sound, auditory input also fosters motor development. As we know, auditory input also plays a highly significant role in speech development.

Play music for your baby. Soft music is often calming to babies. There are great music tapes for infants and young children on the market. Classical music, in particular, is calming at nap- and bedtime. It is the tempo and rhythm of this music that helps organize and calm babies. If you can get over your self-consciousness and remember the lyrics, sing lullabies to your baby. You'll find it as relaxing and as much of a bonding experience as he does. (And your baby won't care if your pitch isn't perfect!)

When showing pictures of animals, tell the name of the animal and imitate the sound the animal makes. Place a bell around your baby's ankle. Every time he kicks, the bell will ring. Most infants truly enjoy instigating this cause-and-effect cycle and will repeat it endlessly. Use your baby's name when speaking to him. Not only does this foster autonomy by teaching him that he is a person, too (he will begin to recognize his name, and yours), but it also helps your baby localize to your voice.

Place small rattles of different shapes and sizes in your baby's hands. This works on his ability to grasp. In addition, the sound encourages arm movement, midline play, and transferring objects from one hand to the other. It also generates initial cause-and-effect play; he shakes the toy and he gets a sound as a result.

Use musical instruments or toys. They don't have to be fancy—a kitchen pot and spoon make a great instrument. Use your sound-making toys to encourage movement. When your baby is on his stomach or in a supported sitting position, hold the toy in front of him and slightly above him and to the sides. Your baby will turn to look toward the noise. Encourage him to reach for them as well. As he reaches for it, name the toy ("You reached for the bell!").

The Well-Balanced Checklist

What You Can Do:
One Through Six Months

- Develop routines for your baby: naps, bath time, feedings.
- Floor play is key to development. Play in all positions—supine, prone, side-lying, and supported sitting.
- Provide movement through space (proprioceptive and vestibular input).
- Allow your baby to explore toys orally.
- Make sure to give your baby the opportunity to hold and play with different textured toys.
- Sit a younger baby in an infant seat or bouncer for feedings.
- Make sure your baby can sit unsupported with a straight spine before using the high chair for feedings.
- Play with cause-and-effect toys to instill object permanence and causal relationships.
- In terms of communication: talk, talk, talk to your baby. Unless he is giving you clues to indicate that he's tired or stressed, he's always listening to you. In addition to the auditory input, you'll be enhancing his cognition. Smile a lot. You will be amazed at the smiles you get back! You'll also be teaching your baby about causal relationships.
- Continue to massage your baby daily or twice daily. This will help calm him in addition to enhancing his tactile sense. Of equal importance, it provides a wonderful bonding experience for both of you.

Olfactory Input

We all know what type of effect various odors have on us. Since infants' sense of smell is generally heightened, it is important to keep your baby away from noxious odors and to let him experience pleasant ones, such as breast milk, good food, and flowers. Just like puppies, babies are comforted by the smell of their parents, as well as the familiar smells of their environment. Keep in mind that some smells that we find pleasant—such as perfumes, cologne, or after-shave—can be irritating, unpleasant, and/or overwhelming to our babies.

As he progresses in these months, your baby will start to use his sense of smell as a protective mechanism—becoming fussy or turning away from things that are noxious to him such as cigarette smoke or spoiled milk. Remember to watch for his cues.

Gustatory Input (Taste)

At this stage, your baby has started putting his hands in his mouth along with all types of toys—creating lots of anxiety for you. Nevertheless, you should encourage this activity, because all this mouth play desensitizes the mouth, decreasing your baby's sensitivity to food, brushing, and mouthing objects. Furthermore, chewing and sucking on toys helps develop the oral-motor muscles that are needed later on for more developed chewing and speech (see Chapter 5 on oral-motor development), as well as teach about textures, shapes, and sizes. Sucking increases digestion by activating the digestive enzymes and it helps babies learn how to provide their own tactile input. Babies also learn about taste at this age by experiencing the different tastes of breast milk, formula, and water. Along with the sense of smell, taste plays a key role in the introduction to new foods.

Once semisolid foods are introduced between four and six months, both tastes and smells will be expanded. Your baby will soon be telling you (in a not so pleasant way—spitting out food at you) that he doesn't like certain tastes, textures, or smells. It's another one of his concrete ways to express his opinion (fussing and turning his head being other ways).

Cognitive Input

Cognitive abilities at this age are generally measured by motor abilities (banging and reaching for toys) and expressive abilities (vocalizing sounds, showing signs of pleasure and discomfort, laughing, and responding to parents).

Most of the activities we have discussed so far enhance cognitive development. Visual tracking, smiling, and reaching for objects are all signs of cognition. Each time your baby picks up a toy and drops it, he is developing his understanding of object permanence. Each time he smiles at you and you smile back, he is learning about causal relationships.

Practice object permanence: drop a toy. Your baby will watch it drop and, seeing it on the floor, can now understand that it still exists—it is the same object that you dropped. Babies love the thrill of this "game" and want to practice it on their own constantly. And be sure to play "peekaboo." Cover and uncover your eyes as you recite "peekaboo!" Your baby will love this game, which enhances object permanence as well as causal relations.

And Always Remember . . .

- *Do activities to your baby's tolerance; don't exercise him the way we would exercise ourselves. Think about frequent periods of exercise for smaller amounts of duration.*
- *Repetition is important. We may get tired of the same activity over and over again, but our babies don't. Repetition helps lead to mastery of all sorts of developmental skills.*

CHAPTER

4

Sit, Squat, Stand

Physical Development and Activities for the Second Six Months

The period between seven and twelve months is one of great transition. Your infant's growing sense of autonomy, along with the continuing mastery of her movements, will thrill and surprise you on a regular basis. You'll see clearly how your baby's volitional movements now overcome random ones. For instance, she can now reach for an object with one hand while her other hand is busy exploring her mouth, playing with a foot, or rubbing her tummy.

Since your baby's movements are now volitional, her limbs become more functional. Her arms help her to increasingly perceive her world. Her hands are her instruments for life. Indeed, we use our hands to learn (about shapes, structure, and texture and to interpret sensory information); for function; to share our emotions; and for our livelihood. We also use our hands to organize our bodies. When your baby is lying on her back and clasps her hands on her chest, she is organizing and thus calming herself. Even when your baby grasps your finger she is comforting herself. In contrast, when she is upset she will flare her arms away from her body.

Hand and Finger Dexterity

Motion increases dramatically during your baby's second six months. You might even get exhausted watching just how often she changes positions—from being prone to getting up onto all fours, to sitting, and then going back to belly play—over and over and over again. From her initial accomplishment of rolling, to the mastery of crawling and then creeping, then to pulling to stand and cruising, she will finally graduate to the true independence achieved by walking. All this within these second six months! Imagine if you had a fitness trainer who told you, "In the next six months I'm going to get you to bench-press 100 pounds before breakfast, run 10 miles before lunch, and swim 100 laps after that, and then we'll throw in some tumbling routines that include double back flips after a floor pass of back handsprings." That's the equivalent of what your baby is accomplishing—and that's just the physical side of things! In doing so, she has seen to it that her ability to explore her world will now be limitless. This new autonomy will eventually lead your infant into the trials and tribulations of toddlerhood as well as the "terrific twos."

In order for your baby to use her hands she needs good postural tone, stability and mobility, and an intact nervous system. She also needs properly developed hand-eye coordination, visual perception, and cognition. That's a long list of accomplishments for someone who's only been around for six months (and counting). Yet it doesn't have to be daunting, because her movements, themselves, are what help her develop all these requisite abilities. For example, the simple act of reaching and grasping stimulates her brain and enhances hand-eye coordination.

Your baby has purposeful control of her arms and hands before her legs. This development is possible because of the shoulder stability achieved from all of your baby's floor play during the first six months. (In general, we need to gain stability in order to gain mobility.) We get stability in our arms from our shoulders, and we obtain stability in our fingers from our wrists and palms. The shoulder blade provides stability so the arm bone can move. The elbow then grades the arm movement so hand movements can be more precise. The forearm helps to *position* the hand while the wrist provides the *stability* and *mobility* for the hand. It may seem exhaustive to talk about distal (hand) development in such detail, but it's not when you remember how critical our hands are, and how intricate every movement is that we make. For instance, think of the different wrist positions we use: when we write, our wrist is extended; when we eat, our wrist is in a neutral position; and when we zip our pants, we flex our wrists.

During this period your baby's finger dexterity increases dramatically. You can notice the development of her finger-isolation ability. The Cheerios that she initially raked across her high chair tray will, by 12 months, be daintily picked up between her thumb and index finger. Of course, there is a developmental progression of ability—and as with most of your baby's accomplishments, there's a lot more to it than meets the eye. At nine months she may be picking up small objects by using a lateral pincer (using her thumb and the side of her index finger), while shortly thereafter progressing to an inferior pincer (using the pads of her index finger and thumb). At the same time, she may be clapping and beginning to wave bye-

bye. You may be surprised to see that your infant has now become a collector—or better yet, a hoarder—trying to grasp and hold several objects at the same time.

This increased ability to manipulate small objects boosts sensory input by enabling much more detailed exploration and manipulation of all sorts of things that attract your little one's attention. The release of small objects also becomes more purposeful. Remember how tightly your baby used to grasp your finger but then wouldn't let go? Now she can, because the automatic grasp reflex has faded and been overtaken by volitional movements. By 11 months, you will be amazed at how your infant is sitting and amusing herself while filling containers and dumping them out, and how she loves to drop her toys. She is also frequently pointing and poking, and is able to finally get that brightly colored ring off of the stacker! Her inferior pincer grasp has now developed into a true pincer grasp (she uses the tips of her thumb and index finger). Manual exploration now takes over for oral exploration. Your little one also loves to imitate you at this stage. She might begin scribbling away on your papers or babble with the phone receiver in her hand. Give her a spoon and she'll stir her own pretend tea.

First Things First

We keep talking about how important fine motor skills are to physical development and our ability to learn. Before our babies acquire strong fine motor skills, however, they need to have developed the following abilities.

- Stabilization of the shoulder and wrist (from all the upper extremity weight-bearing activities).
- Good thumb development. We need our thumbs for proper grasping, pinching, and sensory preparation for the hand. This means we need good thumb opposition, which occurs when the thumb is abducted, or moved away from the hand, and the distal thumb joint is flexed—think of the position of your thumb when you hold a pen.
- Development of the arches of the hand. Try making the letter C with your hand and noting the position of the palm of your hand. Or note the position of the palm when you are holding a pen. This is an arch of your hand. One way that arches develop is when a baby creeps while holding on to a toy.
- Appropriate strength of the hand and finger muscles, mostly achieved by the many manipulation activities that we do a bit later on, between the first and second year of development (coloring, playing with modeling clay, etc.).
- Touch pressure, which involves holding on to toys with just the right pressure—not too strong and not too weak.

Your Seven- Through Nine-Month-Old's Development

Floor Play/Skills

All of the floor activities that your baby has been mastering in the first six months—and will continue to master in these next six months—help to prepare and strengthen the shoulder girdle and trunk for greater postural control, hand function, and balance. These activities include prone or belly play, prone propping, side-lying, balancing on all fours (or the quadruped position), rocking on hands and knees, belly pivoting, belly crawling, and creeping (which we'll discuss in the section on locomotion).

Prone and Supine Play

By now your baby most likely prefers to play on her belly rather than on her back. This is a good thing, because belly play is far more functional at this point. Belly play increases the use and strength of the shoulder girdle, hip extensors, and the abdominal muscles, which are necessary to maintain good alignment in all positions. Your baby might be pivoting on her belly. At seven months, she might even be belly crawling. Not all babies actually belly crawl, but it requires the same components as creeping on all fours. To be able to belly crawl your baby needs to weight-shift the upper trunk onto the supporting arm, with the other arm reaching forward. Simultaneously, the lower trunk weight-shifts onto the bending (or flexing) leg opposite the outstretched arm. The oppositional arm and leg will move forward when the trunk weight-shifts onto them, and so on.

At this stage it's important to encourage prone pivoting, or having your baby play on her stomach and move around in a circle (see Figure 4.1). This activity is good for the co-contraction, or activation, of muscle groups as well as abdominal control. To encourage this activity, try putting toys near the side of your baby but far enough away so that she has to move and/or reach to get them. Move the toys in a continuous arc (making a circle) in both directions. Be sure not to move the toy so far away as to frustrate your baby.

At around seven months you may also notice that your baby has perfected her balance reactions in supine (back) play. She can maintain a ball-like position without falling over to the sides, even with her feet in her mouth. This tells you that your baby has good abdominal tone as well as a growing proprioceptive sense of where her body is in space.

Common Concern

My baby gets so bored playing on her belly. She fusses all the time. She's much happier if I pick her up so she can look around. Why is that a problem?

For one thing, because babies don't get "bored"—they get frustrated and have short attention spans. Nevertheless, it's critical to continue floor play in order to improve your baby's core (trunk) development. If her trunk is weak, her posture could suffer. In addition, more advanced motor skills—such as walking, running, and future sports activities—can suffer. Part of the reason that low back pain in adults is so prevalent is weak core muscles and poor postural control. Let's try to educate our children early, and perhaps we can prevent them from having excessive back pain later on.

FIGURE 4.1

Prone Pivoting

FIGURE 4.2

Lateral Propping

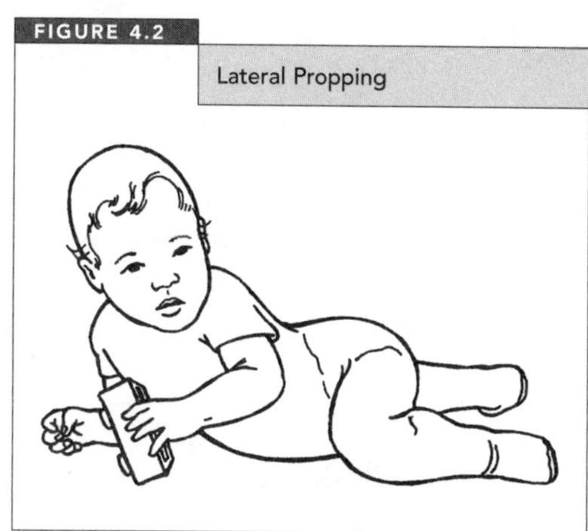

Side Propping

Whereas before side-lying served to work the front and back muscles, side propping now becomes a functional play position. Your baby can now prop up on one arm and manipulate objects with the other, while simultaneously maintaining her head in an upright position and not falling over (see Figure 4.2).

Side propping is a wonderful play position because it requires a lot of weight bearing through one shoulder, nice trunk elongation (lengthening) on the weight-bearing side, and what we call "lower extremity dissociation" (when one leg is bent and the other leg is straight). This posture is also important for pelvic mobility and rotation, which helps to prepare the body for more advanced activities such as walking. It takes great control and balance to maintain this position while playing. If you practice yoga, you'll know this position as a variation of Side Plank. If you are unfamiliar with it, try it. Either way, you'll immediately understand how difficult it is to hold this position. Imagine how much effort it takes for your baby!

Side propping is important for improving shoulder strength and the co-contraction or activation of the flexor and extensor muscles (i.e., having the front and back muscles work together, as described in Chapter 1). If your baby does not yet play in this position it could mean that she is still working on trunk stability, or that she may not yet have enough shoulder stability to support her weight through one arm: you can see lack of trunk stability when she sits and puts one hand down (to stabilize herself) while reaching or playing with the other hand. From side propping, babies often go into belly play, or onto their hands and knees when they are ready.

The Quadruped

Some babies may already be pushing onto their hands and knees, known as the *quadruped position*. At first, a baby's elbows are often locked when she is on all fours. In addition, when a baby is first beginning to get her belly off the ground, the belly tends to sag and the back arches. This is due to weak abdominal muscles or too much separation

FIGURE 4.3 Good Quadruped

FIGURE 4.4 Bear Walking

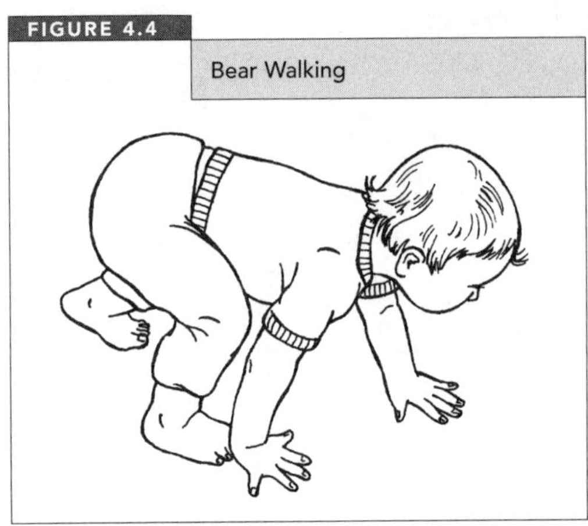

(abduction) of the legs, or a combination of both. But soon enough, rocking on her hands and knees becomes a new pastime, allowing your baby to play with the range of motion of her arms. Rocking provides both vestibular and proprioceptive input to the weight-bearing joints. It also provides good sensory input into hands and knees.

At first, in quadruped, the hips and arms aren't strong enough to support the weight of the body. With time and practice your baby's hip and trunk control as well as shoulder stability will improve (see Figure 4.3). In addition, all the weight bearing into the hip socket helps to develop the hip joint. This development is crucial to the ability to creep and walk. (If a hip socket is underdeveloped due to a birth defect or neurological problem that inhibits weight-bearing motion, it will be shallow. Consequently, the leg bone can slip out of it—or dislocate—easily).

The Bear

By nine months your baby will be able to make the transition from being prone or sitting to being in quadruped more smoothly, due to better motor control and better hip mobility. Some eight- or nine-month-old babies can get into the *bear* position without any help. They push from their hands and knees onto their hands and feet (see Figure 4.4). This is a harder position than the quadruped because it requires excellent shoulder girdle stability, and more control of the lower extremities, knees, ankles, and feet. Attaining this position will give your baby a great upper body workout and will also help elongate her hamstring muscles. Once your baby has started to stand, the bear position will also help protect her from hurting herself when she falls: she can fall into the bear position and thus stop herself from hitting the ground. If your baby is not moving into this position, don't worry. There are a number of suggestions on how to facilitate it for her later on, when she's a bit more mature.

Pelvic Mobility

As with the hip joint, the pelvis changes a lot during the first year of life. For one thing, the mobility of the pelvis increases. You'll see an anterior (forward) pelvic tilt when your baby pushes onto extended arms during belly play and a posterior (backward) pelvic tilt when she plays with her feet during back play. When she begins to side-sit, you'll notice pelvic rotation. Creeping also encourages pelvic rotation. By nine months, you'll see even greater amounts of rotational movement.

When a baby first stands she doesn't rotate her pelvis, but moves it from side to side as she shifts her weight. But once she begins to let go of the table or sofa with one hand, you'll begin to see the pelvic rotation occurring (because one foot externally rotates).

Think of all the simple things we do that require pelvic movement. Just to sit down we need posterior pelvic tilts. For standing up we need anterior pelvic tilts. Both stair climbing and walking also require pelvic rotation, as does turning around to talk to someone or to see something.

Sitting

Once in quadruped, a baby can get into the sitting position, which we will simply call "sitting." This is a big milestone! Remember all of the times you rolled her into sitting? Now she has some independence and can do it herself. Usually she will achieve this by pushing her weight backward over her legs and using trunk rotation to complete the motion. This is when we first begin to see the emergence of trunk rotation, which is crucial for almost everything we do—moving into and out of positions (transitional

FIGURE 4.5

Ring Sit

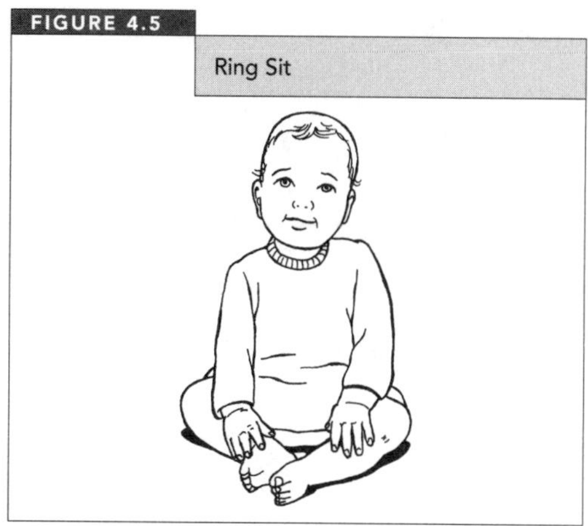

movement), reaching across our body, walking, running, and balancing.

Once sitting, your baby might fall over at first—especially if she shifts her weight too fast. If her extensors are stronger than her flexors, she might fall backward or place a hand out to the side to stabilize herself. Similarly, if your baby's trunk control is not mature enough, she will either fall to the side or put out her hand. This response is known as *lateral protection*. But if her trunk control is good, a balance response occurs, and your baby will be able to sit. In order to sit without falling, your baby also needs strong stomach muscles (to keep her back straight) and good head control (so it doesn't fall forward or back).

Most babies are now able to use their legs in different positions while sitting. However, some babies may still use the ring position (with their hips abducted and externally rotated, and knees flexed, for support; see Figure 4.5). This new mobility makes it easier for your baby to move into and out of sitting. She will still use lateral protection to stop herself from falling over if she is knocked off

FIGURE 4.6

Modified Ring Sit

FIGURE 4.7

Long Sit

balance. Lateral protection also enables her to weight-shift while reaching for an object. Her more developed balance reactions also allow her to reach from sitting and begin to rotate in sitting without falling. The combination of better balance and a freer range of leg motion frees up your baby's hands to manipulate objects—and thus receive additional sensory input (which enhances cognition).

By eight months sitting is usually perfected and is the preferred position. Your baby does not have to use the ring position anymore because she can use her trunk as a way to stabilize herself (see Figure 4.6). You can see her legs moving closer together and her knees straightening (see Figure 4.7). However, your baby may go back to ring sitting when doing fine motor activities (such as working with blocks) for better stability. In sitting, your baby can now rotate her spine with good back extension. (For good rotation she also needs diagonal control through her oblique abdominal muscles.) This newfound ability enables her to reach in any direction while seated and get into quadruped and back into sitting without difficulty. She will also need her rotation for good balance and mobility. As adults, the need for good spinal rotation is readily apparent, as well. If you have ever had the unfortunate experience of back pain or injuries requiring you to guard your spinal movements, then you should know how limited your mobility and functioning can become. Like so many things regarding movement, we take our abilities for granted until we don't have them. This is all the more reason to pay close attention to your child's physical development. By nine months your baby might be stable enough to side-sit and play. She doesn't need her legs for support.

Children with low muscle tone, however, have difficulty sitting with good alignment and with incorporating trunk rotation into their movement pattern. Trunk rotation requires a balance between working flexor and extensor muscles, which these children might not have yet. If your child isn't sitting with legs forward and a straight back by nine months, you might want to ask your pediatrician to check her muscle tone.

Common Concern

I've noticed that my baby always shifts into an awkward sitting position where her legs are in a W. It looks like it must really hurt her knees! Why does she do this?

Some babies continuously get in a *W* sit position, in which their legs go behind them (see Figure 4.8). Children who generally lack trunk stability use this position. By having their legs behind them, they are increasing their base of support. Consequently, they don't have to worry about their balance. However, their pelvises are blocked in one position, making it difficult to rotate into or out of the *W* position, or to rotate while playing. Some children who consistently sit in this position may have low muscle tone and may be delayed in creeping or walking. Sitting in this position can also affect the hip and knee ligaments and bone structure. If your child is often sitting in this position, bring her legs forward and say, "Legs in front" to her. You can also try shifting her hips to one side (with her legs together and bent) and see if she will bring her legs forward from that position. In this way, she'll also get a sense of what it feels like to shift her own weight. After a while you will just have to say, "Legs in front," and your child will shift them herself.

FIGURE 4.8

W Sit

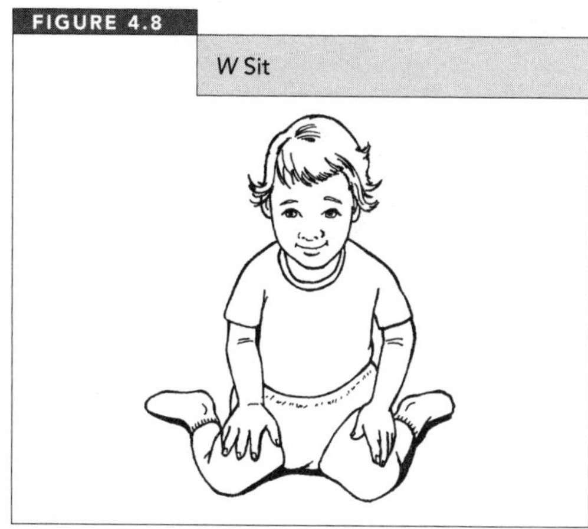

FIGURE 4.9

Baby Leaning Back

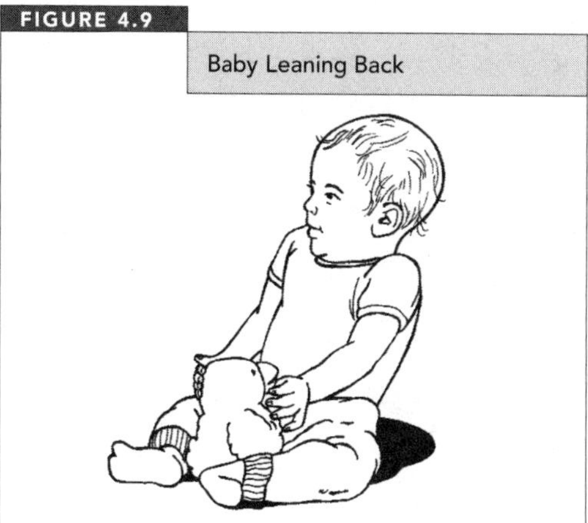

If your baby has a tendency to lean back and scrunch up her shoulders when she is sitting (see Figure 4.9), try to give her some support by holding her trunk and encourage her to reach forward by playing with toys in front of her. Notice if her back and shoulders relax. The higher up on the trunk you place your hands, the more support you are providing (see Figure 4.10). The lower down on the hips that you hold her, the more your baby is working her trunk muscles and balance

FIGURE 4.10

Holding High on Trunk

FIGURE 4.11

Holding Hips

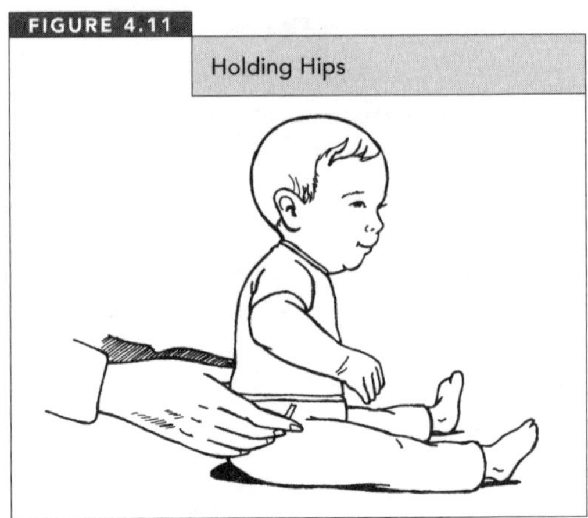

reactions (see Figure 4.11). You may need to rest your hands on her shoulders to gently bring the shoulders down (see Figure 4.12).

Common Concern

My baby's spine is rounded when I sit her. Is this normal?

Yes, all babies begin to sit with a rounded spine. First they prop up by putting their hands down on the floor in front of them for support. As the spinal muscles strengthen, they begin to sit straight and don't need the additional arm support. What we don't want to do is sit our babies too early. Your baby should be using her back muscles properly in early floor positions first. For example, she should be able to prop from her belly and stabilize herself. You should also see good head control and abdominal activation, such as playing with her feet when she is supine.

FIGURE 4.12

Gently Pressing Shoulders

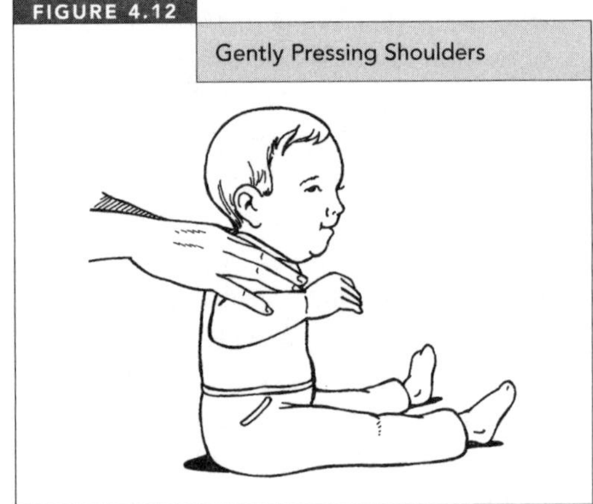

During this period, it may seem to you that your infant either has decided to be a gymnast or is prone to thrill seeking. She loves to thrust her head and torso back against her high chair, or bang into you while you are holding her. This is all part of the strong extensor activity that naturally occurs while your baby is learning about limitations and ranges of movement. She is testing how hard she can push off surfaces and where it will take her. Consequently, she's getting terrific sensory input from her efforts. While all of these forceful movements may be initially nerve-racking to you, just know that her flexors (abdominal and front muscles) will modify this activity by providing opposing force to her extensor movement. Extensor activity occurs before flexion and provides the stability we need to stand. But it is flexion that gives us balance and control. This flexor activation (abdominal in particular) stabilizes the rib cage and shoulder girdle.

Locomotion

Creeping, kneeling, pulling up to stand, and cruising are all types of locomotion that occur at this stage of your baby's development. Remember that what you might consider "creeping"—the act of crawling forward on your belly—is *not* creeping; it's "commando crawling." What most people think of as crawling—moving on all fours—is truly known as creeping, which is what we will be referring to here.

Creeping

From sitting, your baby can now go forward onto her hands and knees (in quadruped) and start to move from this position—or creep. Shortly after your baby has become comfortable in quadruped and rocking back on all fours, she will begin to creep. At this point, many babies are using creeping as their primary method of locomotion. Some babies may even be creeping backward. Actually, this is very common. To encourage creeping, try placing toys out of reach.

Once your baby becomes mobile, life gets truly exhausting for you! Babies on the move are not easily distracted—they hone in on their destination, and nothing (short of being physically picked up) will deter them from their course. By 10 months, they'll even creep out of your sight, relishing their independent excursions while being oblivious to your momentary terror of "losing" them. Turn around for one minute and who knows what infant investigation could be getting your baby into trouble. You'll be on the phone, only to drop the receiver mid-sentence as you chase after your little one who is about to slam her finger into her favorite cupboard door. Or perhaps she is busy pulling at the phone wire you had tried to obscure. More nerve-racking, your baby has now become a human vacuum. She loves picking up the smallest particles off the floor and putting them into her mouth. Candy wrappers, loose change, torn bits of paper, her older sibling's Legos—they all get mouthed and, if you're not quick enough, ingested on occasion. More unsettling, this behavior might not stop for years. Nevertheless, this stage of development is a particularly exciting one for the whole family—and one that you'll boast of and fondly remember for years to come. But if you are thinking that the stages of commando crawling and creeping (not to mention walking!) sound like a vigilance marathon, know that they are all critical stages of your child's development.

Creeping in particular facilitates the left and right sides of the brain working together; assists with sensory integration and cognitive skills; and increases strength and coordination, especially in the shoulders, wrists, hands, fingers (needed for later manipulation skills), and hips. Creeping also puts weight on the ulna border (the pinky side) of the hand, which helps

Developmental Benchmarks for Your Seven- to Nine-Month-Old

- Is able to get into a sitting position.
- Goes from sitting with support (at seven months) to sitting independently (at nine months).
- Indicates wants.
- Responds to "no."
- Says *baba, dada, mama.*
- Creeps.
- Explores the environment.
- Pulls to stand.
- Stands holding on to someone or something.
- Understands object permanence; plays peekaboo.
- Bangs things together.
- Can finger feed herself.
- Holds two objects (one in each hand).
- Transfers objects from one hand to the other.
- Waves.
- Has lateral (sideways) and forward protection reactions.

prepare the hand for later refined skills, such as writing.

Common Concern

I read that babies don't need to creep—that their development won't be hindered if they skip this stage. Is this true?

It's true that gross motor activities, such as walking, are not necessarily affected by a baby's lack of creeping—indeed, many babies don't love to creep and you can't force them to. However, as parents we need to look at the bigger picture of our babies' development. Maybe your child will walk "on time"—but that doesn't mean her shoulder, arm, and trunk strength will be sufficient to help her climb, hop, skip, grasp, and manipulate small objects. Putting a baby on the floor is very necessary to build up proximal (shoulder, trunk, and hip) strength and distal (limb and hand) strength, and these strengths are critical to your child's development.

If your baby doesn't want to creep initially, there are various activities and games you can play with her to help increase muscle strength. We will be reviewing them in later chapters.

During reciprocal creeping—or creeping as we know it—one side of the body is lengthening while the other side is shortening (see Figure 4.13). The body uses this motion for many higher-level motor skills. When abdominal muscles, shoulder muscles,

FIGURE 4.13
Reciprocal Creeping

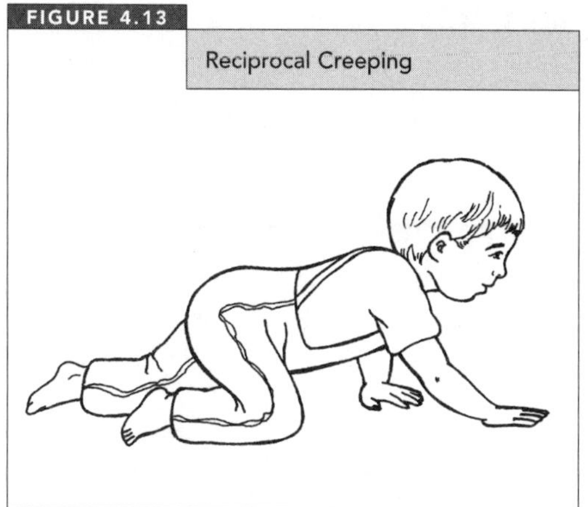

FIGURE 4.14
Unilateral Creeping

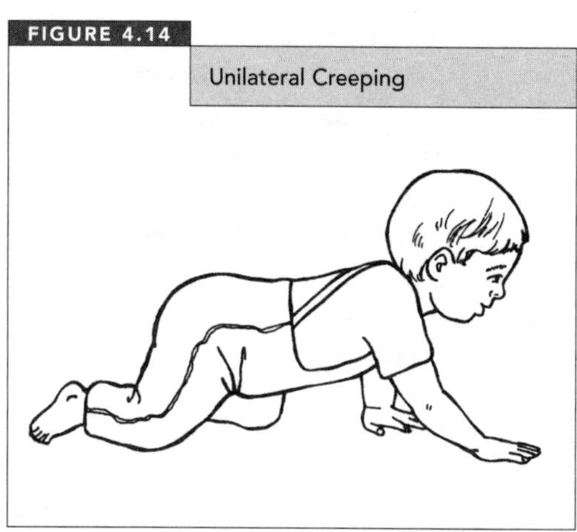

and hip extensors are weak, we tend to see a creeping pattern in which the knees stay tucked under the hips (minimizing the use of the hip extensors), and the weight stays behind the shoulders (thus taking the weight off the shoulders). This does not allow for optimal muscle use or efficiency. If the shoulder girdle can't support the countering forces that occur during reciprocal creeping, a baby might move forward using the same-side arm and leg simultaneously (unilateral creeping; see Figure 4.14). One way to strengthen your baby is to encourage reaching with one arm while in quadruped. It requires control and stability, and practicing improves shoulder and arm strength as well as builds trunk tone and balance.

Babies love to creep under tables and into boxes. So the next time you receive a large package, save the box. You can open both ends, creating a wonderful tunnel or a private spot for your baby to rest in. Watching your baby figure out how to get out is also fun. To encourage further exploration, you might also want to put low baskets or bins containing different toys around in various rooms.

During this period of development you may be concerned about your baby's knees—especially if you have wood or tiled floors. Having your baby wear long pants or leggings is often enough to guard against sore knees. But some babies need extra protection. Putting wrist sweatbands over your baby's knees can do the trick.

A fun activity to work on is having the baby climb over you or objects (such as large pillows from the sofa). This is great for balance and coordination and also works her muscles. It takes control, weight-shifting abilities, and forward movement of her trunk—abilities that will also be needed for walking.

Kneeling

At eight or nine months, some babies are able to assume the kneeling position from quadruped or creeping. They pull up on a piece of furniture, or you. In order to accomplish this they need good trunk and hip control (children with low muscle tone do this activity much later on). Once they are kneeling, babies practice a little "tushie-dance," moving their hips forward and back. This motion works on hip mobility and strengthens the hip extensor muscles that are needed for good creeping and later for walking. If your baby's buttocks remain sticking out in this position, give a little tap to help them go in. This keeps the back straight and works on proper alignment and the use of appropriate muscle groups (see Figure 4.15). If the buttocks continuously stick out and your baby cannot hold her pelvis straight after playing in this position for several weeks, mention it to your pediatrician. Your baby may have underlying low muscle tone and may not be using her muscles effectively.

Common Concern

When creeping, my baby tends to keep her weight behind her shoulders—as if she's a kitten or puppy getting ready to pounce. What does this mean?

Your baby might have some upper body weakness. To improve the strength in her arms, play games like wheelbarrow walking (you hold her legs up while her hands remain on the ground) or airplane (you "fly" her through the air and she lands on her hands while you support her body), or do other upper arm weight-bearing exercises such as bear walking (see p. 66) or rolling over a 12- to 14-inch ball on her stomach while you hold her legs.

FIGURE 4.15

Good Alignment with Buttocks In

If your baby tends to keep her toes tucked under her feet when kneeling, correct her position by putting the top surface of the foot flat against the floor. When your baby keeps her toes tucked under, she must shift her weight forward onto her knees, thus not using her lower leg for support. Chances are she won't have the stability to remain upright and will sit down, with her buttocks touching her heels. In her attempts to remain upright she'll try to straighten her hips by increasing the arch in her back and thus overuse the back extensors to stay up. All these compensatory movements place unnecessary strain on her muscles and joints.

Placing your infant in kneeling too early can cause increased lumbar *lordosis* (an excessive arch in the lower section of the spine; see Figure 4.16) and hip flexor tightness. So be sure to let your baby pull into this position on her own.

Pulling Up to Stand

Your baby may be pulling up to stand. To do so she needs a support surface to hold onto as she pulls up. When babies first start to pull to stand they use their arms to pull

FIGURE 4.16

Increased Lordosis with Buttocks Out

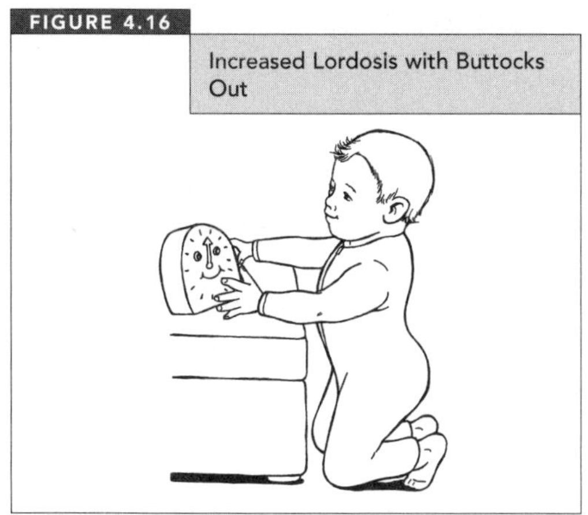

FIGURE 4.17

Half Kneeling

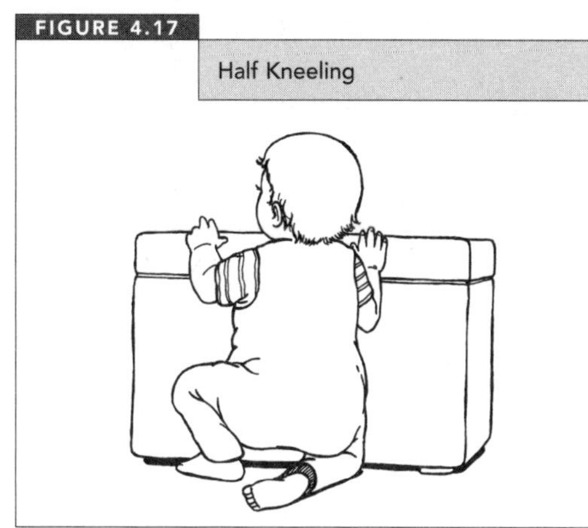

themselves, then they bring both legs up under them. A more mature method would be going through a half-kneel position. In the half kneel, the baby places one foot on the ground from the kneeling position (see Figure 4.17). This requires a lot of spinal and hip mobility, as well as weight-shifting abilities and enough stability to support themselves on one leg. At first, your baby won't have enough control to take all the weight on the supporting leg in the half-kneeling position. Consequently, she'll still need some support to help her pull up. If a child continues to pull up to stand using two legs, she may have other issues going on, such as weight-shifting difficulties or low muscle tone.

Once standing, babies tend to use a wide base of support to increase stability, relying more on their legs than their arms. Don't worry if your baby's feet are turned in or out at this stage. Funny foot positions are a normal part of development (see Chapters 5 and 6). Babies can't weight-shift yet in this position—meaning they can't lift one leg up. Some can bend and straighten both legs (doing slight bounces), while others just leave their legs straight. Soon they will have enough stability to hold the support surface with one arm and reach with the other, thus rotating their trunks when standing. If your baby is not sitting independently or creeping yet, don't allow her to frequently play in stance (standing), as she needs to further develop her core muscles.

Common Concern

Now that my baby is pulling up to stand, she doesn't want to do anything else. She used to love playing peekaboo and hide-and-seek games. Now she just looks away when I try to play these games with her. What's going on?

When a baby stops progressing in one area, it can often indicate that she is focusing on another area of development. For example, a baby who is just beginning to walk might not manipulate toys as often because she is concentrating on this new task.

To Baby Proof or Not to Baby Proof

Now that your baby is creeping around, she may continuously go back to a "favorite" spot such as your bookshelf or a particular low drawer. She might even like one special kitchen cabinet. None of these fixations will make you too happy. Over and over again, your baby will pull the books down from a particular shelf, or take the clothes out of a particular drawer, or remove all the pots from that special cabinet. But try not to say no all the time. Save it for potentially dangerous situations . . . not merely annoying ones. Babies need to explore. If you are tired of putting the books back all day and refolding your clothes, try slightly rearranging these areas. In addition to books, try placing a few favorite toys on the shelf. Instead of clothing that needs to be refolded, place old scarves in that drawer. Instead of getting frustrated, go with the flow. Each stage of development goes by so fast—enjoy it.

That being said, there are other basic areas that you might want to make safer for your baby. You might consider putting up gates to prevent accidents, especially near the stairs. Special outlet covers are available so your baby can't put her fingers into sockets. Many companies sell rubber/elastic siding to put around sharp edges (such as your coffee table). Locks and latches are readily available for kitchen and bathroom cabinets, not to mention toilets. Doors should have latches out of reach, or locks, particularly screen doors. In any event, don't leave cleaning agents or medications within your baby's reach. Electrical wires can be covered or rerouted, if they are out in the open. All toys with small pieces belonging to older siblings should be put away. Stove knobs can also be locked or removed.

There are actual baby-proofing companies that will come to your home, check it out from a baby's perspective, and give you recommendations on how to make your home safer. Most companies can install what they suggest, but much of it will be simple common sense, and you will certainly be charged for their help. If you spend some time down on your hands and knees, you'll see what could be dangerous to your child. You don't need an "expert" to dictate the obvious. But you do need to take the time to address these hazards.

Cruising

Shortly after learning how to pull to stand, your baby will begin to cruise or walk along, holding onto furniture. As with creeping, you can encourage this by placing toys slightly out of reach. Cruising helps strengthen the abductor and adductor hip muscles and also helps shape the *acetabulum* (the part of the pelvic bone that the leg bone, or femur, fits in). Babies initially cruise sideways (facing their object of support); then they begin to turn in the direction they are moving. This helps rotate the pelvis over the legs and activates the muscles in preparation for walking.

When your baby takes her first step independently, she is discovering a whole new world. Most parents can't wait for this to occur and are just as proud as their infant is.

But it's important not to just jump right in and lead her from a first step to walking across the room in one day! While some babies do this, most don't. (In fact, some babies aren't walking until they are between 14 and 18 months old.) Consequently, taking both of your baby's arms over her head and walking her is not really helping her become an independent walker with good posture and motor control. Instead, allow her to push her push-toys or push a child-size chair. This gives her a sense of independence as well as uses her muscles in a more effective way.

While it's a fun activity to pull your baby to standing, try not to indulge in it too often. It might be easier for her to stand against gravity than working all her muscles on the ground—but it's not better for her. Her own abilities of creeping, kneeling, and pulling to stand (and later squatting to stand) are extremely important to her development. Bear with her frustration at working her way through this sequence. And she *will* want to stand more often than not—after all, it opens up a whole new world for her to experience.

You might notice that your baby initially has a "funny" walk—somewhat like a march. This is due to her wide stance, the external rotation of her hips, and excessive knee and hip flexion (which brings her legs up high). As your baby gains better control, balance, and self-confidence, this stiff-legged gait will fade away.

For tactile input, it's important to allow your baby to stand barefoot on various surfaces: the floor, carpets, grass, sand, and so forth. New standers like to explore their range of motion, pushing up against gravity and using their leg muscles in new and exciting ways. It's common to see babies standing on their toes. But toe-walking should not be continuous—babies need to put weight on their heels for proper muscle activation and later for proper walking mechanics. If toe-walking does continue, consult with your pediatrician.

Common Concern

My nine-month-old baby just learned to pull to stand. But once she's standing, she stays on her toes. Is this a problem?

Many new standers begin on their toes. After playing for a minute or so, your baby should relax her legs and feet, coming down onto her heels. If she doesn't, you can help her by gently holding on to her hips and slowly shifting her weight back onto her heels. The sensory feedback from the floor up through the heels might be enough to keep her heels down. If, after several months, your baby continues to stand, cruise, and/or walk on her toes a majority of the time, there may be an underlying reason (such as low muscle tone or an underlying sensory issue). Consult with your pediatrician.

Pre-Sitting, Sitting, and Kneeling Activities

The following paragraphs highlight play exercises that you can do with your baby at this stage. Included here are baby leg presses, sitting exercises, ball exercises, and kneeling activities.

Baby Leg Presses

Have your baby push her feet into your hands or chest while she is lying down on her back. This helps work the abdominal muscles, elongate the spinal muscles, and flex the head. It also provides pressure—good tactile stimulation—into the feet.

Lap Sitting

Sit your baby on your lap facing away from you, while you are sitting in a chair. Hold her near the hips. Slowly lean her forward and back. This helps work the spinal and stomach muscles. You can feel this yourself: When sitting or standing, lean back and you will feel your stomach muscles working. Lean forward and you will feel your back muscles working. When sitting with your baby on your lap, though, try not to cuddle her at all times (I know that can be difficult). The further out on your legs that you hold her, the more work she has to do for herself.

Long Sitting Between Your Legs

Sit on the floor with your legs straight and abducted (open). Sit your baby between your legs. Let her rest her back lightly into your chest, without rounding her spine. When you move slightly to the side, your baby moves to the side. In this way, you can help her learn to weight-shift, with support. From this position, you can also have your baby reach for toys in front of her and to the sides.

Sit on the floor with your legs straight out in front of you. Sit your baby sideways on your thigh. Hold her tummy and back. You may want to sit near a sofa or a wall to support your back. Slowly tilt your baby backward. This will help activate your baby's stomach muscles. The higher up on the trunk that you hold her, the more support you are providing. As she gets older, lower your hands to the hips. This makes her body work more.

Now, straddle your baby over your leg. Have your baby reach for your toes. She can use her arms to help push herself back into sitting while simultaneously using her hip extensors for dynamic spinal control. While your baby is pushing back up into sitting, weight is being transferred through various parts of her feet. This helps to prepare the feet for transitions up to standing and later to walking.

For similar responses, go back to having your baby sit sideways on your thigh. Have her reach down for a toy and come back up again. However, reaching all the way down to the floor may be difficult for some babies to do at first. You may need to place a toy on a low bench or on blocks. This allows the baby to strengthen her back muscles in shorter ranges.

Hugging the Ball

Sit your baby on the floor with a ball between her legs. The "Gertie Ball" (mentioned in Chapter 3) works well because it's soft and easy for little hands to hold on to. As the ball moves between your baby's legs, it works her trunk muscles and balance reactions. When using it, try to keep your baby's knees (and thus legs) straight. If the toes are turned outward, then the legs are externally rotated. You can tell that the legs are aligned straight, or in neutral, when the toes are pointing upward. It's best for your baby's spine when the legs are in neutral. If the legs are turned outward, the pelvis tends to go into a posterior (backward) tilt, which rounds the spine a bit.

Kneeling

Once your baby begins to pull to kneel, it's nice to have a carton of toys for her to creep up to. A great kneeling activity is for you to take a toy out of the carton, place it on the floor, and have your baby reach down to one side to get the toy. She should then put it back in the carton or hand it to you. Don't forget to do this to both sides. Another activity is to place magnets on the fridge and have your baby reach up in kneeling to get them.

Try to get your baby to push Mom or Dad over. Get on your hands and knees and encourage your baby to knock you over. In addition to working core strength and balance, this pushing motion gives proprioceptive feedback into the joints.

For greater input into the joints and to help improve shoulder and arm strength, try doing the wheelbarrow walk with your baby. This puts maximum weight on the upper body. From the hands-and-knees position, lift your baby's legs off the floor while holding her hips or trunk. If your baby tolerates this position, try setting up a tower and have her knock it down while she is in the wheelbarrow position.

Your Ten- Through Twelve-Month-Old's Development

The period between 10 and 12 months is one of great exploration. Overall, babies are more daring. They are always on the go. When they sit, they now have full trunk control and can rotate their torsos. The oblique abdominal muscles are working to give support to the ribs and pelvis. They can stand alone using all their weight through the legs, reach for furniture, or even walk unassisted. They may still tend to move quickly when upright because more balance and control are needed to move slowly. When first learning to let go, babies at this age fall a lot; they are not used to balancing themselves. (In fact, their balance reactions aren't perfected until five years of age.) Consequently, when they stand we tend to see their arms go up high. This means that they are using trunk extension for greater stability. They tend to begin independent walking with a waddle gait (a wide base of support). As trunk control improves in standing, less extension is needed, and the arms begin to come down to the sides. Some babies may even have a reciprocal arm swing (the opposite arm and leg moving forward simultaneously). This rather advanced skill can only occur once the trunk is stable, thus allowing counter-rotation of the shoulder and pelvic girdles.

By 10 months babies tend to focus on their fine motor activities. Earlier in development, their arms and hands were used for balance and movement. Then they were used for reaching and mouthing objects. Now they are able to manipulate and explore objects. Good manipulative skills, visual skills, and thought processing involving problem solving all help your baby's cognitive development. When working on fine motor skills, babies may actually go back to a wide ring sitting position for greater stability, allowing them to focus more intently on the task at hand. You may also notice that when your baby reaches for something beyond her grasp, the other arm goes up and back (the scapula adducts), as if she is assuming a fencing position. The baby uses this posture to enhance trunk stability and to prevent too much weight-shifting (so she doesn't fall over).

Common Concern

My baby is 11 months old and is not creeping yet. What should I do?

Does your baby like to play on her tummy? Is she able to sit alone? How is her trunk tone? Is she rolling, or is she afraid of movement? Do you have her spend enough time in prone? If she hasn't spent much time on her belly, try to do activities to improve her propping in prone, such as those mentioned in Chapter 3. These will make her trunk, neck, and shoulder girdle stronger so that she'll be more able to creep. Also play upper body weight-bearing games (like wheelbarrow walking or rolling over a ball). While she's sitting, have her activate her abdominal muscles by doing the activities mentioned in this chapter. Encourage your baby to move toward objects just out of reach when she is on her belly. Remember that visual stimulation is a great motivator for your baby's movement.

Creeping and kneeling are now used much more often, and pulling to stand is mostly completed through half kneeling. Some babies actually have enough control to play in half kneeling without support. When your baby cruises, she incorporates a lot more trunk rotation and can now lower herself to a sitting position as opposed to dropping into one.

Many babies at this age love to climb. Having a small climbing apparatus in your house could save a lot of climbing on beds and furniture. Many children's stores sell mini castles or tunnel slides. Daily walks in the park are also terrific for sensory stimulation and motor skills at this age. Bring a designated bag with you, filled with bubbles, buckets, a ball, large chalk, clean clothes, wipes, and a small first aid kit (antibiotic ointment, bandages, etc.). Place your baby in the bucket swing. Let her climb up low-level slides and ramps. Put her in the sandbox—even though she will want to eat the sand, keep repeating that sand is not for eating. Build castles with her. Pour the sand into buckets. Carry your baby through the sprinkler. Let her smell the grass and flowers.

By the time your baby reaches her first birthday, she'll have both the stability and the mobility to remove pegs, open boxes, dump objects, and perhaps place a circle shape into a shape sorter. She might also show you her architectural skills by building a tower of two cubes. Her release is now controlled enough so that she can drop objects into a cup. Remember when your baby first started to reach for your hair? You were amazed at the strength of her grasp and the hundreds of times you had to repeat "gentle" or "touch nicely." Now your baby has learned graded control, meaning that she can distinguish between the force of her actions—for instance, between holding a block and holding a soft piece of fruit.

Babies at this age love to imitate. While you supervise, let her try to make marks on paper with a crayon. They also love to rip paper. This is a great way to use all of those catalogs you get in the mail. (Some people don't let their children do this because they feel that infants who are allowed to rip magazines might rip their books without knowing the difference. At this age babies will rip whatever they see if they are in the mood to tear. So use your own judgment.)

Common Concern

My baby has outbursts that seem to come out of nowhere. Does this mean he's going to have a bad temper or be constantly out-of-sorts?

Not necessarily. Take notes on the times that your baby has these outbursts. Is it when you are walking fast or slowly? Is your baby teething? Is it after his bath? At new places?

You will be surprised when you notice the consistent responses that your baby has to various activities or situations. Once you are familiar with his likes and dislikes, you can modify your behavior to help him feel more comfortable. If your baby continues to have frequent, unaccounted-for outbursts, consult with your pediatrician.

Sitting, Kneeling, and Standing Activities

The following paragraphs highlight advanced play exercises that you can do with your baby at this stage. Included here are sitting, kneeling, and squatting, exercises, as well as ball activities.

Long Sitting

Have your baby sit on the floor with her legs out straight. Place a toy between them. When she reaches forward to get it, she will be lengthening her hamstring muscles. If the hamstring muscles are tight, the pelvis will go into a posterior pelvic tilt (the spine will appear rounded). Anyone who stretches in this position knows how painful it can be when the hamstrings are tight. For most of us, that's all the time, so help your child now to avoid chronic muscle aches later on.

Playing in Half Kneel

Have your baby reach for toys while maintaining balance in the half-kneel position. If your baby is not able to balance in this position, she can use a support surface such as a coffee table. Some babies are able to play independently in this position at 10 months while others cannot maintain it until 18 months. Needless to say, this position requires a lot of balance, as well as abdominal and extensor control.

Playing in the Squat Position

While squatting, roll balls back and forth to each other. Have your baby reach for a toy above and below her center of gravity. This allows the leg joints to work in different ranges while maintaining good flexor and extensor control (we call this midrange joint control). The goal is for movements to be smooth and balanced, not jerky or ungraded (see Chapter 1).

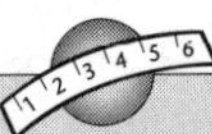

Developmental Benchmarks for Your Ten- to Twelve-Month-Old

- Stands alone.
- Pulls to stand.
- Walks holding your hand.
- Understands object permanence; uncovers toy from under cup.
- Rotates well while cruising.
- Can roll a ball to a person.
- Understands questions in context. "Where is your bottle?" "Where is your shoe?"
- May produce two or three words.
- Imitates activities.
- Uses push toys.
- Points.
- Assists with dressing and undressing.
- Puts a cube into a cup.
- Turns pages of a book.
- Looks for you.
- Shakes her head no.
- Throws objects.
- Can drink from a cup (with some spillage).
- Tries to build a tower of two cubes.

Common Concern

My 10-month-old still does not bear weight through her feet. Should I be concerned?

Some babies aren't interested in this activity yet, and others are not yet "connected" to their feet. If your baby is actively withdrawing her feet from the ground, it's an indication that her sensory system may not be mature. Try to do some feet-tapping games and use deep pressure on the soles of the feet. By 12 months, if your child still isn't bearing weight through her feet, consult with your pediatrician. There may be some underlying issues.

Bench Sitting

Have your baby sit on a small step stool or sweater box. Her feet need to be on the floor (which is the support surface) so they can work, or push, against it. Her hips and knees should be at 90-degree angles. Her back has no support. From this position your baby can pick a toy up from the floor, which will cause her weight go over her feet, thus preparing the feet for standing activities. She can then sit back up again, activating her back extensor muscles. You can also have your baby use both hands to reach for toys or a ball to each side, at about head height. This works on crossing midline, bilateral hand use, and trunk rotation.

Ball Play

Again, playing on a gymnastic ball (22 or 26 inches) is both fun and good for joint proprioception, movement, balance, postural alignment, and muscle tone. Have your baby lie on her stomach on the ball. You can move the ball in different directions and at various speeds. Be aware of your baby's temperament. Some babies are frightened of being on the ball at a young age, or of being moved too quickly.

Ball Sitting

This is a more advanced position than bench sitting and requires more balance. Have your baby sit on a 12- to 14-inch ball. Once on the ball, your baby can do some small bounces. She can also move the ball in different directions to work the trunk and abdominal muscles.

Push and Play

Encourage your baby to push herself on sit-and-scoot toys and to push toy strollers or shopping carts. Toys toddlers can ride on are great for motor planning (in terms of figuring out how to get on and off), balance, proprioceptive input (into the feet), and coordinated leg work. Push toys also provide proprioceptive input, as well as improve balance.

Walkers, Exersaucers, and Jumpers

Exersaucers and baby walkers are popular items used by many parents and caregivers. Over two million are sold annually. In fact, over 70 percent of infants are placed in them prior to unassisted walking. In other words, infants are upright long before they actually learn to pull up to stand. If almost every expectant parent in America either receives one as a baby gift or buys one, perhaps you feel using one is inevitable. However, cliché or not, just because everyone else is doing it doesn't make it right.

Why, then, are exersaucers or walkers so bad? Let me first answer why parents tend to use them. The most common reason is that they believe these devices help strengthen their baby's leg muscles for walking. Babies also tend to love exersaucers, and many parents have told me that they feel their babies are bored when they are not in it. Others have said that they use the exersaucer to keep their baby out of trouble when they can't watch them closely.

Of all these rationales for using an exersaucer, the latter is a completely valid reason. But here's the bad news: While I have never read a study proving the benefits of walkers or exersaucers, there are many studies showing that their use may actually have adverse effects on your child's health or development. One study performed an electromyograph (EMG) on six sets of fraternal male twins at 10 months of age. One twin spent a total of two hours per day in a walker while his sibling had no specific training, but no walker use. The purpose of the study was to determine if muscular activity was different between the two groups. The results showed significant differences between them. Those infants placed in the walker walked independently later than their siblings not placed in the walker. There was also less use of the gluteus maximus muscle (a hip extensor muscle) and of the quadriceps (the muscles responsible for knee extension) in the walker group. Overall, the 1977 study by Ira B. Kaufman and Marcella Ridnour found that "the use of infant walkers modified the mechanics of infants' locomotion markedly."

Overuse of an exersaucer can result in poor posturing that may affect later development. Some of these unwanted positions include head/neck extension, shoulder elevation, and scapula retraction (the scapula adduction that occurs when the arms are in an up-and-back position for added balance). There are also propensities toward increased lumbar lordosis (poor abdominal use) and stiff knees (extended legs). There is weight bearing on toes, which can lead to later toe-walking and overdevelopment of the calf muscles (extensor leg muscles). Finally, the baby's center of gravity shifts forward as the baby leans forward, which interferes with the development of her balance.

Before the exersaucer, there was only the walker. My mother put me in a walker. I fell over and received about 15 stitches over my left eye. I was lucky. Yet upon our arriving home from the emergency room my mother put me right back in the walker. Ironically, while many people acknowledge the effects of activities that may be harmful to infants and children—such as not using seat belts, ingesting toxic substances, and not wearing helmets during certain activities—far fewer acknowledge the number of accidents related to the use of infant walkers. Accidents have included tipping over of the walker, falling down stairs, banging of the child's face, skull fractures, head trauma, tooth avulsion, concussions, broken limbs, and abrasions. There have been so many emergency room visits due to infant walkers that in the early 1990s the American Medical Association (AMA) petitioned the Consumer Product Safety Commission to ban the walkers. While they were not banned, more stringent safety requirements were instituted. Consequently, the walker design was adjusted, allowing infants the ability to be upright but not mobile. The resulting product—the exersaucer—has become the predominant type of "walker."

Although *Consumer Reports* magazine recommends exersaucers, the magazine's nod of approval is based on safety measures (over the walker), not developmental ones. While the mechanical and stair dangers have been reduced or eliminated, the motor and cognitive consequences remain.

Studies show that prolonged use of an exersaucer or walker may affect cognitive development. A child may see something across the room but cannot get to it, explore it, and manipulate it. She has to wait until a toy is placed on the tray in front of her. It is this interference of exploration that may affect cognitive development. Some professionals have argued that babies do catch up cognitively once they are walking independently. However, I strongly believe that vital floor play is missed forever, and all the benefits associated with floor play cannot be reclaimed. Generally speaking, once an infant is upright she does not like to go back down. Consequently, the use of these devices can contribute to skipping of creeping. (Creeping, as discussed earlier in this chapter, is important for upper body development, left and right sequencing, wrist stabilization, and finger elongation.)

Taking in all of the previous arguments, it's clear that the exersaucer is the lesser of two evils. But even with the advent of the exersaucer, the walker hasn't disappeared. In fact, many people still buy both. The exersaucer is large and can't fit into many places, while the walker is more compact and easier to travel with. Buying both is an accident waiting to happen.

It's understandable that, as parents, we all need a safe place to plunk down our babies when we can't keep an eye on them—or even during those times when we are too frenetic or too exhausted to play with them. The problem is the *overuse* of exersaucers—once you start using one, it's easy to rely on it too much. Often, parents and caregivers are loathe to give up its convenience. One mother actually assumed I was *not* a mother because I suggested that she substitute the exersaucer with the floor, a high chair, a swing, and—yes—even a playpen. She was outraged. "Anyone with children the same age as my twins knows how bored they get with the same toys, or with being in one position—and how frustrated they get when they are on the floor. As for the swing idea, *you* can try to lull my child to sleep as an alternative to his boredom. I find that ridiculous." So do I. As a mother, I do realize that one cannot provide input or entertain a baby all day long. But between feeding time, naptime, dressing, changing, and bedtime we need to find some amounts of playtime throughout the day. When we can't play one-on-one with our babies, we can use alternatives to the exersaucer. I did not place either of my babies in the exersaucer and I never assumed they were bored because of it. I can't stress enough one of the core tenets of this book: having the ability to explore the environment enhances cognitive and motor development. Please do not deprive your baby of her floor play. There are, of course, excellent alternatives to using an exersaucer or walker. Try leaving your baby on the floor while keeping an eye on her. Use a playpen or a gated area for safe play. And, finally, try using the baby swing.

Door jumpers offer problems similar to those of exersaucers or walkers. Parents tend to put very young infants in them, usually when their baby is not yet sitting or creeping. Allowing a baby to be upright at this age causes her extensor muscles to be overdeveloped in addition to the postural issues noted earlier with exersaucers. Therefore, there is no developmental advantage to using a door jumper.

Lest you think I'm alone in my point of view, here's a word from a pediatrician who relocated her family from a city to a suburb: "I have never seen so many parents with so many gadgets to sit their babies in. When do these kids have a chance to move and develop?" She was referring to a typical day in the life of a baby—going from the infant seat to the car seat to the shopping cart, back to the car seat, back home, and then being placed in an exersaucer or swing or walker—and later taken out again to go for a ride in the stroller. Think about it, and see if you are overusing these devices in caring for your little one.

Sensory Activities for Your Seven- to Twelve-Month-Old

At this age it's still very important to use sensory activities to continue development of your infant's visual and cognitive abilities as well as her vestibular and proprioceptive senses. Touch, hearing, taste, and smell are all developing at a rapid pace.

Visual and Cognitive Input

Babies at this age are visually oriented—it is what they see that helps to motivate them to move and explore. They will examine an object's size, shape, and texture, and they are beginning to understand that objects have sides (front/back, top/bottom). Continue to read to your baby daily. This enhances not only visual input but also auditory input, memory, and hand-eye coordination (babies are beginning to point to the pictures). At this age, your baby loves to drop items and then look to see where they went. To demonstrate object permanence, hide toys under a cloth, or block them with some obstacle, and see if your baby can figure out how to find or get the toy. By eight months, your baby should be able to find a hidden toy in your closet or inside a pot with a lid. Your baby will happily engage in social games now—play puppet and peekaboo games with her.

At this point you will have been making sounds for your baby to imitate, which also serves as a form of social interaction. Now you can add the physical component and hand her a toy. She'll want to keep it. Coax her to hand it back. Then give it back to her, and so on. By nine months, a baby understands the purpose of an object: a cup is for drinking, a rattle makes noise. You can place any number of objects in front of your baby and help her make the appropriate associations.

Vestibular and Proprioceptive Input

Your baby is improving her proprioceptive and vestibular senses through her movements on the ground and through space. She is learning about her limitations in range of motion, as well as her body in relation to other objects. So move with your baby!

As long as you aren't abrupt, engage in roughhouse play with your baby. Most parents (especially mothers) worry about this type of play. But in truth, babies love to flow through the air or to be rocked quickly from side to side. Dance while holding your baby. Hold your baby on your lap and move her both up and down and laterally (side to side). Play "airplane" and "seesaw" with your baby. While lying on the floor, have your baby on top of you and hold and rock her. Play "this little piggy" with your baby's toes to increase awareness of her feet.

Give your baby a pony ride: sit in a chair with your legs crossed, put your baby on your ankle, hold her hands, and raise and lower your leg. If you feel comfortable, give your baby a ride on your shoulders. Babies and toddlers love this vantage point and it's good for balance and trunk control. Play "rock the baby" by using a sheet: place your baby in the middle of the sheet. Hold both ends up (you need two people to do this) and gently rock your baby and sing songs. Or push balls, cars, and other wheeled toys. Play with different size balls, and begin throwing the ball back and forth. This is good for balance, coordination, and interactive play. At 12 months, your baby might enjoy swimming classes. Swimming is a wonderful activity to promote movement, sensation, and proprioceptive and vestibular awareness, as well as socialization and bonding for the two of you.

Tactile Input

To help your baby enjoy the sense of touch, continue to massage her daily. Let your baby self-initiate touch with her hands. Place objects in her hands and on her feet and stomach. Place pressure on the soles of her feet and palms of her hands (especially if she appears sensitive to touch). Continue to give her new experiences of textures—different types of rugs, grass, mud, and so forth.

At this age, your baby is not just holding and mouthing objects. She is actually able to rotate objects in her hand (which means she can purposefully turn her hand upward and supinate the arm). Encourage fine motor activities and enhance fine motor skills by increasing your baby's awareness of her hands and body. Playing in midline helps accomplish this. You also want to increase hand-eye coordination, as well as increase her exploration of objects through manipulation of them (which will improve her bilateral hand use). Let your baby have the opportunity to hold small objects to explore, throw, bang, drop, twist, squeeze, and shake. Self-feeding also enhances fine motor skills. Let your baby bang a pot or two—banging is great for midline play, bilateral upper extremity use, and eye convergence. Vertical—or up-and-down—banging will occur before your baby will bang two objects together.

You can also work on the following motor skills. Filling and dumping are good for hand-eye coordination and size awareness. Have your baby pour and stack. (Infants at this age are just beginning to stack; elaborate "cities" come later.) Fit appropriately sized beads together (the plastic pop beads are great) and pull them apart. Have her pick up and hold two objects (one in each hand). Try finger painting by putting yogurt or spaghetti on the high chair tray and letting your baby smear it all over—a Picasso in the making! Let your baby play with all kinds of foods—from ice to pasta. This is great for exploring textures, as well as for enhancing fine motor skills and exploration. Your baby can press levers and turn knobs (at this age babies love to explore and master things). Put Cheerios in a small jar or container and have your baby figure out how to get the Cheerios out to eat. Practice cup drinking. Create poking activities by poking holes in the top of a cardboard egg carton and having your baby poke her fingers through the holes. Use a peg board—putting the pegs into the holes helps isolate your baby's index finger from the rest of her hand.

Auditory Input

Enhancing your baby's auditory input is essential at this age. Continue to talk to your baby. Imitate her sounds and ask her to imitate yours. Again, read to her every day for *short* periods of time—she also wants to be on the move. Label and point at all objects and body parts as they come into context. It is also nice to begin to talk about the sequence of events—or point out details—to your baby. For example, rather than saying, "Let's change your diaper," say, "We are going to change your diaper. First we need to pull off your pants; next we need to open the diaper, then clean you, dry you, put the new diaper on, and then get you dressed." Instead of saying, "Look at that picture," say, "Look at the blue sky in that picture and at the girl's face."

Gustatory and Olfactory Input

At this age, your baby's senses of taste and smell are expanding rapidly. The introduction of new foods on a regular basis is a constant source of sensory input. Remember, though, that it's important to watch for any

Recommended Toys for Your Seven- to Twelve-Month-Old

- Cause-and-effect toys: Pop-up boxes and spinning tops.
- Toys your baby can ride for balance, coordination, and a sense of adventure. I prefer the ones with a narrow base that your baby's legs can fit over while her feet can reach the ground.
- Push toys to encourage walking and that give a sense of accomplishment. (Appropriate for babies who are pulling up to stand, cruising, and showing a desire to move forward.)
- Activity tables to pull up on and play.
- Cubes and cups for stacking.
- Stacking rings.
- Dolls.
- Plush animals (both large and small for tactile input, hugs, and imitative play).
- Books: Flap books, peekaboo books, alphabet books, picture books—colors, farms, and animals.
- Musical instruments for listening and imitative skills.
- Musical tapes with children's songs (Raffi; Joanie Bartels; Tim Cain's *Travelin' Magic*, *Lullaby Magic*, and *Dancin' Magic* tapes; *Baby Dance*—a toddler's jump on the classics).
- Bubbles: Good for visual skills and cause-and-effect play.

adverse reactions following the introduction of any new food.

The Soles of Our Existence: Your Baby's Foot Development

Throughout Chapters 3 and 4 we have talked about different activities that help prepare the feet for later walking: Each time your baby plays with her feet, bends them to fit into her mouth, or bangs them on the floor, tactile and proprioceptive input is occurring. Each time your baby rolls over her foot, sits on her feet, or uses them for support (when she is side propping, kneeling, or crawling) she is helping to shape her feet.

A child's foot is very different from an adult's foot. Besides being smaller, it is flatter and more flexible. Its arch is hard to detect due to the thick, fat pad that covers the sole of the foot. (In addition, the arch may be low until about age three.) Your child's foot undergoes many changes, resulting in foot positions that can make her appear bowlegged, knock-kneed, pigeon-toed, or flat-footed. In fact, most babies will appear bowlegged until about 15 to 20 months of age. Once your child starts to stand, she toes out in order to increase her base of support and help with her balance. As she begins to walk, your toddler's feet will straighten out. During the various stages of growth and development, some children become knock-kneed but self-correct by five to seven years of age.

Continue having your baby play in bare feet to help strengthen all of her foot muscles.

The Well-Balanced Checklist

What You Can Do:
Seven to Twelve Months

- Continue to massage your baby.
- Continue all floor activities.
- Encourage creeping.
- Concentrate on weight-bearing activities, especially for the upper body.
- Play a lot of reaching games while your baby is on her hands and knees (quadruped).
- Try to incorporate sitting activities into daily routines.
- Remember not to stand your baby frequently—let her pull to stand.
- Try to avoid the "exersaucer trap."
- Sensitize your baby's feet to different surfaces.
- Encourage manipulation skills.
- Try to make daily outings to a local park.
- Encourage finger feeding and open cup drinking with your guidance (you can introduce open cup drinking at seven to eight months).

It also helps develop balance reactions in the feet. In addition, riding on scooter toys helps strengthen the foot muscles. Try not to have your baby wear socks—they are slippery and can cause her to fall. It's also difficult to work on balance reactions when wearing socks. Skid-proof booties can be worn on cold floors. Finally, massage your baby's feet—it does more than soothe tired little muscles; it helps provide tactile input to feet that might otherwise be hypo- or hypersensitive to touch.

Developmental Warning Signs in the First Year

The following warning signs are often indicative of low muscle tone and can also be symptomatic of sensory integration issues. If your baby is exhibiting a number of these behaviors, you should increase your vigilance over her motor skills and sensory input. It's important to find out why these delays could be occurring.

- Early rolling at one to two months. (Can indicate that your baby does not like the feel of the surface or is sensitive to a particular position.)
- Your baby's head is not able to stay in midline (the head rolls to the side) by a few months of age.
- Her hands are mostly fisted.
- She cannot extend her arms to reach.
- She reaches or grasps with the same arm continuously.
- She exhibits hand dominance prior to 18 months (may be indicative of weakness on one side).
- She does not roll.
- When she brings her feet to her mouth while playing on her back (at five or six months), her legs stay very externally rotated. This is cheating; your baby is

not getting a good stretch of the hamstrings, and not really working her stomach muscles.

- She curls her toes under frequently when sitting and when standing. (Curling of the toes is often a sign of using increased tension in the legs to compensate for low trunk tone, or of inadequate balance reactions.)
- She pulls to stand when you try to sit her (she wants to be standing instead of sitting).
- She frequently sits in *W* position.
- Rather than creeping, your baby is bunny hopping (moving both legs forward at the same time rather than one at a time).
- She continuously creeps with her hands fisted and/or her feet off the surface to avoid touching the surface.
- She persistently walks on her toes instead of bearing weight through the soles of her feet.
- She has difficulty progressing from semisolid to solid foods, or may not chew table foods presented to her.

And Always Remember . . .

- *As frustrating as it might be for you, tolerate your baby's need to explore every nook and cranny. At the same time, take obvious safety precautions.*
- *In addition to the sensory input it provides, floor play helps a baby learn to move. Creeping develops upper body strength and allows for early exploration so your infant can learn from his or her environment.*
- *Praise the "deed" and not the "doer": try not to say "good girl" or "good boy." Say "good job" or "that was great crawling."*

CHAPTER

5

From Cooing and Babbling to Sucking, Swallowing, and Chewing

Your Baby's Oral-Motor Development in the First Year

The Foundation of Language

Language begins at birth. A cry is language, a smile is language, and the opening of your newborn's mouth when he looks at you is language. In its most complete sense, language is defined as how we communicate with each other through touch, facial expressions, body language, and speech. Language is both receptive and expressive. Receptive language refers to the way we take in information that we see, hear, and touch, as well as how we comprehend this information. Expressive language refers to the way we share information through speaking, writing, or gesturing. From early on, your infant begins to use all of his senses for language development. In addition to his senses, other critical factors come into play as well. Just as movement is dependent on genetic makeup, muscle tone, and environment, so is the development of speech. It is also dependent on auditory abilities and intellect (while earlier I mentioned that there is no correlation between intelligence and early walking, there appears to be a strong correlation between speech and intelligence).

During the first year of your baby's life, his oral-motor development is exponential. From initially responding to sounds by startling, at 12 months of age he understands catchphrases such as "Clap your hands!" "So big!" and "Bye-bye!" (all of which have been repeated to him many times before). Your newborn knows you by voice (not just by vision or smell) and communicates to you in a number of ways. He coos when you speak to him. He may tell you when he hears something by his eye movements. He will blink, but he is unable to localize to sound at this stage. Clearly, though, your baby is using vision and sound together. He is also visually attracted to toys that make noise and is discriminating among their sounds. Your newborn's oral reflexes, such as the rooting and the suck-swallow reflex, are also used for communication, as well as for helping work the oral-motor muscles for later speech. These reflexes are present from birth to about three months. Our gag reflex, which is more of a protective reflex, lasts with us throughout life.

By the time your baby reaches one month of age you can begin to differentiate your baby's cries. You can notice the difference between the "I'm hungry and tired" cry and the "I've got a wet diaper" cry, or a cry of discomfort and an "I need some attention" whine. Your baby will offer different reactions to varying sounds. For example, he may startle at loud, sudden noises and simply stare at you (momentarily at this age) when you speak softly to him. You might also notice how he turns his head to gaze at several people. He'll also be making sounds to signify pleasure.

Between two and four months, your baby may be making single vowel sounds produced from the back of the throat: */ah/ /oo/ /uh/ /aw/* (*ah* as in *father*, *oo* as in *foot*, *uh* as in *cup*, *aw* as in *ball*). While these vowels might sound purposeful, at this point they are more reflexive. Your baby's facial expressions will tell you how he is feeling. They're also great photo opportunities—the yawns, the scrunching up of his face in displeasure, the little "O" of curiosity—are all trademark looks you'll remember. Soon your baby will be laughing and squealing—especially when you continue to make all those silly faces at him.

At three to four months you may notice various intonations as your baby coos or cries. He is now able to turn his head and even smiles when you speak to him. He might quiet to your voice. Consonant sounds may begin to emerge, and he usually enjoys practicing one at a time. He may even begin to use a combination of consonants and vowels: *baba-ahah-mama*. This is known as two-syllable, or reduplicated, babbling. Many babies do not achieve this until six or seven months.

By five months your baby may respond to his name by localizing (turning his head to your voice). True babbling develops shortly thereafter (at six to eight months), and your baby is now using vocalization as a way of social interaction—he both imitates you and responds to you. He might even speak to himself when he sees himself in a mirror. He'll string syllables (such as *ba-ba-ba*) together, sounding as if he's singing. He may also begin to respond to "no" (while he might, in part, understand the context of the word, he's also responding to the change in tone of your voice). Consonants arising from the back of the throat such as *K* and *G* are now heard as well as consonants originating from the tip of the tongue (*T, D, N, R, L*). Your baby is also changing sounds when he puts his hands in his mouth. Watching (and listening to) your little one as he stuffs a fist into his mouth and works sounds around it—getting louder and louder—is like watching a comedian making weird sounds into his mike.

At seven months your baby is also experimenting with sound—its production is beginning to occur separately from movement. In other words, he no longer has to be moving to make sounds. He appears to be having a conversation (using sounds, not words) as his intonations begin to vary even more. Babbling continues for at least three seconds and can last as long as three minutes. Your baby clearly listens when spoken to, or when others are speaking. He might even stop all his activity to listen intently. He could also begin to babble to you when his name or other familiar words are called. Babies at this age will often produce sounds ("speak") after being spoken to in order to continue the "conversation." Your baby will respond by gesturing (waving his arms, for example) to familiar statements such as "how big?" "wave bye-bye," and "come here." In this way, he is communicating to you that he understands what you are saying. He can mix consonants and vowels originating from different areas of the mouth, the lips (*P, B, M*), behind the teeth (*D, T, S*), and near the back of his throat (*ah-oh*).

Between eight and twelve months, although your baby may not be pointing, he seems to make wants and desires known by sound production (*uh-uh* or *eh-eh*). Babies at this age tend to chain their vowel sounds: *aaaa, aa, aaaa*. He babbles continuously now. Some babies begin to "sing" along with music. Gesturing and mimicking are now commonplace. Your baby shakes his head no, waves and lifts his arms up, and perhaps even tugs on you for attention. He starts to use inflection when vocalizing and is beginning word approximation (for instance, "wa" means *water* and "ba" means *ball*). He could already have one or two words—*mama, dada, baba*—and loves to imitate sounds such as clucking, fake coughs, and blowing raspberries (clusters of small bubbles). Your little one also loves to perform by responding to simple questions and requests through his gestures—"Blow a kiss to Mom," "Eyes—where are your eyes?" He can also respond when asked to say something—such as "Bye-bye." Clapping games are generally favorites, as well.

Between 11 and 12 months, your baby will be able to respond by "singing along" if you sing to him. At this age, babies tend to practice lots of vocalizations by "talking" to their toys, pets, and other people throughout the day. Your baby can now calm to your voice even when you are out of sight. He also knows when you are happy, sad, or mad by the tone of your voice. Children at this age are very good at telling where sounds are coming from. Even more exciting, sounds have meaning. A closing door may mean that Mom or Dad is arriving home or going out; the coffee grinder means someone is awake. While babies often imitate new words at this age, they might not talk as much when they are practicing to walk because they are focusing heavily on this new motor skill.

By 12 months of age your baby will probably be able to say two to five words besides *mama* and *dada*. Fifty percent of infants say their first word by 12 months, 90 percent by 18 months, and 7 percent by 20 to 22 months. Speaking words is no small accomplishment—it requires significant trunk and respiratory control. For speech production we need to have control over our inhalation and exhalation. For the ability to produce words, we also need trunk control. When trunk muscles are weak, respiration is weak. When we breathe in, the thoracic diameter increases (our rib cage moves up and out), giving us the ability to produce sounds on exhalation. An infant's rib cage is flatter and higher than an adult's rib cage. As an infant's trunk begins to develop, the rib cage gets "pulled down," giving him greater room for inhaling and exhaling.

Common Concern

When we are outside our home, our baby will not speak or show off what he knows. Is this common?

This is a very common occurrence, and it's hard on parents, especially since we are all very proud of our children's accomplishments and want to show them off. Some children tend to take in all new information before they respond to any of it, and are usually very busy exploring their surroundings. In addition, your child may need time to warm up in a new environment. This is why, at well-baby visits, pediatricians don't place much emphasis on the child's behavior, but rather rely on the parents' *report* of their child's behavior in addition to his milestones. (However, if concerns are present, a good pediatrician will give the child time to warm up and adjust before making any assessments.)

Activities to Enhance Sound Production

There are many different games and activities that you can use to engage your baby in "conversation." All of them will help stimulate the production of his own sounds. Remember, he wants to communicate with you!

For the Newborn These activities are designed to enhance your newborn's language acquisition. Sing nursery rhymes and use rattles to make your baby follow the sound. Speak to your baby, in a soft, pleasant tone, even when you are not directly in front of him. He will soon learn your voice. To heighten his auditory awareness, you can vary your intonation patterns. Also speak from behind him, or from out of his line of vision. Check to see if your baby is listening to you. Make sure he makes sounds and looks at you.

For One to Three Months Engage in back-and-forth play by imitating your baby's sounds. Let him make a sound. Then you repeat the sound. Wait for a response and begin again. Your baby is following you both visually and auditorily. Talk to your baby as you move from side to side. Continue to sing to him—"Twinkle, twinkle, little star," "Mary had a little lamb," and "Rock-a-bye baby." Use sound toys to get

Language Development Benchmarks for Your Baby's First Year

Newborn
- Startles at loud noises.
- Appears to listen to you.
- Makes sounds to indicate pleasure or contentment.

Newborn to Three Months
- Attends to sounds and voices.
- Recognizes your voice.
- Produces vowel-like sounds, or coos.

Three to Six Months
- Produces different cries.
- Produces more vowel sounds.
- Laughs.
- Coos.
- Responds to "no" by vocalizing.
- Responds to his name.
- Searches for sounds that he hears but can't see (door slamming, dog barking, phone ringing).
- Uses some consonants.
- Is beginning to babble (closer to six months) and stops babbling when another person vocalizes.

Seven to Ten Months
- Recognizes familiar objects/responds to familiar words.
- Babbles continuously.
- Talks to toys.
- Imitates sounds.
- Mixes consonants and vowel sounds.
- Gestures and mimics.
- Starts babbling when another person stops talking in order to keep the "conversation" going.

Ten to Twelve Months
- Listens to stories.
- Produces two to five words other than *mama* and *dada*.
- Expresses himself when objects are taken away—sounds his displeasure.
- Turns to the sound of his name being called.
- Understands and enjoys imitation games (peekaboo and patty-cake).

your baby to follow. If your baby is not interested in one particular toy, try another one. Use your baby's name. Call out to him before he sees you. This helps him to become familiar with your voice, and to recognize you by voice.

For Three to Five Months By now your baby can turn his head to the sound of a bell or rattle, and will continue to look at it and study it. Use different intonations and loudness levels, such as soft, loud, or playful voices. Encourage sound production (*oo-oo-ee-ee*) by using words with these sounds so your baby can repeat the sounds. The more talking you do, the more your baby will do (but try not to get into the habit of anticipating your baby's responses and saying them first). You want to encourage talking, not hinder it.

The Well-Balanced Checklist

What You Can Do to Enhance Language in the First Year

- Finding the right time to work on communication is just as important as finding the right time for visual or motor input. Your baby needs to be receptive. For communication, that time is usually quiet time when you are reading or even in the bath (as stimulating as a bath can be, it's also wonderful for sound production).
- Talk to your baby when he is playing. For example, if he is pushing a car, you can say, "The car goes vroom-vroom." If he is playing with a plush animal, name that animal and make the animal sound. Also, describe what your child is feeling if the object is soft, hard, cold, or hot.
- Label objects when your child is pointing to them.
- Expand your child's knowledge—if he sees a cat and says, "meow," you can say, "Look at the cat—he is black and white and his fur is soft."
- Keep activities age-appropriate.
- Don't make your child repeat sentences—or "perform"; all activities should be fun, not work.
- When reading to your baby, remember that there is a difference between your child's naming the picture and understanding what the picture is. When you point and say, "What is this?" and your child answers you, he is labeling, naming, and using his words. When you ask him, "Where is the bird?" and he shows you, it indicates that he understands the question.

You can use sound to enhance motor skills as well. When your baby is playing on his belly, use the sound of the rattle to encourage him to lift and turn his head. When you build a tower of blocks and knock it down, say, "Uh-oh! All fall down!" You are demonstrating expressions that your child will begin to use and understand the meaning of. Try lip patting—sit with your baby on your lap (facing away from you) or with your baby in the high chair and gently pat his lips. This provides sensory input to close the mouth. Consonants that need lip closure are *B*, *M*, and *P*. You can also help your baby to pat your lips as you say *m-m-m*, *p-p-p*, and *b-b-b* so that he feels the vibration of the sound. You might also want to put the object near your mouth as you label it. This helps your baby associate the sound with the object. Play peekaboo for reciprocal interaction.

For Six to Eight Months Bath time often stimulates sound production. The splashes of the water cause lots of laughter (which increases the activity of the abdominal muscles while inhaling and exhaling), and the deep breaths help with phonation. Label everything—dress, top, pants, body parts, animals, people, everyday items (phone, pen, pot, spoon, food). When outside, point and tell your baby all the different sounds that you hear (wind, trees blowing, sirens, birds chirping, dogs barking). An action accompanied by sound helps foster language development. You can generate this circumstance with just about anything. For instance, when something drops, say "uh-oh," or when something tastes good, rub your belly and say "mmm—good."

Babies at this age are interested in back-and-forth games (communication by body language). A nice back-and-forth game is "[Andrew] has a hat. Take it off and give it to Mommy." You take off the hat and place it on your head, then give it back to your baby. Continue back and forth. Keep singing! Babies at this age love animals: sing "Old McDonald." You can practice singing, then stopping, then resuming, then stopping abruptly, leaving a word or phrase out. This will encourage your child to vocalize by "filling in" what you left out. Use a play phone and hold it to your baby's ear. Play talk with one another. Talk through a paper towel ring. Make funny sounds. Your baby will love it.

For Ten to Eighteen Months Imitate sounds that you both hear—cars, boats, airplanes, sirens, phones, splashing, kissing, blowing, and humming. Use all kinds of puppets to make up stories. Set up a stage when playing—create a farm, water park, dance studio. Be creative. When you are driving in the car, talk to your child in the backseat and label the things you see as you drive. Use prepositions—"the bus is next to/behind/in front of us." Older children love to play various car games, such as counting cars of a certain type, "I spy," and singing games.

The Foundation for Feeding Skills

Babies are born with the innate ability to suck and swallow for survival. The strong sucking pattern most newborns have is partly due to mechanics. The oral cavity is small and the tongue fills this cavity. In addition, the "chipmunk" look your baby has is actually due to sucking pads located on the inside of his cheeks that help create stability of the mouth. The combination of the small oral cavity and these sucking pads creates compression and enables your baby to draw liquid from a nipple.

The palate is what divides the oral cavity from the nasal cavity. It provides a resting place for the tongue and prevents liquids and foods from entering the nasal cavity. (Infants born with a cleft palate—one out of seven hundred births—have difficulties with feedings because they have a hard time achieving enough negative pressure to draw liquid from a nipple. Consequently, liquids can enter the nasal cavity as well.)

Just as a baby's movement begins randomly and unrefined, so does the development of his mouth and surrounding areas. His jaw movements are initially uncontrolled, and his tongue moves with his jaw as a single unit. Consequently, when your infant first begins to chew, his tongue moves vertically with the jaw. (For instance, babies at this stage will gum crackers in an up/down movement pattern.) As your infant's jaw becomes more stable, his tongue begins to move independently and he can move his lips and cheeks more readily. As semisolids (such as baby cereals) are introduced, food moves from one side of the mouth to the other and the tongue begins to move laterally. Rotary movement of the tongue develops as your baby begins to chew real foods.

The sensory input your baby receives in his mouth also affects his motor function. Since an infant's tongue takes up his entire mouth, he is receiving constant tactile input from all sides. Even as he gets older, he gets constant tactile input from anything introduced into his mouth. Some babies and children are far more tactile sensitive than others. If a sensitive baby doesn't like the texture, taste, or temperature of his food, he will quickly shift the food around in his mouth and swallow it, as opposed to properly chewing it and using rotary movements. He might also chew or swallow food with his mouth open (thus not using his oral-motor muscles) if he can get away with it. However, when he realizes that the food falls out of his mouth if he leaves it open, he will then close it. (He might also opt to spit the food out and refuse to eat it.) We'll discuss oral sensitivities throughout this chapter.

Common Concern

My daughter is four months old and I just weaned her from the breast to the bottle. I'm noticing that she leaks quite a bit of liquid from the sides of her mouth when I feed her. Should I be concerned?

There are several factors to consider when a baby is leaking liquids from the sides of his or her mouth while feeding. The type of sucking pattern a baby uses is slightly different between the breast and bottle, and it may take an infant some time to get used to. It's not uncommon for babies to initially choke or gag when making this transition, because they suck in more liquid from the bottle than they are used to getting (using the same amount of exertion) from the breast. Also be aware of your baby's position during bottle feeds. In general, a baby who is nursed on the breast tends to have his or her chin tucked, with the head in a slightly flexed position, when feeding (we discussed this briefly in Chapter 3). This automatically creates a stronger seal and sucking pattern, and less air gets in with each draw on the nipple.

Meanwhile, bottle-fed babies tend to keep their necks slightly extended and extend even farther back to empty the bottle. If your baby has this tendency, using an angled bottle can be helpful to decrease this head-back pattern. (You can find angled bottles at most baby supply stores.) Remember, if the ears are behind the shoulders, more neck and head extension is present, making it harder to get good lip closure and a strong seal around the nipple. Generally, by six months of age, most babies stop losing liquid from the sides of their mouths when they are drinking. Some babies continue to lose liquid when the nipple is pulled out of their mouths until nine months of age.

Premature babies, babies with low muscle tone, and babies with anatomical or neurological impairments

Pre-feeding and Feeding Benchmarks for Your Baby's First Year

Newborn to Three Months

- Brings hands to mouth.
- Belly plays—face, cheeks, and lips get lots of tactile input, helping prepare the mouth for sensory and motor skills.
- Holds toys and brings them to his mouth.

Four to Nine Months

- Hands-to-mouth play continues.
- Introduction to semisolid and solid foods.
- Begins to gum baby crackers/ Cheerios (lateralization of tongue).
- Lips begin to close around a spoon.
- Chewing behaviors begin, progressing from vertical to diagonal to rotary movements (around seven to eight months).
- May begin to drink liquid from a cup.
- May begin to finger feed himself.
- Holds spoon.

Ten to Twelve Months

- Self-feeds finger foods.
- Assists with cup drinking by holding the cup.
- May hold his own bottle.
- Imitates spoon stirring (with a cup and spoon).
- Eats a variety of textures.
- Attempts to feed himself with a spoon.

tend to have difficulty with good lip closure, suck-swallow coordination, and the ability to develop a strong suction pressure to draw the liquid out from the nipple. Contact your pediatrician if, by six months, your baby is still leaking a significant amount of liquid.

Making Mealtime Enjoyable

To help to make mealtime more enjoyable for both you and your baby, you need to be able to communicate together. Understand your infant or child's body language. Try to pay attention to how your baby expresses his wants and needs. Does he need you to feed him at a slower or faster pace? How does your infant tell you when he is finished?

Keep in mind that babies pick up on their parents' and caregivers' moods—just as older children do. They might not be able to speak yet, but they can sense every kind of emotion. For this reason it's important that you try not to engage in a potentially frustrating or anxiety-producing activity—such as feeding—if you are in a tense, rushed, or simply bad mood. Of course, we all have our moments, and sometimes we can't act on the best of our intentions. So don't be too hard on yourself, either!

Make sure your baby is ready to eat and the environment is set up for feeding. For example, when feeding your newborn, try to be comfortable. Lower any music or the TV, and try not to be interrupted by phone calls or other disturbances. As you progress to semisolids, try to prepare your food and have it ready before getting your baby situated in his bouncer seat. For a busy baby or toddler on the go, you might want to try giving him a few Cheerios on his high chair tray in order to entertain him while you continue to prepare his meal. Every child is different, and it is up to us to be aware of our child's desires, likes, and dislikes if we want to create a well-balanced child. You may want to keep a written list of foods that your baby enjoys and those he spits out. You can even try to reintroduce a food several weeks later and take note of your baby's response.

When the Going Gets Messy: The Introduction of Semisolid Foods

Pediatricians recommend beginning the new and exciting phase of feeding semisolid foods (cereal) at between four-and-a-half and five months of age. At an earlier age, reflexive movements are still dominant. Consequently, babies will tend to push the food out of their mouths. Nevertheless, you should check with your pediatrician before beginning these foods.

Your baby needs to be developmentally ready for this next stage of eating. He should have good head control and sufficient oral-motor control (some infants with low muscle tone or neurological impairments may not be ready to begin spoonfeedings at this age). Once your baby is ready to begin spoonfeeding, there are several preparatory steps that may be helpful.

Just as the position in which you hold your baby during breast- or bottle-feeding is important, placing your baby in the infant, car, or bouncer seat is important for spoonfeeding. The support provided in the semireclined position not only frees up your hands to do what you need to do, but it also provides added stability for your baby as he learns a new and sometimes daunting activity. (In addition, it fosters communication between the two of you and allows him to see the food entering his mouth!) Spoonfeeding does not come naturally to every baby. Following are some tips to make this challenging and exciting phase pleasurable for both of you.

- Place your baby in a reclined seat.
- Place your baby at eye level—for example, on a tabletop. Never leave your baby unattended while on the table.
- Stand or sit in front of your baby. This helps keep the head in midline position for better lip closure and swallowing.
- Make sure your baby's head is bent slightly forward (also for better lip closure and swallowing).
- Most parents tend to place the spoon in the mouth and "scrape" the food off the spoon by lifting upward on the upper lip. This is not the ideal way to achieve good lip closure and/or optimal control of the oral-motor muscles. It is best to use firm pressure, pushing downward on the tongue and sliding the spoon outward on the bottom lip. This causes the upper lip to come down rather than retract upward. Consequently, the lower lip can hold the spoon while the upper lip uses a sucking motion to get the food off the spoon and into the mouth.

Common Concern

My four and a half-month-old began semisolid feedings a week ago. I'm confused about the consistency of the formula when he drinks it. Couldn't he choke on it?

This mother had put her baby's cereal into his bottle. She thought her pediatrician had said to add the cereal to the formula, rather than add the formula to the cereal. A baby should *not* have cereal in the bottle unless there is a medical necessity.[1] Food should be taken by spoon-feeds, and formula or breast milk by bottle. By your mixing cereal in the bottle your baby is getting mixed messages on sucking. The mixture makes it difficult for him to extrude the liquid from the cereal, resulting in understandable frustration. He is also missing out on early oral-motor activities such as chewing and tongue movements, which are crucial for oral-motor development and later for articulation of words.

If your baby is not used to putting things in his mouth (such as his fingers and toys), he may be sensitive to the spoon in his mouth as well. Therefore, you may want to "prepare" the mouth first by rubbing your fingers around it. Rub downward on the upper lip. On the cheeks, rub toward the lips to obtain lip closure. You can place your whole hand—four fingers—on the lips for the same response. Also rub upward from the lower lip. While doing this you want to be careful not to thrust the neck back into extension—this makes lip closure difficult. These motions help prepare the oral-motor muscles to work. You can also put only your index finger in your baby's mouth. Rub it along the gums, moving from the back of the gums to the front and from the top of the gums down toward the teeth. You might want to provide deep pressure on the tongue with a tapping motion. Use your index finger on the center of the tongue—but not too far back. You don't want to elicit a gag response.

Another way to desensitize the mouth is to use a "finger toothbrush." This toothbrush is worn over your finger, and it can be found in most drugstores. You can use it to begin "brushing" your baby's mouth. It's a nice activity, especially for babies with oral sensitivities. It's also a good way for your baby to experience tactile input in the mouth prior to spoon feeds. In order to minimize the association between oral input and feeding, some therapists feel that oral "preparation" should not take place at feeding times.

Your baby may initially push the food out of his mouth with his tongue. This is natural, since his tongue movements are not yet organized. Remember, food is a new sensory experience—consequently, your baby might initially push all new foods out of his mouth. Your baby's mouth will adapt to spoonfeeding over time, and food spillage will decrease with practice. Your patience and perseverance are crucial to making the initial stages of solid feeding nonstressful (if not fun) for both you and your baby.

1. If your baby has *reflux* (a medical condition in which he vomits up his formula), your pediatrician may tell you to put cereal into the formula. The thicker feed helps prevent the baby from refluxing. Severe reflux may require additional intervention.

Common Concern

My baby seems to turn away each time I try to put the spoon near her mouth. Why does she do this?

There could be a number of reasons why your baby is unwilling to eat. We need to establish several things: Is she awake and alert? Is she hungry? Is she comfortable with new objects being put in and around her mouth? If the latter is a problem, try to desensitize the mouth first. Or she may simply not be ready for spoon-feeds yet. Try postponing it.

If your baby is six months old and you have tried to introduce solids at different times during the day, and you have prepared your baby but she still will not take the spoon, there may be some underlying issues. For example, there are infants who have hyperactive gag reflexes or oral-motor sensitivities that can cause them discomfort when certain textures or tastes are in their mouths. There could also be underlying medical problems, such as reflux or poor sensory organization, that are causing your baby's unwillingness. These kinds of concerns can be helped by a pediatric speech or occupational therapist trained in infant feeding and oral-motor input. Never force-feed your infant, and consult with your pediatrician if ongoing spoonfeedings are not a pleasurable experience.

High Chairs, Cheerios, and Eating Like a Grown-Up: The Introduction of Solid Foods

Solid foods are often introduced by six months of age. Parents may first give their infant a graham cracker, Cheerio, or baby cookie. Generally, a baby will suck and chew these foods until they are clumps of mush before he'll swallow them. By eight months there is even more shifting of foods in the mouth, as well as an emergence of rotary movement in the jaw. Your baby's upper lip is even more active and cup drinking is better coordinated. As his jaw stability increases over time, you'll notice less drooling. You'll probably give your baby more finger foods (such as chopped vegetables, teething biscuits, boiled chicken, and cheese cut into strips or cubes) now that he has better sitting ability. He is better able to shift foods in his mouth due to increased lateral tongue movement, and there is more activity of the upper lip.

While many people introduce "stage 3" baby foods during this period, I think that they are often confusing for new munchers. Stage 3 baby foods are clumps of solids mixed in with a lot of liquids. This is a combination of two very different types of tactile experiences that require different patterns of sucking, chewing, and swallowing. So how is a little one supposed to manage? I personally feel if an infant is ready for stage 3 baby foods, then he is ready for homemade mashed, moist table foods.

Between nine and ten months your baby's lip closure over the spoon is terrific, and there is even better rotary movement of the jaw. Your baby will imitate sounds and they become more purposeful.

The Well-Balanced Checklist

What You Can Do to Enhance Feeding in the First Year

- Try to have quiet time prior to feeding.
- Set an environment conducive for feeding.
- Optimal positioning for both you and your baby helps foster a pleasurable feeding experience for both of you.
- Be consistent in both your actions and your scheduling of feeding times.
- When beginning semisolids, place your baby in an infant seat—especially if you have a squirming baby. The seat provides stability, helping your baby feel more secure during this transition.
- Remember, your baby will "tell" you when he is ready to sit upright in a high chair.
- Check with your pediatrician before introducing any new foods (your child might have allergies).
- To help familiarize your baby with new foods, place them on the tray of his high chair so that he can see and feel them prior to putting them in his mouth.
- Encourage your child to experience new tastes, but don't force him.
- Don't use food as a reward.
- Model good behavior, and try to ignore undesirable behavior in your baby.
- Try not to become a short-order cook.
- Don't give your child too many calories through juice and other drinks.

By 11 to 12 months most babies like to feed themselves, but they tend to lose a lot of the food to the floor. Most babies of this age generally prefer "table food" (soft meats, fish, and chopped, cooked vegetables). At this point your baby will have good lateral tongue movement to help shift (or transport) the food for chewing. He will be able to transfer foods from the center of his mouth to either side, and will be able to swallow foods with greater ease.

High Chairs

Since some babies are sitting before others, it follows that some babies are ready for high chairs before others. If your baby is pulling forward in his infant seat, he might be telling you he wants to sit upright. Once your baby can sit upright or push into an upright sitting position when in a reclined seat, then he is ready for a high chair. By seven months some babies are ready. Some are sitting in a reclined position while others are sitting upright. Be sure that your baby's hips are all the way back in the seat, with his pelvis in the neutral position. Keeping his hips and trunk in alignment helps activate muscle tone. To help secure this position, towel rolls can be placed on the sides of the chair (especially if it is large). Your baby's spine should also be straight, with good head and neck alignment, which helps maintain the esophagus and airway in proper alignment.

There are many types of high chairs on the market. The old-fashioned wooden ones look beautiful, but they are not very functional. First of all, they tend to be larger than other types of chairs and your baby will have difficulty maintaining himself upright. Remember, he is just learning to use his trunk muscles to hold himself upright, as well as learning how to eat. The carvings in the wood make the chair very difficult to clean, and it doesn't have wheels, which makes it difficult to adjust positions when you need to. The newer, plastic-coated models come complete with adjustable positions, padding, wheels, and footrests. You can even buy high chairs that accommodate your baby's growing needs—they recline for younger babies and adjust to upright positions for older babies.

Footrests actually help keep proper alignment. Once your baby is sitting in the high chair in the upright position, you want to see "90-90 angles"—90 degrees at the hips and 90 degrees at the knees. The footrest helps give your baby the needed support from a surface to maintain this position. Think about it—when you are sitting and your feet are off the ground, it is much harder to sit upright. However, when your feet are on the ground it is easier to maintain proper alignment.

The Wonderful World of Cheerios

If your baby is in a high chair and eating solids you may be interested in the world of Cheerios—one of the only "safe" foods that allow your baby to practice his fine motor skills. (Graham cracker bits are another good choice.) At first he will try to scoop up the Cheerios, but eventually (though perhaps not for months) he will develop his pincer grasp so he can pick the Cheerios up individually and navigate them into his little mouth.

It's often hilarious to watch a baby's initial attempts at gathering Cheerios. More cereal bits end up on the floor than in the mouth, particularly when watching the cereal bits falling to the floor brings much quicker gratification than the task of putting them in the mouth. If you have a dog in your house, he will be sure to snatch up the offerings—further delighting your child and annoying you—unless you think of the dog as an efficient way to clean up the floor.

You may want to check with your pediatrician before introducing Cheerios. Make sure that a hyperactive gag is not present and that your baby's swallowing mechanism is working well. You may feel more comfortable if you dip the Cheerios in formula or water first, to moisten them. However, your baby's saliva does the same trick—the Cheerio becomes mush prior to being swallowed. Place only a few Cheerios on the tray at any given time, and for the first several attempts, stay close to your baby. Watch as your baby regards the Cheerio, then attempts to "rake" it into his palm and bring it to his mouth (moist Cheerios also adhere to the hand). Once the Cheerio makes it into his mouth, your baby will use his tongue to move the Cheerio around. Since babies like to imitate us, you might want to model chewing for him. Watch as he swallows it. If your baby cannot get the Cheerio into his mouth, help him. Put the cereal bit on the inside cheek of his mouth, not in the center. This helps prevent the Cheerio from being swallowed too quickly, and it also gives the oral muscles a chance to work more.

Common Concern

My 10-month-old seems to drool all the time—we have to keep a bib on him all day. Is this normal?

Yes. Swallowing saliva (as well as liquids and food) requires oral organization. It is a sensory-motor phenomenon—just as all development is. The jaw stability it requires takes time to achieve. Yet even though newborns lack oral stability, they don't drool much until later on. This is because they spend much of their time in the reclined position; thus gravity helps them swallow their saliva.

All babies drool when teething, when achieving new developmental skills, or when they are tired, stressed, or sick (colds can create nasal congestion, which may result in increased drooling). It's also common to see a child with slightly low muscle tone drooling due to postural instability (where the shoulders are elevated and his head is slightly extended, with the mouth slightly open—making swallowing more difficult). Drooling also occurs in babies with a diminished oral-sensory awareness. A child may not realize that he is drooling, that there is wetness around the mouth. If drooling continues once a developmental skill is mastered and your baby is not ill or under stress, you might want to address it with your pediatrician. He or she may want to request an evaluation with a feeding specialist or pediatric speech therapist.

Eating Like a Grown-Up: Independent Eating

In order for a child to be able to eat independently, he needs to have reached several developmental milestones. First, he should have enough postural control to sit without support. He needs shoulder stability and mobility, as well as graded muscle control for smooth movements (having the ability to control the movement of the utensil from the bowl to his mouth).

As he continues progressing, he'll need the following utensils to help him on his way. The first utensil introduced is usually a spoon. A flat spoon makes it easier for a new feeder to remove the food from his bowl. A deeper, or bowl-shaped, spoon (like a soupspoon) makes it easier for the older, more experienced self-feeder to keep the food on the spoon while trying to get it into his mouth. Along with the spoon comes your baby's first bowl. Slip-proof children's bowls help steady the bowl for a new self-feeder. Finally, it's time to introduce a fork. Those with wider handles can help little hands grasp more easily.

From Spills to Sippy Cups: The Introduction of Cup Drinking

Usually by six or seven months your baby will try to take your cup from you while you try to take a drink. Undoubtedly, when you hold the cup up to his mouth, most of the liquid will dribble down his chin. By 12 months, your baby can hold a small cup with one or both hands (some spillage will occur). By two years of age a child can generally hold and drink from a cup with little leakage.

Infants are usually introduced to cup drinking by nine months, most often with water. Normally, a baby will open his mouth wide upon seeing the cup approach his lips, which helps provide jaw stability. As his jaw stability improves, he won't need to open his mouth so widely. Some babies will then bring their tongues out and place them on the cup, as they would for a nipple. Then they will try to suck the liquid in (or it will pour in—in which case your infant will cough or gag). Keep in mind that just as babies sometimes backtrack in their motor development when learning a new motor skill, the same thing can occur when learning new oral skills. An infant who has mastered nipple sucking may actually cough or choke when learning to drink from a cup. This is very common, until the infant learns a coordinated sucking pattern that accompanies cup drinking. Be careful not to pour liquid into your baby's mouth—we want his lips and jaw to be active, and to encourage his lips to come down onto the rim of the cup.

By one year of age, babies tend to demonstrate a more mature drinking pattern with improved, coordinated movements between the tongue and the jaw. They have good lip closure over the rim of the cup, making sipping easier. Consequently, less liquid is lost during this drinking process. By two years of age, enough jaw stabilization is present that your toddler no longer has to bite down on his cup or use his tongue for tactile input or stability. As with chewing, the type of sucking pattern a child exhibits during cup drinking also depends on the taste, temperature, and texture of the liquid.

Common Concern

My baby seems ready for cup drinking. Should I use a closed, spouted cup (like a sippy cup), or an open cup?

A new cup drinker will use the spout like a nipple and will continue using a suck-swallow pattern similar to that of breast- or bottle-feeding. An open cup provides the new cup drinker with an opportunity to learn how to actually drink from a cup. It also allows him to use his oral muscles in a more mature way (because he is attempting to draw in the liquid instead of sucking it). Of course, the advantage of spouted cups is that there is less of a mess to clean up, since your little one can actually carry spill-proof sip cups. If your child shows no signs of oral-motor sensitivities or difficulties, then you can use spouted cups along with open cups. However, it's important that your child gets experience with open cup drinking, even if it's only during mealtimes, when he is seated.

Activities to Strengthen Your Baby's Oral-Motor Muscles

There are a number of ways that you can help strengthen the muscles in your baby's mouth, to facilitate eating as well as language production. Allow your child to chew on "chew toys" (those rubber toys from the pet store mentioned in Chapter 3). Textured fruit teethers (which come in different colors, shapes, and sizes) are also terrific. Play blowing games with bubbles, blow toys (whistle-type toys that react when you blow into them), and whistles. Give your child age-appropriate foods that require chewing—bagels, meats, and vegetables in small pieces. Have him drink thick drinks, or yogurt, from a straw. Use twisted or funny-shaped straws to drink from (these require a slightly greater sucking pattern).

How the Sensory System Affects Eating

Input from all the senses can (and will) impact your baby's concentration when he's feeding. Let's review how each one contributes to his diversion.

Visual and Olfactory Input

The sight or smell of food may make your baby become excited about eating. You may see him bounce in his chair, point, or smile and coo. However, the sight or smell of a particular food he doesn't like may cause overt reactions of withdrawal or crying. Also be aware that visual stimulants (such as a television) during mealtime can distract your child from eating. (Some parents, however, feel that this distraction helps them feed their child more easily.)

Try not to have your baby exposed to offensive odors such as cleaning solvents and cigarette smoke during mealtimes. These can distract him from feeding. Pleasant smells, on the other hand, can help make feeding more enjoyable.

Vestibular Input

An infant who is held in an awkward or uncomfortable position while bottle-feeding might not be able to suck properly on a nipple. Similarly, a baby placed in an overly large high chair might worry about falling, or might be distracted by constantly having to adjust his position in order to remain upright. In addition, he needs to concentrate on what his limbs are doing in space, which could make him feel disorganized or possibly anxious. Slow rocking prior to mealtime can help calm and organize a baby so that he can suck and swallow more efficiently. A firm hug also helps. Children who are fussy may also find gentle rocking or swinging to be calming prior to mealtime.

Tactile Input

When we think of the tactile system as it relates to feeding, we need to think of the taste, temperature, and texture of foods. Foods that are sweet, salty, sour, or bitter (such as fruit, saltine crackers, lemons, and pickles) tend to be more awakening (in the sense of surprising) to the system than bland foods (such as cereal and cottage cheese). Foods at extreme temperatures are more alerting (in the sense of warning) to the system than neutral ones. Crunchy foods are more awakening to the system than mashed foods.

Children have a greater number of taste buds than adults. Consequently, they don't need spicy, sweetened, or salty foods in order to enjoy eating. However, a low-toned child with decreased oral-motor control may respond better to sweeter, saltier, or bitter foods—as well as those that are chewy—since they have a heightening effect to taste. At the other extreme, children can be hypersensitive to tastes and textures in the same way that they can be hypersensitive to touch and smell.

Warning Signs for Oral Defensiveness (Hypersensitivity)

It's important to note if your infant or child tends to overreact to sensations that generally would not bother others. If he seems constantly out-of-sorts at mealtime and you have made sure that he is comfortable, rested, and focused—and you have a good sense of his gustatory likes and dislikes—then he could be orally defensive. Following are some signs to look for.

- Progression to spoon-feeds remains difficult over an extended period of time.
- Your child never or rarely mouths toys, fingers, or objects.
- Your child dislikes tastes, textures, or smells of certain foods over an extended period of time.
- Your child resists solid foods (chewable table foods).
- Your child appears to have tactile sensitivities in other areas (doesn't like certain clothing, doesn't like skin exposed, doesn't like the bath, etc.).

"You get your lips after your hips." This is a little phrase we like to use in therapy. Parents are often concerned when their child is not speaking as well, or as often, as his or her peers. Remember, you need adequate muscle tone and postural control for phonation and you need oral-motor control for word formation. Therefore, once you have enough motor control in your trunk (hips) you will also have enough oral-motor control (lips) for speech.

And Always Remember . . .

- *Have the right environment for feeding times: make sure your baby has had some quiet time, and have his food ready prior to sitting him in the high chair. Turn off loud, jarring music, the television and videos. Make sure the vacuum isn't running in the next room, and remove all his toys. Also, try not to have your baby exposed to offensive odors such as cleaning solvents or cigarette smoke, which can distract him from feeding. Pleasant smells, on the other hand, can help make feeding more enjoyable.*
- *Try not to become frustrated—an infant quickly picks up on and reacts to stressful signals.*

PART 3

Able to Leap Tall Buildings

Your Child's Development from One to Five Years Old

CHAPTER

6

Your Mobile Explorer

Development of and Activities for Your One- to Three-Year-Old

Between the ages of one and three your baby will become a true playmate and an avid explorer. She is beginning to master her body, continuously refining and learning new skills. Your new walker will soon be running, walking backward and sideways, and climbing stairs. Those little hands of hers are now very good at manipulating and will soon be sorting, building, and beading. Just a few months ago, stringing beads could only be accomplished with large beads. By two and a half to three years your baby's little fingers are sturdy enough to string one-inch beads. And while grasping a crayon began with a whole fisted clasp around the crayon, by the time she's three your child will be able to grasp the crayon like we do. This becomes possible, in part, because your child's wrists have greater mobility now—particularly the ability to rotate.

As an explorer, your baby is busy getting into everything—opening and closing doors, squeezing toothpaste, playing with the water in the toilet. Whatever you imagine (and even some things you can't!) *can* actually happen. Your baby's exploration gives her knowledge, and knowledge leads to language, which is critical to the development of intelligence. By two years of age your baby's language is exploding. She probably knows hundreds of words, can carry on a conversation, and can even follow directions. That being said, your baby also has a distinct personality by now—and often that means she will try to stand up for herself. "No" is a very common phrase.

Many babies are still crawling at 12 months and may not walk independently until 16 or 18 months. Nevertheless, you'll have a curious crawler on your hands. She'll practice pulling to stand by pulling up on anything, including objects that are not sturdy enough to be pulled upon. Consequently, even a crawler is a climber—her exploration doesn't end on the floor. Babies *love* to be off the ground. So don't be surprised where you find your baby sitting—perhaps on a low chair or sofa, or even on something higher. Even if she can't walk yet, she can still get herself into a heap of trouble.

During her second year, your baby will have a better attention span. She'll continue (with even more intensity) to be fascinated by small objects. Crumbs, dust, and even bugs will mesmerize her. She'll explore these objects just like she explores her toys—putting them in her mouth, throwing them, crushing them, banging them, and examining them. However, all these sensory-motor experiences now become functional abilities to explore, learn, and use objects appropriately. During the first year of life your baby was developing a refined grasp—now she's using that grasp to learn what to do with objects in addition to playing with them. For instance, a spoon may not just be for banging and making noise, but is beginning to be used for feeding. As manual manipulation improves and your child becomes more interested in what an object actually does, her mouthing of objects will decrease. Nevertheless, keep in mind that babies like to use their mouths for exploration to up to two years of age. So don't let up your vigilance of what your child appears to be sucking on—or swallowing.

Between two and three your child becomes familiar with what she is allowed to touch, explore, and play with throughout the house (although that doesn't stop her from trying to take apart the VCR or play with the CDs). She'll love to explore in cabinets and closets. I will never forget the time I opened my closet door, left the room for a moment, returned, and closed the closet door—and then realized I could not find my daughter. After what seemed like a long time, I found her happily playing in the closet. From that point on, the closet became one of her favorite spots (but I left the door open).

Throughout this period, simple everyday activities for us can be building blocks for more complicated tasks our children will accomplish later on. For example, let your baby play with a pen. Let her figure out how to hold it, mark paper with it, and so forth. Help her (gently) turn the pages of your book. Show her a picture with her in it, and she'll be able to recognize herself. Provide her with a play kitchen or a broom and she will imitate you. Remember, your baby is constantly watching and observing you. She loves to be around Mom or Dad all day, so allow her to be with you as much as possible. When you're in the kitchen, let her explore in one or two cabinets. Let her bang pots together and put lids on them in order to figure out what these objects do. Do they roll, bounce, or clatter?

Much of your toddler's day is also spent trying to get objects to change shape. For instance, she'll be fascinated with crumpling up pieces of paper. It's a nice hand activity and throwing the paper into a bin is also a good visual-motor skill. So give your child old magazines and catalogs to play with. Tearing paper (a favorite amusement between two and three years) is another great hand-strengthening activity. Toddlers also love to play with tape (ages two to five). Just give them a long piece of masking tape and watch them have fun. They can also play for hours with a few rolls of toilet paper. Older kids (between ages four and five) will create mummies, decorate the swing set and the bushes, or even create a path of paper leading to a box of "treasure."

By three your "terrific" two-year-old will enjoy helping you and will love getting praised for both her efforts and her skills. She is much more coordinated and her balance is much improved. She can now run around obstacles with ease and loves to jump (from anywhere, much to your dismay). She can gallop and is beginning to have the ability to hop (although she might not actually hop for another year). She can climb stairs, taking alternative steps, but continues to use a step-to-step method for descending them.

The Soles of Our Existence, Revisited

From the moment we walk, and for the rest of our lives, our feet bear the brunt of our load. In addition to carrying our weight, our feet allow us to adapt to a never-ending change in the surfaces that we walk on. Walking requires delicate control of, and coordination between, all of our muscles and joints—from our feet up through our trunk—and the timing of our movements needs to be just right. As adults, we take this control, balance, and timing for granted until we have a problem, such as a pain in our foot or knee, hip, or back. Only then do we realize how one small problem affects the entire way we walk. We're so used to walking that we pay no attention to all the components of our gait, which is divided into two phases: the stance phase and the swing phase. To take a step, we need to shift our weight forward, balance on one leg, and adjust our bodies so our foot can hit (or strike) the floor. In order for this motion to occur, as our pelvis rotates and drops, we need to keep our toes up on the reaching leg, while the knee flexes on the standing leg.

That's an awful lot for a toddler to accomplish! It's no surprise, then, that it takes some time for her to learn to walk steadily. Unlike an adult, when a toddler takes a step, her whole (flat) foot strikes the ground, with her knee bent. (Adults strike the ground, heel first, with their knee extended.) Unlike the adult knee, the toddler knee may then extend or remain flexed. It is this knee motion in toddlers that causes their bobbing appearance (the up/down movement). Toddlers also do not have full hip extension (during stance phase), which causes them to have a shorter step. Toddlers don't usually swing their arms reciprocally, as we do, because they need to hold them out wide for balance. Also, as we've discussed, a toddler has a wide base of support (her feet are wide apart to help her balance). The combination of these compensatory movements is what causes toddlers to "waddle."

Between two and three years of age, a toddler begins to use the adult gait pattern: heel strike, foot flat at midstance, knee flexion and extension, decreased base of support, and reciprocal arm swing. By age seven the child has mastered the adult gait pattern. Children's feet continue to grow until they are between 12 and 14 (for girls) and 14 and 16 years old (for boys).

Some common orthopedic conditions are discussed in Chapter 11.

Selecting Shoes

What is the best shoe for your baby? For young infants, no shoe is the best shoe. Its only purpose is for protection outdoors. In fact, I recommend bare feet in the house until a child is at least five years of age. (Skidproof socks or booties in colder weather will do just fine.) Bare feet are the best for freedom of movement and perceptual awareness. In addition, walking barefoot allows for the development of both the intrinsic foot muscles (the small muscles in the feet) and balance reactions (by allowing the foot to react from the surface). It also provides sensory input while standing or walking on different surfaces (wood floor, carpet, grass, and sand).

When it's time to put your child in shoes, don't get hard-soled ones. Many parents believe a hard-soled shoe provides the stability that their little one's feet are lacking. In truth, a hard-soled shoe actually inhibits foot development. A toddler cannot use the various parts of the foot for balance reactions. She can't learn to push off with her toes and she needs to keep using a high-step gait pattern to clear the surface (since she can't bend the foot).

A physician may prescribe hard-soled shoes for special circumstances. If your child toes-out, your doctor may prescribe stiff shoes worn on the wrong foot (as a corrective device) for several hours a day. A high-top, flexible shoe may be warranted for the infant who has ankle rolling. This condition is seen mostly with *hypotonia* (abnormally low muscle tone), when the ankle is actually rolling in during weight-bearing activities. In this case extra ankle support is helpful to ward off overstretching of the soft tissues in the ankle joints.

Common Concern

My 18-month-old daughter has been pulling up to stand, cruising, and using push toys to walk for almost three months. She'll also walk holding my hand, but she won't let go of it in order to walk independently. Shouldn't she want to walk on her own by now? My mother rolls her eyes at me when I bring this up and tells me I'm being neurotic—am I?

There are many possibilities as to why a child may not be progressing in what is considered a "reasonable time frame." One possibility is that she is just not ready yet, or she is concentrating intently on another area of growth. However, other underlying possibilities need to be explored: Have other transitions been slow or difficult? Is she able to weight-shift? Is rotation not in her repertoire of moments (is she only moving in straight planes)? Could she have underlying low muscle tone? Are there motor-planning issues? Does she become easily upset or frightened during roughhouse play or when someone accidentally knocks her off balance? If any underlying issues such as these are noted, it's possible that she will continue to have fears, frustrations, and difficulties as she attempts new and more challenging activities through her early years. Consult with your pediatrician if you have any nagging concerns. Maybe your child is simply going through a phase, or maybe she needs a little extra help. Either way, don't second-guess your instincts. Asking questions is always more productive than staying in the dark.

Just as we tend to choose sport shoes that are biomechanically correct for ourselves, we need to make the same considerations when buying shoes for our little ones. Shoes need to fit well. If shoes are too large, slippage and toe jamming can occur. If shoes are too small, your child's toes will also be jammed, affecting balance reactions. So be particularly careful about using hand-me-down shoes, which are often a bit too large or too small. Don't guess on your child's shoe size even if it's easier than encouraging her to try on different pairs at the shoe store. An experienced salesperson can ensure that your child gets the right shoe. Remember, then, that, in general, shoes need to fit and be, flexible, durable, and lightweight.

Activities and Play for Your One- to Three-Year-Old

We all understand the importance and benefits of play—how it enhances concentration, communication, dexterity, and cooperation. We need to keep in mind that play is also important for sensory input—helping children improve their balance, coordination, and motor planning. While all play at this age provides visual and cognitive input, different types of play provide increased benefits to the various senses (tactile, vestibular, etc.). We can break down play and activities that young children enjoy into different categories.

Physical Play/Vestibular and Proprioceptive Input

Life seems more frenetic if you have a high-energy toddler—especially when he or she doesn't want to do anything except run around and climb on everything. When other children sit in a group and listen to music or a story, your child is the one trying to climb out the window. While it does appear true that boys can be more active than girls, plenty of girls are high-energy. In any event, there are a number of ways to cope with a very active child.

First of all, stick to routines. They provide structure, which helps to organize and calm your child. Be predictable and prepare your child for the day's activities. Help your child feel secure by giving her lots of affection—even if she's too busy to return it. Hugs can help a child to feel grounded. Finally, encourage your child to play with you. Let her choose activities that the two of you can enjoy together, such as block building, dramatic play, or creating your own zoo in the corner of a room.

Since fine motor skills are important, try to encourage your active toddler to practice them by finding the right time of day to

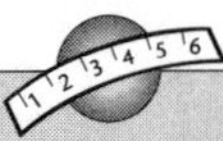

Developmental Benchmarks for Your One- to Three-Year-Old

Please keep in mind that the following chronological markers are *average* guidelines based on standardized tests and screenings. Children can develop these skills outside of this continuum.

- Walks independently (12 to 18 months).
- Kneels (13 to 14 months).
- Creeps upstairs (14 to 16 months).
- Walks backward (12 to 21 months).
- Pulls a toy (15 to 18 months).
- Fast walks (14 to 18 months).
- Walks sideways (14 to 15 months).
- Imitates scribble (12 to 15 months).
- Has forearm rotation by two years.
- Helps with his dressing and undressing by two years.
- Can build tower of six cubes by two years.
- Throws overhand (16 to 22 months).
- Runs (18 to 24 months).
- Throws a ball into a bin by two years.
- Can get into a chair independently (18 months).
- Enjoys finger painting, modeling clay, and paints (18 months to 5 years).
- Places shapes in form board (circle by 18 months, square by 21 months, and triangle by two years).
- Can string beads by two years.
- Enjoys roughhouse play (throughout development).
- Jumps (two to two and a half years).
- Can use feet to ride on toys with pedals by (two and a half to three years).
- Stands on one foot for about three seconds (two to three years).
- Knows six body parts by two and a half years.
- Can use feet to ride on toys with pedals (two and a half to three years).
- Knows various rooms in the house (two to two and a half years).
- Builds a tower of nine cubes (three years).

work on these types of activities. When is her concentration level best? If your toddler refuses to sit at a table for fine motor activities, then let her stand up beside the table or lie down on her belly.

Physical Play

No matter if your child is high-energy or not, the following activities will help with her gross motor skills. Roughhouse play and "crashing," as well as pulling and pushing games, actually help organize the body. Jumping, climbing, and hide-and-seek are terrific activities. Do lots of running. Play chase games. Toddlers love to be chased and love to chase you. A new runner will have stiff legs and will only be able to go a short distance before she falls. But don't worry, she'll quickly get up and try again. Continue to use ride toys, which are great for balance and coordination.

Common Concern

Why doesn't my daughter want to use a scooter?

Riding a scooter may not be fun for your daughter—it might be too much work. Perhaps she can't figure out how to get on it and then push it, using two feet at the same time (she might have motor planning difficulties). She might also have a hard time using her feet (balance and tactile issues). You might want to try tapping games—using deep pressure—on the soles of her feet to help desensitize them. Have her stamp her feet on the ground to increase body awareness (proprioception). Try working on getting your daughter to figure out how to get on to the scooter. Once she's on correctly, give her a ride so she can feel how much fun it is to move on it.

Though your toddler is walking, don't forget to continue working on other skills. Play games where your child gets to crawl under tables or fit into small spaces. This helps with perceptual awareness, that is, "How much space do I take up?" Crawl through tunnels. You can use a store-bought one, or just use a large box open at both ends. This is great for balance and depth perception. Some children are afraid to go through the tunnels. If this is the case with your child, try putting it away for a few weeks and try again later. Make an obstacle course by moving furniture, toys, and pillows. You can go through the "course" first and have your toddler follow you. This is a great activity for motor planning, balance, and coordination.

There are several different types of walking games: pivoting, walking on large cardboard bricks (made by Ready Set and Grow), walking or creeping on firm pillows scattered on the floor, and going up and down the stairs and curbs. These are all great activities for balance reactions. Games involving walking backward, tiptoeing, and duckwalking (walking on the heels of the feet) also help with coordination and balance. Kneeling and half-kneeling play (when one knee is on the floor while the other foot is planted firmly on the floor) are great postures to enhance balance. Work on ball throwing and reaching games from these positions.

Common Concern

I take my toddler to a mini sports class once a week. Most of the kids enjoy it, but my son doesn't like to participate and whines about going. Frankly, it's an exhausting experience for both of us. Does he really need to go to a program like this? Can't I just let him do the activities he enjoys, like computer games, puzzles, and blocks? I feel like I'm pushing him for no reason.

If a child continues to sit out in a class, becomes withdrawn, or can't participate once the class begins, then he is telling you that it is not the right class for him. However, it *is* important to be physically active—to work on movement, balance, coordination, and strength—as our nervous system is maturing.

Some classes are more challenging than others. It is our job, as parents, to discover which activity works best for our children, and at what level of difficulty. The mini sports class may be good for one child but may be too fast, rough, large, noisy, or advanced for another. Karate, gymnastics, dance, or skating might be better suited for him.

If we allow our children to drop out of all activities they don't like, they will never gain the confidence to try. Focus in on what makes your child unhappy about a particular activity, and then be persistent in finding the right activity for him to participate in.

Ball Play

Ball rolling is the beginning of cooperative play, but it quickly becomes a game of throwing by 14 months of age. Teach your toddler how to kick a ball. By 18 to 20 months, most children can kick one. At first, your child may overshoot the ball or only touch it slightly with her feet. She might even fall. But soon this skill will be perfected—and then watch out! To teach your toddler how to kick, first have her practice while holding onto a piece of furniture for balance. Then have her practice kicking in the middle of the room, without support. This is a wonderful skill for balance and coordination, as well as encouraging running skills by getting the ball after she kicks it. Leg strength also improves each time your child squats down to pick up the ball. Use a soft ball to "hike" the ball like a football player (eighteen months to five years). This game is great for balance, as well as developing strength in the leg and foot muscles.

By three a child is able to throw balls of different sizes into boxes and pails. Play with textured balls such as kick balls (about 11 inches in size), tennis balls, Ping-Pong balls, and footballs. All have different properties of movement and provide a multitude of proprioceptive and vestibular input. They also teach your child about depth perception. Hang a tennis ball on the shower rod in your child's bathtub. She will love to swat at it while she sits in the tub. Having your child push around a gymnastic ball (about 26 inches) is great for building upper body strength. These types of play help all visual motor skills.

Outdoor Play

Parents frequently say to me, "I know I should go to the park, but I hate it." Nevertheless, outdoor play is a very important part of development, so partake in outdoor activities as much as possible. Take your toddler out of the stroller and let her walk and explore a bit. Take your toddler for walks, barefoot, on the grass and sand—both are great tactile experiences. Work on balance when walking on curbs. Work the leg muscles by climbing up hills. If you have the means and the space, buy a climbing structure for your home. It does not have to be an elaborate piece of equipment, just a small ladder with a slide and perhaps a space to crawl through. Kids love these structures and they are wonderful for muscle toning as well as vestibular and proprioceptive input.

Bench sitting happens to be a great way of improving postural control. As discussed

Recommended Toys for Your One- to Three-Year-Old

- Toy strollers to push.
- Ride toys.
- Pull toys. You can buy these or make them yourself (using paper cups or large beads on a string).
- Bath toys.
- Small, one-inch cubes.
- Crayons.
- Puzzles. Individual-piece puzzles are fine at first. Between two and three years of age, four- or five-piece puzzles are appropriate.
- Balls of various sizes.
- Animals.
- Stickers (ages two to five). Toddlers love stickers, but watch closely or your walls and furniture will be re-covered as well.
- Nesting cups. These help a child learn about size differences.
- Shape sorter. By 18 months, a toddler can usually get the rings on in the correct order.
- Foam puzzles by Lauri. These require a certain amount of strength to pull the pieces out and push them back in.
- "Magna Doodle" by Fisher-Price (between two and three years). Interlocking blocks such as "Duplos" or "Gears" (by International Playthings).
- Ball tracker by Tag or Battat. These are great for pounding, visual tracking, and hand-eye coordination.
- Wood pegs. Push them through a wood bench with holes, which is good for pounding and hand-eye coordination.
- Beading. Use either large wooden or plastic beads, or spools, and thick string (ages eighteen months to two years).
- Lock boxes (ages two to three and up). Children love to lock and unlock things, opening them up and finding surprises inside.
- Between two and three years, key toys and twisting toys are favorites, especially because incorporating wrist rotation is easier now. The same is true for the monkey barrels, which require wrist rotation to open (not to mention sturdy hands that are needed to hook the monkeys together).
- Felt boards and Velcro boards. These are good for the imagination and very useful during car rides.
- Toys that imitate things that you do (such as garden tools, kitchen utensils, phones, and dolls) are usually a big hit at two years of age.
- Simple matching games. Ravensburger makes nice ones.

on page 82, your child should sit with her hips and knees at 90-degree angles, with her feet flat on the floor. Have your child reach for a ball slightly to one side of her and then to the other. Hold the ball about (her) arms' distance away, at head height. As your child reaches for the ball, try to encourage her to use both hands. This causes the abdominal muscles to work and encourages trunk rotation. You can also encourage your child to reach down to the floor to pick up blocks or some small toy to help strengthen the lower back muscles.

Heavy work activities are good for propriocepitve input. Ask your toddler to help you push filled boxes or to carry a handful of books for you. Also continue to do wheelbarrow walking. By the time your toddler is 18 months old, you can begin to play tug-of-war games with a hand towel (you hold your end up and pull a bit). During activities like this one, muscle contraction against resistance helps muscles to work more, and thus become stronger. Jumping on a trampoline or swinging from a bar (for the two- to three-year-old) is another great activity for strengthening muscles in this manner.

Common Concern

When I am out with my two-year-old daughter, she tends to cling to my leg. Most of the other children her age are running around or playing games. What should I do?

Every child has his or her own comfort level—physically as well as emotionally. If your toddler is clinging to you in a playground, for example, there are a number of variables to consider. Is this a new environment or experience for her? Perhaps the stimulation is initially overwhelming. But if she clings to you no matter how often she comes to this particular park, then you need to consider if she is comfortable with the various activities. Is it the sandbox she finds "icky"? Does the slide scare her? Remember, children can *seem* shy or stubborn, when in fact they are neither. Your child might have tactile sensitivities, or have minor developmental lags in her gross motor development and/or vestibular/proprioceptive senses that make her feel insecure when trying various activities (slides, swings, etc.). You need to compare her behavior in different environments with her behavior at home. Pay close attention to how she handles new tasks within the comfort of her own space. What is her temperament on a daily basis?

If your baby is the quiet, fussy, and/or shy type, she might not explore as freely as the more outgoing, energetic child. Therefore, it's important to foster this exploration and help her out. Talk her through a new activity or two. Play with a toy first and explain what you are doing. "Look what I have—a small ball. It fits in the tunnel. Watch it go! Now, you try it."

Encourage your child's curiosity by asking questions. Go outside and ask, "Where is the sun? How does it feel outside—cold, rainy, hot?" Join her in feeling the grass, smelling the flowers, playing in the sand. You'll be helping your child experience and enjoy novel things.

Playground Safety

Playgrounds—whether in a backyard or in a local park—are a wonderful, important, and integral part of a child's weekly (if not daily) routine. Playgrounds help our children socialize, strengthen their bodies, and provide total sensory stimulation. However, playgrounds can be needlessly hazardous. In fact, the majority of reported playground injuries are due to falls that often could have been avoided with proper supervision.

Between ages two and five, children begin to explore independently, and can become forgetful. You should check on them frequently (four- and five-year-olds in particular), especially when they are playing in your own yard. Clothing should be comfortable and safe. For girls, pants are better than dresses, which may get caught in chains. Shoes should be flexible, with rubber soles, and toes should be covered—especially for little ones who often trip and fall. While this can seem like a problem in the warmer weather, you can find sandals that are woven so they are open, yet with toes protected. Shoelaces should be double-knotted. In colder weather, scarves should be left at home. Use neck warmers instead. Scarves can easily get caught in links and chains, causing avoidable accidents.

Be especially vigilant when playing in public parks. The swing areas there are often enclosed, so please remember to close the safety gate behind you. On jungle gyms or monkey bars check to make sure that all screws are secured and that there are no rungs missing on the climbing apparatus (this may cause a child to lose her balance). Try to have your toddler stay on climbing equipment that is age-appropriate—and always spot her. Remember, toddlers love to imitate. If they see an older child sliding down the fire pole, they want to try it. However, they often misjudge the distance the pole is from the platform and cannot hold on long enough to get all the way down. In addition, young children become easily distracted and can lose their balance or grasp.

When snacks or lunch are given, firmly encourage your child not to run around with food in her mouth (chewing while moving around can be hazardous). Always wash your child's hands prior to eating. If an injury occurs, follow the R.I.C.E. rule: **R**est, **I**ce, **C**ompression (applied pressure—not like a tourniquet), and **E**levation. If sand gets into your child's eyes flush them out with water—do not rub them, since the sand can scratch the corneas. Call the doctor if:

- Numbness or tingling occurs.
- Your child is in severe pain.
- She can't move a body part.
- Swelling does not go down within 48 hours.

A simple park safety kit might come in handy: adhesive bandages, antibiotic ointment (such as bacitracin), iodine swabs, cotton balls, a small water bottle, and an antiseptic solution (such as Purell) for those times when hand washing is impossible. With proper vigilance, most park accidents can be avoided. We must do what we can for our children both for their safety and for our peace of mind.

Manipulative Play/ Tactile Input

Manipulative activities play a very important role in building your child's fine motor skills.

Modeling Clay Recipes

Mother's Recipe

Mix in a pot:

2 cups flour
1 cup salt
1 tbs. cream of tartar

Mix together in a clear jar:

2 cups water
½ cup oil
Several drops of baker's food color gel

Slowly pour the wet mix into the dry one and mix all together in the pot.

Cook over a low heat, stirring constantly. The mix will slowly get stiff. When it gets quite stiff and dry, remove from pot onto a board dusted with flour. After it cools a few minutes, knead it.

Gingerbread Play-Dough

A recipe from the Chicago Children's Museum

4 cups flour
¾ cup salt
2 tbs. ginger
2 tbs. instant tea
2 cups water
½ cup oil

Mix dry ingredients together in a large bowl. Add wet ingredients and stir. If the dough is sticky, knead in enough flour to make it the desired consistency. Store in an airtight container.

As parents, we love to use products that keep toddler (and parental) frustration to a minimum, products such as Velcro closures instead of buttons and laces, washable markers instead of colored pencils and crayons, and precut stickers instead of cutting and pasting shapes. But because these items require minimal time and effort from your child, they detract from the use and development of her fine motor skills. However, there are plenty of activities you can both enjoy that give your child the manipulative input she needs.

Art Projects

Art is a cause-and-effect activity. It helps develop hand-eye coordination, which later on helps a child to write. Do not expect a Renoir, but enjoy your child's creativity and sense of expression. Any type of art project should be simple at this age. You can keep art supplies in a large sweater box containing paper, paints, sponges, smocks, plastic cups, paintbrushes, old photos, glue, large-size crayons and markers, and a plastic tablecloth for the table or floor.

Painting and Drawing While setup time is minimal for a painting project (grab some paper, smocks, paints, and sponges), the project itself may last five minutes or one hour. Spill-proof paint bottles to dip brushes in are great. Easels are also wonderful. It is easier for a toddler to use easels than to paint or draw on a flat table. Their arms don't smear the page, and it makes it easier to see the picture. It also promotes a better arm position because it strengthens the arm and encourages wrist extension. Also, toddlers who love to stand can do so to paint or draw. Adjustable easels are nice to have, but they are more costly.

Crayons and Markers Finger painting is a wonderfully creative activity. You can use pasta sauce, whipped cream, or washable paints. Small hands prefer larger-size crayons, so buy the wide ones. Less tension is needed to hold on to them, which makes marking easier. By age three most children also like to use markers. Again, try to use wide markers over thin ones, and make sure they are water soluble.

Glue By three years of age children love to glue. You can give them discarded family photos and familiar pictures cut out from magazines to work with. Cut out the pictures in advance, so your child doesn't lose interest in the activity. Keep the pictures in a box for a rainy day and have your child glue them onto paper. Then help your child name the pictures. As your child gets older, add other fun objects to the box to glue (such as glitter, feathers, felt, ribbon, pipe cleaners, leaves, and shells).

Puzzles
Puzzles are great for perceptual awareness, language development, and wrist rotation. The easiest puzzles are those having individual pieces that fit into a specific hole. Your child learns about shape and size from them (which piece fits into what space). Knob puzzles make the pieces easier to pick up. More complex puzzles contain four or five pieces that fit together to make a picture. Add the level of difficulty in proportion to your child's concentration span and frustration tolerance.

Hiding Small Objects
The old game of hiding the coin in your hand and guessing which hand it's in is excellent for dexterity. First you do it, and then have your toddler (not under two) hide the coin from you. This activity sends toddlers into peals of laughter—they love "tricking" you—and it also occupies them during long waiting periods.

Building Blocks
Block building is great for enhancing visual motor skills such as spatial perception, organization, and later arithmetic skills. It is endlessly fun, no matter what the child's age, and always works with the child's own creativity. I like to work with wood blocks; however, many other types of blocks exist: cardboard, foam, and plastic blocks come in all different shapes and sizes as well.

Modeling Clay
Modeling clays such as Play-Doh are very tactile substances that are good for hand and finger strengthening. It's appropriate from about 15 or 16 months on. Keep a modeling clay box in your home. Add cookie cutters, play knives, designs, and so forth. Let your child experience the medium by mashing it, rolling it, changing its shape, and even mixing the colors. It is

also easy to make your own modeling clay, but beware—the food coloring may stain your hands for a while.

Sand Play

Playing in sand is also a very tactile experience. At this age, most children will put the sand in their mouths because they are still exploring most objects orally. (If sand is a new experience for them it will most *certainly* wind up in their mouths.)

You can change the texture of the sand by wetting it. Experiment with silkier, dry sand on to heavier, moist sand. Most children love playing in mud, and thus love making mud pies and dribble castles out of dripping-wet sand. Have some sand toys ready as well—wheeled cars or trucks, cups for pouring, a shovel, a sifter, and a bucket are all good to have on hand.

Indoors, when sandboxes are not convenient, you can try to make your own tactile box. Fill a shoe box–size or sweater box–size plastic container with a mixture of rice and some dried beans. Bury small objects inside (clothespins, nuts and bolts, and small cars). Have your child place her hands inside the box and find as many objects as she can. This activity needs to be closely monitored—all children will try to eat the rice, beans, and small objects.

Clothespins and Sock Puppets

Old-fashioned clothespins are also great for hand-strengthening activities. Clipping them onto the sides of a plastic container may sound easy to you, but watch your child hard at work (this activity may be better suited for the two- to three-year-old). And save all those single socks for play dates and rainy days. Children (at closer to three years of age) love to draw and glue on the socks, then wear their puppets on their hands. They can then make up simple stories using their new puppets.

Musical Instruments

Create your own musical instruments—whistle blowers, noisemakers, and shakers are especially fun. Blow through cardboard paper towel rolls. Put dried beans into plastic eggs and glue them shut. Put dried beans or popcorn between two paper plates and staple them closed. Film canisters also make great shakers. Be sure to glue the tops on to prevent children from swallowing small pieces inside. Older children can help you make these items. All are great for sound production and auditory input, in addition to enhancing fine motor and oral-motor skills.

Water Play/Tactile Input

Babies and toddlers love water. So much happens—it makes noise, it can be messy, and objects can float and sink in it, and even squirt because of it. Turn an everyday bath into a wonderful sensory experience by using silly foam or bath paints for children to paint themselves with. Some children may find the silly foam too much of a tactile experience at first. If this is the case, put it away and try again in a month.

Bubble blowing is also a fun activity to do in the bathroom, in the bath, or outdoors. Chasing and popping bubbles is great for visual-motor coordination. Reaching for bubbles in the tub can also facilitate trunk rotation (something we need for almost every activity we do).

If you have a yard or you are at the beach, fill a large bucket of water and give a cup to your child so she can scoop up the water and then pour it out. In your kitchen or bathroom, have your child pour water from one container to another. Watch her expression as she sees how the same amount of water fills up different shapes and sizes of containers.

One reminder when playing with water: everything gets wet. Be prepared.

Imaginative and Symbolic Play/Auditory and Cognitive Input

Children love to use their imagination to create scenarios with play animals, dolls, blocks, and rocks. You can also use puppets and make up "plays," as discussed in the section on manipulative play.

To further enhance creativity, let your child assist you in the kitchen. Make sandwiches, fruit salad, and blender drinks. These foods require no wait time and children receive immediate gratification. Use play food as well. Children love to cook and serve play food.

Play "dress up" with your child. It's good for body perception, among other things. Keep a basket of dress-up objects including old work shirts, pillowcases, pieces of fabric, and scarves. These are all wonderful objects that can be transformed into many things. Go shopping: give your child a large shopping bag and let her go around the house collecting things.

Some people believe that dolls are structured toys that children become easily bored with. However, playing with dolls can be a wonderful way for boys and girls to use their imagination and work out issues of concern to them. Unstructured toys (blocks, crayons, paints, etc.) are better for the imagination (and usually cheaper) than brand-name ones advertised on TV. Children also tend to play with them for longer periods of time.

Playgroups

Small playgroups can be a nice way for your child to make friends, learn to cooperate, and have a sense of independence. There are any number of organized programs to join that offer music, gymnastics, dance, or story time (to name a few). But you can organize your own small groups as well. Either way, make sure that the class is not too long (30 to 45 minutes is plenty of time) and that it is convenient to get to. Classes and playgroups should not interrupt nap or feeding schedules.

Whether with her playgroup or with just the two of you, be sure to take your toddler on outings. Children between the ages of two and five love going to the firehouse, museum, and library. Let them collect things. Toddlers love to collect and are proud of their findings (even if it is a bunch of sticks or rocks).

Language Play/Auditory and Cognitive Input

In order to stimulate your child's language development, continue many of the activities you started when she was younger. Continue to read board books. Continue to point to the pictures as you read, or make animal sounds when animal pictures are shown—help her learn that pictures represent *things*. This fosters language skills. Label everything, even body parts. This helps your child get to know her body. Play "Simon Says." ("Stand on your toes; find your belly button; sit down.") This game helps a child connect words and labels to actions.

Between two and three, children love flap books—reading them is like playing peekaboo. Kids get to open the flaps and discover what is underneath them. By two years of age, try to encourage your child to turn the pages of a book, one page at a time, while using two or three fingers (rather than the whole hand).

Hiding things and having your child find them is both fun and good for problem solving. Put a ball in a box, or cover a mirror and have your child uncover it—surprise! She can see herself! Children love having the ability to find things, and you can help them with language by naming what they find.

Feeding Your One- to Three-Year-Old

Between one year and 18 months babies continue to take in "adult" foods, and by 18 months they prefer to eat what we eat. At this time your toddler is able to eat independently with a spoon. As she eats foods that are more challenging for her (harder foods that require more chewing), your child's chewing abilities will continue to improve.

Common Concern

My 18-month-old still loves his pacifier, and I see no reason to deprive him of it. But my friend saw him with it the other day and told me to wean him from it immediately. She says it will ruin his bite and cause him to have braces.

Many parents believe that a baby should never be given a pacifier, while others believe that the pacifier has saved them from many sleepless nights and noisy days. There is no right or wrong reasoning here. Pacifiers should not be used to constantly quiet a crying baby. It is our job to understand why our infants are crying and to address their needs. In addition, most pediatric dentists will give you many orthodontic reasons why pacifiers should not be used.

That being said, pacifiers are self-soothing and self-regulating. They help calm infants while at the same time provide oral-motor and sensory input. A three year old, however, doesn't need to be walking around all day with a pacifier in his mouth. Constantly sucking on it could hinder your child's expressive language development at this age. If your child is between two and three and can't seem to give up his pacifier, there may be underlying reasons why he needs the constant oral input. You might want to mention it to your pediatrician.

Feeding Benchmarks for Your One- to Three-Year-Old

Twelve to Eighteen Months

- Feeds herself with a spoon using a palmar grasp (her palm is facing down). Because her wrist movements are not refined (stable) yet, food will spill out of the spoon as she turns it to put it in her mouth (oops!).

Eighteen to Twenty Four Months

- Most infants give up the bottle and prefer cup drinking, although many children continue to take a bottle at naptime and bedtime, under stressful situations, or when they are ill.
- Feeds herself with a spoon or a fork (a child is now able to accomplish this task with her palm facing up).

Two to Three Years (and up)

- Feeds herself with little spilling off of the spoon or fork.
- Can stab food with the fork.

If you choose to give your baby a pacifier, it should be a safe one with no loose parts and it should fit your baby's mouth in order to provide the sensory input that he desires.

By 18 months your baby may not want to sit in the high chair. If this is the case, you might think of getting a booster seat, a sassy seat, or your child's own table and chairs. You'll notice that when your child first tries to get into a chair on her own, she will face it, then kneel or stand on it. Eventually she'll learn to hold it behind herself and wiggle into it.

The advantage of having pint-size table and chairs is that your child can have a greater sense of autonomy and independence. The disadvantage is the same—your child has a greater sense of autonomy and independence. She might not want to sit through an entire meal. So consider your temperament and your child's before making a decision on what kind of seating makes the most sense.

By two years of age, your toddler can hold food in her mouth (without losing it) and swallow parts of the total amount in her mouth. This of course takes greater control and skill. But while a two-year-old has the motor skills and coordination to eat any type of food, what she actually eats and how she eats it is another story. (Social graces are a topic to be addressed in your home—and in another book.) In general, the most difficult foods for toddlers to manage are fruits with the skin left on, soups with chunks of solids (such as chicken noodle soup), and cereals with milk.

Your One- to Three-Year-Old's Language Development

Between 13 and 18 months there is a wide range in language development. Some toddlers continue to gesture with sounds or pointing, while others may have a range of words and are combining two or three words ("give me," "no-no," "doggie-woof/woof," "all gone"). By 14 months, babies are learning and comprehending new words each week. They are also beginning to understand the various intonations that people use to give meaning to their words. Children at this age will come close to having the proper pronunciation, but sound errors/substitutions are still common. During this period it's important to be sure that your toddler is able to understand or comprehend what you are saying. Also make sure that she is listening to you, and that she is communicating with you by facial expressions, gesturing, or babbling/jargonizing.

By 18 months most children have five to ten words, can identify one or more familiar pictures (mom, dad, sibling, pet, bottle, ball, car, etc.), and can point to one or more body parts (eyes, nose, mouth). By this age most children are also able to follow simple commands, such as "Show me your shoe," "Get the ball," and "Bring Mama your book." Around this time babies are beginning to use words—either alone or accompanied by gestures—to express their wants and needs. They are also saying words that they hear in their environment.

The Cell Phone Phenomenon

As you walk down the streets of any city, you will see scores of people talking away on their cell phones. Often, they are talking through microphones—appearing as if they're just babbling out loud to themselves. Mothers, fathers, and caregivers can be seen walking through parks, streets, and stores, talking on their cell phones while pushing a toddler in a stroller. They are chatting away in their cars with a child strapped in the backseat. Let's face it: most of us are guilty—even if we are unaware of it. But what's so important that it can't wait until we are at home or in our offices?

"Being" with a baby or young child is an active process that demands attention and communication. We all need to be interested in talking to, and engaging, our children. It's a large part of how they learn both language and concepts. So try to refrain from being another "talking head" on the streets—and talk with your child, instead.

Between 18 months and two and one half years there is usually an explosion of vocabulary. Your child might say or use up to three hundred words and could comprehend yet another one hundred to three hundred words. She is also beginning to use pronouns such as "me," " I," and, the big one, "mine!" In addition to following simple directions, your child might begin to ask you questions such as "What's that?" "Where is . . . ?" and the dreaded "Why?"

Language Development Benchmarks for Your One- to Three-Year-Old

One to two years

- Points to things he wants.
- Can point to pictures of objects in a book when you name them.
- Points to a few body parts.
- Continues to build vocabulary (moving toward three hundred words).
- Begins to put two words together—"More milk," "No more," "Mommy car," "Eat cookie," and "Daddy go" (closer to 16 or 18 months).
- Uses the pronouns "I," "me," "mine," and "you."
- Understands simple commands—"Come here," "Give a kiss"—and simple questions—"Where is your shoe?"

Two to three years

- Uses three-word sentences.
- Names pictures when you say, "What's this?" (as you point).
- Identifies familiar pictures (when you say, "Find the cow," for example).
- Understands and follows two-part requests—"Get the block and put it on the chair."
- Vocabulary increases—might have as many as five hundred words.
- Uses plural words.

Between ages two and three is a big time for imaginary play—setting up tea parties, cooking, playing trains, and so forth. Most three-year-olds use complex sentences and have an expressive vocabulary of up to five hundred words while their receptive vocabulary (what they understand but cannot say) may be up to eight hundred words. Your child is now able to carry on a conversation with you. She is able to understand prepositions such as "up/down," "on/off," and "top/bottom" and verbs such as "jump," "walk," and "run." She is also forming longer sentences and may begin to use plural words ("more cookies") to describe things. She knows the words to songs and what certain objects are used for. Language is mostly used in a concrete fashion—she is not yet creating stories. However, children at this age generally love to have stories read to them and enjoy picking out their favorite books for you to read. They are also beginning to understand taking turns (although they may still have difficulty waiting their turn). Children are also beginning to refer to past and sometimes future events at this time.

Warning Signs for Language Acquisition Impediments

In order for proper speech and language to develop, prerequisite skills need to be in

The Well-Balanced Checklist

What You Can Do: One to Three Years

- Allow ample time for exploration.
- If your child is not walking yet, but is cruising (at 18 months), try not to walk her by holding her hands—give her push toys instead for upright, independent mobility.
- If your child is walking, continue to play games that require upper-extremity weight bearing.
- Set up activities that will challenge her motor and balance abilities (but not to the point of frustration).
- Focus on manipulative skills (such as coloring, pasting, and beading).

place. A child needs to have appropriate cognitive and auditory function. In addition, as she begins to use words, she'll need to have a good repertoire of vocabulary items—such as nouns, verbs, and pronouns—before she can use two-word combinations. Furthermore, a child between the ages of two and four might experience a period of incongruence between what she hears and understands and what she articulates. In other words, her receptive language abilities are more advanced than her expressive language abilities.

Consequently, she can have difficulty expressing her ideas—which is very frustrating to her. If such a stage persists or gets worse, you might consider consulting with a professional speech therapist. Following are some warning signs for language acquisition impediments.

- Your infant is not making sounds or engaging in sound play by 10 months.
- Your child is not using a variety of consonant and vowel sounds by 12 to 15 months.
- Your child is not gesturing by 18 months.
- Your child does not progress in a variety of sound play by 18 months.
- Your child continues to use only single words by 18 to 24 months.
- Your child does not increase the size of her vocabulary by 18 months.
- Your child does not understand simple commands or questions by two years ("Give Mama your shoe" or "Where is your shoe?").
- You still need to gesture or point to make your wants known to your child (for example, if you are pointing to your shoe as you say, "Shoe—give Mama your shoe") by 18 to 20 months.
- Your child is not combining words by two years.
- Your child has difficulty communicating her wants and needs from early on (e.g., a lack of gesturing) and later through speech.
- You (or other people) have difficulty understanding your child's words by two years.

- Your child continues to omit beginning and/or final consonants of words ("aa" is what he says for *ball*) by two to two and a half years.
- Your child is not using two- or three-word sentences by two and a half years.
- Your child can't follow a two-step direction (e.g., "Get the ball and give it to Dad") by three years.
- Your child can't name specific objects by two and a half to three years.
- Your child's speech is slurred or unintelligible by two and a half years.
- Your child is not speaking in simple sentences (using three to five words) by three years.
- Your child is not using clear speech or adultlike sentences by three years.
- Academic, emotional, or social problems are noted in school by five years.

Undetected language problems will affect your child's ability to understand or express her thoughts. Consequently, if you have any concerns regarding your child's speech development, it's important to see a pediatric speech-language pathologist. He or she can tell you if your child's speech is immature, or your child is not progressing or going through the necessary stages of speech and language development. He or she may also be able to provide you with home activities, or might recommend professional intervention.

The following groups of children are at a higher risk for developing speech delays or difficulties:

- Premature babies
- Children with low muscle tone
- Children with sensory issues
- Children with neurological impairment or immature nervous systems
- Children adopted from orphanages
- Children with one or both parents who had a speech delay (known as a familial delay)

And Always Remember . . .

- *Imitation is important for learning.*
- *If you are in sync with your baby's moods and schedules, you'll be more able to help her through new transitions.*
- *Don't second-guess your instincts. If you feel that something "is not quite right," as Miss Clavel would say—speak up.*

CHAPTER

7

Your Walker and Talker

Development of and Activities for the Three- to Five-Year-Old

Your three- to five-year-old is becoming an increasingly social little person, full of thoughts, emotions—and surprises. He's a wonder, and he might seem to be three children, not just one! Although he engages in a greater amount of cooperative play, he enjoys playing alone as much as with others. He also loves new environments. While he is becoming increasingly independent, he still loves to snuggle and cuddle, and won't want to stray too far from you.

Between the ages of three and five, your child's motor planning abilities become much greater. He has mastered walking and running, and can now easily stay focused on one or two activities for a significant period of time. There is less running around to every object in a room. He is better coordinated and can follow directions more easily. That being said, you may find that your three- to three and a half-year-old is falling or tripping more frequently. This is due to the fact that his muscle maturity is not completed, and he is often trying to do more difficult motor tasks—like running faster, walking farther, and climbing higher—than his legs can manage. When your three- to four and a half-year-old is lying down and sees something he wants, he can now quickly sit up while simultaneously turning to reach the object and bring it close to him. This skill involves both trunk rotation and good abdominal control. It's a lot to accomplish—even many adults have great difficulty doing this in the gym!

Most children between the ages of three and five achieve another, different kind of milestone: entering preschool. For some children, the transition of being without Mom and Dad is a smooth one. For others, the idea is far more daunting. Similarly, some parents have a much easier time separating from their little ones than others. For many children, preschool is the first time that their day is structured for significant periods (other than the weekly gym or music class, for instance). This can be either a calming or restricting experience for them, and might take a good deal of time to adjust to. To help them, you can relate the introduction of school routines to your child's routines at home—mealtimes, bath-books-bedtime, and so on. Over time, most parents find that school routines help organize their child in many aspects of his life.

Common Concern

There's a child in my five-year-old son's pre-K class who really annoys all of the parents—not to mention the other kids. He seems hyperactive, but worse, he sometimes bites other kids. I don't think he should be a member of the class if his behavior can't be changed. Am I being too harsh?

There's no right or wrong answer here. If a child's behavior is constantly disruptive to his class, then it needs to be addressed with both the child's parents and the school authorities. In order to help your own child deal with a disruptive child, you first need to discuss the school's position with your child's teachers and then explain the circumstances to your child in language he can understand. Let your child know the school is working hard to help the other child learn to use his words and not resort to physical attacks. Sometimes, a behavioral and neurological diagnosis will need to be made by a psychologist and/or a neurologist. Depending on the circumstances, some children with deficits may have a special education teacher work with them in the classroom setting (these children have been classified by the board of education as having special concerns).

Taking a Fresh Look at the Developmental Continuum

During these years, it's important to keep in mind that all children go through various phases of being shy, aggressive, and constantly irritable. Transitions (such as new routines) can account for changes in behavior, as can shifts in a child's development. Remember, just as fine and gross motor coordination develop along a continuum, so does the sensory system. We all exist on the continuum at different places. Some people excel more at sports, some at playing musical instruments. Some are more sensitive to touch or hearing. Some are more comfortable being in close proximity to other people.

One thing is certain—we all experience sensory overload at various times (think of a loud concert or an overcrowded holiday party and you'll know what I mean), whether we are one, five, or adults. As adults, we can experience sensory overload and know it will pass. We also know what we can do to alleviate it (change venues; take a hot bath; stay in a quiet, dark room; etc.). Children with heightened sensitivities, whether due to overload or something as ordinary as a morning transition, need help in understanding how to self-regulate. If a child is *constantly* in some form of overload and behavioral issues have been ruled out, then he might be suffering from a sensory disorder or dysfunction (see Chapter 10). If that's the case, consult with your pediatrician.

By the time our children are age five we usually begin to expose them to sports (which is different than play or games). Sports tend to be organized, and may be competitive. Sports, like play, can be wonderful; however, sports should not dominate a child's life. In addition to taking up tons of precious time, sports can often be played for the wrong reasons. They should be something that a child wants to do, not something a parent wants to do vicariously through the child.

Common Concern

My five-year-old son wants to participate in many activities like softball, soccer, and rock climbing. However, he isn't as coordinated or as fast as the other children he plays with. Sometimes they even make fun of him. Should I keep him in these activities or steer him more toward activities that he might be better at?

If your child wants to do these activities, he should be given the chance. Your focus should be on his level of *confidence*, not *competence*. You've crossed the biggest hurdle if your child wants to try—and continues to try. I have observed children who appear awkward or uncoordinated who have "stuck it out" because they wanted to—even when their parents wanted to pull them out of a certain sport. When they are allowed to keep trying, these kids improve in *all* areas of their development. You can build up your child's confidence level slowly. If he wants to go bouldering or rock climbing, start by walking up some gently sloping rocks until he feels comfortable with his balance. Or, use a larger (11- to 14-inch) ball when playing catch or T-ball, until he gets the hang of it.

If your child really can't seem to catch up, don't view it as a problem. Your anxiety will affect him more than comments made by his peers. And, you can get help by speaking to your pediatrician and getting an evaluation with a physical or occupational therapist.

Believe it or not, there are some five-year-olds who have begun weight-training programs. While I'm not in favor of young children weight lifting, I do encourage strength and endurance training by using one's body weight through activities such as running, jumping, swinging from a bar (trying to "pull up" while remaining on the bar), and even beginning sit-ups. Unlike organized sports, strength training—or plain old physical "fun" of any form—is something our children could do more of. Typically, children do less physical activity today than in the past. Large amounts of schoolwork and pastimes such as Nintendo, computer games, and online chatting have eaten up a lot of the time that used to be spent running around. This lack of play and exercise is not healthy for your three- to five-year-old. Not only is physical conditioning critical to a child's gross motor development, but it also helps create a healthy self-esteem and elevate his mood, and even helps him sleep better at night.

Partly due to this decrease in physical activity, therapists are seeing an increasing trend in upper extremity weakness, lack of postural control, and back problems in young children. A surprising number of eight- to ten-year-olds are referred to therapy because of postural instability and low back pain. In addition, over the past 10 years greater numbers of children are being referred to occupational and physical therapy for a variety of issues other than those just mentioned—oral and tactile sensitivities, fine motor and visual-perceptual difficulties, as well as clumsiness and low muscle tone, top the list.

This increase in referrals may not just be from children's skipping milestones or having inactive lifestyles, but might be related to increased awareness and proactive measures on the part of parents looking out for their kids' best interests. Sending kids for physical and occupational therapy is not a negative thing, but rather a positive one. Much more is understood today about the sensory-motor relationship and how its integration affects our overall development than we knew even five to ten years ago. If your child exhibits any persistent symptoms of low muscle tone or perceptual difficulties, for instance, you can give him a tremendous advantage by having him evaluated by a therapist—and there's no stigma about it. Imagine if (among other things) the cause of your chronic back pain or "poor" sports performance could have been diagnosed and treated years ago—you might have a totally different quality of life today!

Activities and Play for Your Three- to Five-Year-Old

A more active lifestyle would not hurt anyone. There are many lifelong benefits to active lifestyles: a better fitness level, better general health, a decrease in fatigue, and increased endurance, to name a few. For our children, early activity can lead to better motor control, which can lead to the initiation of more play. This in turn contributes to socialization and may lead to a greater enjoyment of sports later on. And as with adults, physical activity helps children feel good about themselves—from a physiological point of view as well as an emotional one.

Physical Play/Vestibular and Proprioceptive Input

Most of the activities described in this section are great for coordination, body

Developmental Benchmarks for Your Three- to Five-Year-Old

Please keep in mind that the following chronological markers are average guidelines based on standardized tests and screenings. Children can develop these skills outside of this continuum.

- Can drink from a cup independently by 15 months.
- Can dress himself but may need help with buttons and snaps—one day he may do it and the next he'll need you for help (three to five years).
- Can brush his teeth (four to five years).
- Understands four prepositions (three to five years).
- Knows the use of three objects (three years).
- Knows colors (three years).
- Can string small beads (three to four years).
- Can use child's scissors (three to three and a half years).
- Has over one thousand words (three years).
- Can hold a pencil with the proper grip by four and a half years.
- Can draw a person with three to six parts (three and a half to five years).
- Can copy a circle by three and a half years, a cross by four years, and a square by four and a half years.
- Can balance on one foot for about six to eight seconds (four to five years).
- Ascends stairs using a step-over-step pattern (three years).
- Descends step-to-step without support by three years and step-over-step by five years.
- Can jump down a 12-inch step using two feet (three years).
- Skips (four to five years).
- Jumps from table height (five years).

awareness, and motor development in your three- to five-year-old. Also covered are body mechanics, since it is never too early to take care of your body.

Playing for Exercise

Running games are a big hit. To motivate your toddler, incorporate running into everyday activities, such as racing to the bathroom for toothbrushing or racing to the bedroom to get dressed. Flashlight games in the early evening are a fun way to encourage running around outdoors. Encourage hopping and ball kicking for balance and coordination. Practice stair climbing—a three and a half-year-old is now able to descend by using a step-over-step pattern.

Have your child kneel on the floor. While he's holding a ball with two hands, have him lower himself down to one side of his legs, then go back up to kneeling, then down again to the other side. This activity is good for pelvic mobility, balance, and abdominal control, and it strengthens the muscles around the hips. Have your child sit with his legs out in front. Hold them up until your child starts to tilt back a bit. You can make up a game ("rock the boat"). This is also a good activity for the abdominal muscles.

Play games where your child has to walk or run on uneven surfaces. Practice walking on a beam—this can be a curb, railroad ties, or even the play cardboard bricks that were mentioned in Chapter 6. Encourage climbing. When at the park, try to find some large rocks to climb on for upper body work. Walk up hills to work those leg muscles and build endurance. Swing sets, merry-go-rounds, and slides all provide vestibular and proprioceptive input. Children at this age love crashing games. Continue with rough-house play and wrestling.

The three-year-old is now ready for a tricycle. You will be amazed at how quickly your child learns to maneuver around corners and obstacles. A four-year-old can be introduced to bikes with training wheels. By five some children can ride a two-wheeled bicycle. Scooters and in-line skates are big hits with young children. Both are great for coordination, endurance, and strength training. Remember that proper protective gear should be worn at all times. Helmets should be worn during all wheeled activities.

Let your child practice walking on a straight line by putting masking tape down. Have him practice walking backward. Dance around the house for balance, coordination, and fun. Play "follow the leader," and try to let your child lead as well. Do different things such as clapping hands, singing, banging toys, and jumping. Set up your own obstacle course. Have your child step over a bucket, walk on blocks, crawl under a table and through a box, and jump into rings laid on the floor. These are great activities for motor planning and balance reactions.

Create your own bowling games with milk cartons, which is good for hand-eye coordination, aiming, and visual tracking. Play basketball games by using a hamper or wash basket. Start close and have your child move farther away after each shot. Play T-ball or baseball (these sports are great for bilateral skills). Play games of kick ball, which are also good for balance and aiming (aim for objects). Introduce a jump rope. At age five, some children are able to jump while holding the rope by themselves.

Continue with ball play. A child can now catch a ball with his arms straight out in front of him. A child at this age can use a 16-inch ball to throw and catch, while a younger child finds it easier to use the 11-inch ball. In recent years, "fitballs," or exercise balls, have become increasingly popular as a workout tool for grown-ups. But they're also terrific for children and can be used for many activities. Sit your child on the 16- or 20-inch size and have him bounce around in a circle for proprioceptive input, as well as for balance and conditioning. Also using the 11- or 16-inch ball, have your child lie on his back and hold the ball between his legs while he tries to lift his legs up and get the ball with his hands. He can also try to hold the ball between his legs while he moves them from side to side (a familiar exercise if you've ever used any kind of fitball). While he's standing, have your child try to maintain an 11- or 16-inch ball under one foot for balance.

The 24- to 26-inch ball is great for balance and conditioning activities as well. With your help, your child can lie on the ball on his stomach while you hold his feet. You can play "Wonder Woman" or "Superman" in this position by having your child lift his arms and trunk upward. Once his hands go forward and down onto the floor, your child can walk out on his hands. The farther he walks out on his hands, the greater the amount of weight is taken through the arms. The trunk muscles are needed to assist in balance. From this position, you can have your child reach for objects that you place in front and to the sides of him. A great motivator is a felt board. Ask your child to grab different pieces that you name or he names off of the board (placed in front of him). This not only works all of his muscles, but helps foster language development as well. Sit your child on the ball while you hold his legs or feet. Depending on how much support he needs, the farther away from the body you hold him, the greater the amount of work he has to do to maintain his balance. You can move his legs slowly from side to side. This is also good for balance, trunk activation, and abdominal control. Put the ball up against the wall at your child's waist height. With his back against it, have your child circle around the ball without letting it fall to the ground. This is a nice activity for spinal control.

Push and pull games also stimulate proprioception. Tug-of-war, pulling wagons, and pushing light furniture or toy grocery carts are all good games to play. Interlock outstretched arms with your child and take turns pushing each other forward and backward.

Try ribbon dancing. Have your child dance around while holding a long piece of ribbon in each of his hands. This is a lovely activity for bilateral arm use.

Body Mechanics

As a physical therapist, I know that an ounce of prevention goes a long way. Children need to be educated about body awareness and body mechanics from an early age—people should not wait until they are injured before learning how they could have prevented their injury. Many children today tend to sit and watch television, or play video, handheld, and computer games. Often poor posture and poor body mechanics are used while playing with these items. All of this can and will lead to later postural problems as well as back pain. Most often a five-year-old is still quite active. However, between eight and twelve years this activity level is on a steady decline—which is why I raise the issue now, before lethargy sets in! Children love to learn, so teach them the simple body mechanics that can be a lifelong gift.

Lifting Lifting, in particular, requires good body mechanics to prevent injury. But it's a misconception to think something needs to be heavy in order for us to use care in lifting it properly. Ideally, we want to teach children how to lift even the lightest objects properly, so that the appropriate body mechanics will become natural to them. Following is a list of proper lifting techniques.

- Children should be taught to keep their feet apart when lifting. This helps increase one's base of support and takes the stress load off of the lower back.
- Tell your child to turn his feet toward the object he's picking up. This helps avoid undue twisting of the trunk. Twisting puts stress on vertebral discs.
- He needs to use his legs when lifting—this means squatting first. Never pick up an object with straight legs, which puts a lot of stress on the lower back. Don't let your child bend over at the back; instead, have him drop his buttocks closer to his heels.

- He should keep his head up (straight), not down, when lifting something. This helps to keep the natural spinal curves in proper alignment.
- Tell your child to bring objects close to his body (toward the belly button) first, and then lift them.
- Movements should be slow. Fast, jerking movements put stress on the joints and muscles.

Jumping Since children love to jump, it's important to tell them to land with soft knees. In other words, tell them to land as "quietly" as possible. This simple cue will ensure that they bend at the knees and hips, which allows the legs, and not the back, to absorb the shock.

Sitting When your child is sitting at a computer table or craft table, his feet should be on the floor, or resting on a bench. His back should be straight against the back of the chair (you can use a pillow behind his back if the seat is too deep). His hips should be about one inch higher than his knees. If his knees are higher, then more stress is placed on his lower back (because it's forced into a rounded position). The tabletop or desk should be at elbow level, not chest level, for good sitting posture. If the tabletop is too high, then he'll have to raise his shoulders, and arms to reach the keyboard or objects.

Standing Ironically, we don't really need to worry about young children's posture in standing. They don't stand still for very long, and when they do, they typically have good posture. Their backs are fairly straight and they keep their knees slightly bent. When the knees are unlocked, the back remains unlocked, thus allowing both the back and hips to rest in good alignment. (It's usually in older kids that we see slouched shoulders and hyperextended knees—a sure postural sign of budding adolescence.)

Carrying Backpacks Sooner than you would like to believe, your child will be carrying a backpack. By third or fourth grade a child may be carrying up to 25 pounds on his or her back. There is much controversy over this today. Two solutions are too expensive to explore: one is that schools could provide two sets of books—one for home and one for school. The other is for publishers to divide textbooks in half so that the entire textbook does not have to be carried home on a regular basis. Since neither of these is practical, we need to look at another option—the backpack itself. Wheeled backpacks are the best, biomechanically. Pulling is always better than lifting and carrying. But there appears to be a social stigma against boys pulling their backpacks, and many refuse to do it. The next best alternative, then, is to use a hard-framed backpack with a waist belt. This puts the weight across the hips and not on the shoulders. With weight on the hips your child is actually strengthening his or her legs, which is good. When weight is placed on the shoulders (as is the case with a regular backpack), the shoulders and head have to round forward, causing a kyphotic posture (the rounded shoulders you see in older people)—and a very sore back.

Focusing on good posture now can help prevent your child from acquiring low back pain, disc problems, back strain, and mechanical joint problems as an adult. The time you spend working on these issues with your child is well spent! Prevention is the name of the game.

Manipulative Play/ Tactile Input

Because the three-year-old has increased hand-eye coordination and visual skills, which broadens the range of activities, there is much he can do to enhance his fine motor skills. Try stringing beads or pasta, or creating a shell necklace. By the age of three, you can introduce scissors and gluing—cutting is important for fine motor development and builds the strength needed for other hand activities. Children also enjoy printing and painting at this age. Use potatoes, sponges, and different shapes.

Common Concern

I would very much like my four-year-old to play the piano. What early skills does he need?

The biggest skill he needs is finger dexterity. Play with modeling clay and Silly Putty. Color with crayons, unwrap candy, and put coins in his hand for him to play with. Help him unscrew the lids of jars, unfasten garments, button garments, and lace cards.

A four-year-old is able to hold a pencil. Work on the proper grip (the pencil is between the thumb and forefinger and resting on the middle finger) and suggest that changing his grip may help make drawing a little easier. Use a wide pencil or put rubber bands around the bottom of a regular one, which helps create a larger grip.

Continue block building. The three- to five-year-old loves to create things—cities, towers, zoos, and castles. Your three-year-old may still need to watch you build a three-block structure, but by three and a half years he can model it (i.e., he can look at something and reproduce it). He can also build a tower of ten blocks. Modeling clay continues to be a favorite amusement. You can elaborate on designs by using buttons, bottle caps, and other handy items to make imprints in the dough. You can also use Popsicle sticks to make appendages, houses, and so on.

Children at this age continue to love water and sand play. They love to wash their toys in the bathroom sink. Sewing is also a big hit with boys and girls. There are a number of different types of children's sewing kits on the market today—crocheting, quilting, puppet making, weaving, and pot-holder-making kits, to name a few. You'll need to help out with and supervise these activities.

This age-group loves banging items—whether they are hammering pegs into holes or smashing empty milk cartons into flattened, new shapes. Opening and closing lids on jars is great for wrist rotation, as is screwing and unscrewing nuts and bolts. Collecting all sorts of things—from leaves, rocks, and bugs to trucks and dolls—is a nice way of sorting. This activity also fosters language, since children are proud of their collections and will be happy to share any information they have on what they have collected.

Recommended Toys for Your Three- to Five-Year-Old

- Matching and sorting games. There is a huge variety on the market today.
- Balance boards.
- Zoom ball. This is an old-fashioned pulley game. It's great for bilateral arm use and upper extremity strength and endurance. It can be played indoors or out.
- Gym sets with ropes and ladders for climbing.
- Any tossing game where the ball is gripped by Velcro mitts, or thrown at a Velcro target.
- T-ball (using lightweight bats).
- Soccer ball.
- Football.
- In-line skates.
- Children's basketball hoops and balls. "Hoops to Go" by Franklin is great for indoor use because the equipment is soft and collapsible.
- Beginner board games. The choices are endless.
- Wood blocks.
- Alphabet and number puzzles.
- Large floor puzzles.
- Children's toolbox—tape measure, plastic hammer, screwdriver, etc.
- Art box—paints, markers, colored pencils, watercolors, glue and scraps, etc.
- Felt boards.
- Child's clock.
- Crafts. Curiosity Kits and Alex make a number of good ones.
- "Zolo" by Cozmo Systems. These are interlocking shapes. You create your own crazy things.
- Puppets—both finger and hand puppets are nice.
- Age-appropriate science projects.
- Cash register.
- Beginning lacing and sewing kits. Lauri, Edushapes, and Lights, Camera, Interaction all make great ones in portable packages. There is also a book, *Red Lace, Yellow Lace,* by Mike Casey, that is a wonderful tool to help a child learn how to lace a shoe.
- "Rail-Road Rush Hour" by Binary Arts. This is a nice visual-perceptual activity. A child needs to match the layout of the trains (or cars, zoo animals, etc.—depending on the set you buy) with the corresponding cards.
- "Thin Ice" by Milton Bradley. The tweezers used in the game are helpful for hand strengthening and dexterity.
- Pick-up-sticks. This is an old fashioned game (still available with plastic sticks) that is also very good for finger dexterity.

Common Concern

My son is five and can't dress himself. Why is it so hard for him?

There are a couple of reasons why dressing at this age can be difficult. One has to do with our lack of patience—not our children's. School mornings are frequently too hectic for us to take the time to allow our little ones to try to dress themselves—everyone ends up in a bad mood (and late, to boot). Instead, use evenings and weekends as times for letting your child practice getting dressed. And if he attempts to dress himself at any time, even if he isn't "color coordinated" or quite warm enough, praise his accomplishments and bite your tongue! Let him go to school looking a bit odd—it's his confidence that needs building, not yours.

There's another reason that getting dressed at this age is tough—it requires a number of basic skills we take for granted. Just imagine sitting on the floor and trying to pull your socks off if you didn't have good balance reactions. Well, that's what your child has to deal with. In order to dress himself, he needs intact tactile and vestibular systems. He also needs perceptual awareness of the difference between in/out, on/off, and front/back. In addition, he needs to be able to weight-shift, balance, and display a certain amount of stability, mobility, and finger dexterity. Of course, a dose of patience all around goes a long way!

Language Play/Auditory and Cognitive Input

In order to enhance your child's language development, continue many of the activities you started when he was younger. Of course, continue reading to your child. He is now able to follow stories well and point to all the different things on the page. Children at this age love to hear the same story over and over again, and they have memorized every word. They now know when you try to skip a few lines or pages, so beware! They also love rhymes and poetry. Listen to music and discuss different forms of music with your child. Continue dramatic play. Children can create increasingly complex scenarios, which can last for hours (and might even resume over a period of days) due to their longer attention spans.

And finally and most important, foster communication. Listen and talk to your child now, and you will be stringing the lines of communication for the coming years.

Your Three- to Five-Year-Old's Language Development

Between the ages of three and five, your child will become more social, more curious, more expressive, and even more fun. Many parents find this age to be the pinnacle of their child's "cute years." This is largely because a three- to five-year-old can express his thought process—and its inherent "logic" is often highly amusing and endearing.

Some Tips on Toys

You do not need to buy every character-driven toy from every movie your child sees. Kids quickly tire of these objects. Furthermore, while children may ask for specific toys, in general toys don't need to be gender specific (as in GI Joe for boys and Barbie for girls). Buy toys that aren't locked into a specific form of play. For instance, if you are looking for a castle or a dollhouse, you can try to buy a wooden house that may seem more generic. This way, one day it can be a castle and the next day a zoo or a barn.

It has been said that a two-year-old learns words, whereas a three-year-old uses them. Indeed, your three-year-old is good at articulating his feelings, needs, and desires. His vocabulary and use of complex sentences continue to expand dramatically. In trying to piece together his world, he's full of questions—the *how many, what, when,* and *why* questions abound. He'll also continue to ask many questions that refer to thoughts or events on his mind ("Where do clouds come from?").

He's using proper sentence structure more often—as in "let's do this" rather than "me do it." At around this age, children develop their own conversational style, with favorite phrases and intonations such as "Actually, Mom" and "Well, you *see*. . . . "

By five years, your child is generally speaking to you like an adult. He can discuss a variety of topics at length and in detail. He'll try out big words—"Stop interrupting me," "That particular book is just what I wanted!"—but won't necessarily use them in the correct context—"Don't be demanding me so much!" It's wonderful to witness and listen to these vocabulary extravaganzas, whether they make sense or not. You'll also notice your child's self-confidence growing measurably with the increased ability to articulate his thoughts and feelings. Five-year-olds can sound quite sophisticated—and yet they emotionally revert to being babies when they are tired, frustrated, or scared.

It is also between four and six years that your child enjoys using words that you may not want to hear. We have a saying in our house: "Bathroom words are to be used in the bathroom, not in public." By this age, your child can also manipulate speech to win over his audience. For example, your five-year-old may use baby talk when talking to a baby, use silly voices when making up a story, or use a scary voice to scare you. He'll try to tell you jokes, too.

The sounds *l, J, L, V, ch,* and *sh* are usually articulated by the time your child is five, while the sounds *R, S, Z, th,* and *st* are usually articulated by six years of age. (If, by five, your child is having real difficulty pronouncing sounds or is unintelligible, you should consult with a speech therapist.) Additionally, your child's comprehension of abstract concepts will continue to expand throughout his developing years.

It's amazing how a child's comprehension comes together seemingly overnight: one day he can't articulate the differences among "yesterday," "tomorrow," and "today," and the next day he wants to know his summer camp schedule and the life span of butterflies. While it seems that your child grasps concepts suddenly, he's been imperceptibly collecting data and testing it out on you. In fact, your interactions with your child are highly influential in his language comprehension—so don't take them for granted!

Language Development Benchmarks for Your Three- to Five-Year-Old

Three to four years

- Answers questions "who," "what," "where."
- Can tell you what familiar objects are used for.
- Clarity of speech and pronunciation is improving. (Uses beginning and ending consonants, for example.)
- Vocabulary expands dramatically.
- Grammatical knowledge and proper use of words expand.
- Uses a variety of sentence types as well as inflecting nouns and verbs to enhance meaning ("running," "ate," "completely," "fastest," etc.).

Four to five years

- Communicates easily with family and peers.
- Listens to you.
- Can answer questions about a story.
- Can answer questions to explain causal relations.
- Can form sentences to define words.

Finally, once your child enters preschool or kindergarten, you'll find that getting him to give you information about his day is nearly impossible. You will quickly tire of asking your child how his day was and what he did at school, only to hear, "It was fine," and "We did nothing" or "I don't remember." This stage in your child's life is to prepare you for his teenage years.

There are several strategies you can try to keep conversation flowing with your child. Try asking specific questions that can't be answered in two words, such as, "What art project did you work on today? Did you paint or color? What did you draw?" Or, converse with your spouse on what the best and worst parts of *your* days were. Children will want in on the conversation, and you will soon have nightly roundtable conversations revolving around the best and worst parts of the day. Eventually you will hear things like "Science was great today—we learned about rocks and crystals" or a report about a friend who spilled paint all over the table and they all decided to put their hands in it and paint each other's hair. This technique is language provoking and never dull—you'll be surprised where such a simple conversational frame can lead you!

Developmental Warning Signs and Solutions for Your Child

We *must* be vigilant about our children's sensory-motor development, especially since we *can* help our children have a better quality of life. Whether your child is one or five (or even older), it's never too late to bolster his development and subsequent self-esteem—but it does require keeping an eye out for any potential warning signs that might crop up. By dealing with them early on, you yourself can remedy many of these potential problems.

In regard to your vigilance of your child's development, one point can't be stressed enough: It's important to notice the *quality* of your child's movements, not just the *milestones*. For example, a two-year-old may be walking, stair climbing, and attempting to jump. That's great—except that he's walking in a slightly crouched position with his knees flexed during all of these activities. His feet may be severely pronated (flat-footed) and he could have underlying low muscle tone, making it difficult for him to have good balance reactions and posture. In order for him to progress through these skills (of walking, stair climbing, and jumping) so that they can be *built* on, the underlying issues mentioned previously need to be addressed. When it comes to physical development, sometimes less (when executed properly) means more.

With *all* areas of development, remember that, while progress occurs on a continuum, not all areas of development will progress at the same rate. Certain skills will come more quickly to a child than will others, and skill areas in which your child once excelled may take a temporary backseat to a new, emerging one. For instance, your three-year-old might be climbing everything in sight, but he is less articulate than he was a month ago. Don't worry; he'll resume expanding his vocabulary once he's mastered his new motor skills. Of course, children also progress at different rates overall, and shouldn't be compared with each other (unless you want to make yourself needlessly nuts).

Common Concern

My child always seems to be delayed in acquiring skills, but he always gets there eventually. Should I be concerned?

Not necessarily, since he is achieving skills at his own pace. If he is delayed in his gross motor skills, he might not be a superstar athlete. Consequently, your level of concern might depend on how important you feel it is that your child excels in sports. Some parents request intervention, while others are content to let their child progress at his own pace.

Ideally, on a good day, your one- to three-year-old will be able to make the transition with ease from one activity or place, to another. He will enjoy his new independence and will be interested in experiencing new activities. Your three- to five-year-old should enjoy playing with his peers, creating projects, and moving around. He'll be excited when he accomplishes a new task. By now, he should be proficient at matching activities, and his vocabulary and fine and gross motor skills should be steadily improving. Of course, as we've discussed, he's also going to be prone to behavioral changes due to developmental hurdles, new experiences, and daily transition periods.

If, however, any of the following behaviors are constant and persistent in your one- to five-year-old, you should consult with your pediatrician. For many of these warning signs, activities or guidelines to correct them have been suggested when appropriate. If a couple of these suggestions work for you and you would like further assistance, ask your pediatrician about consulting with a physical, occupational, or speech therapist. Following, then, are some warning signs you might notice.

- *He doesn't want to assist with most daily activities (dressing, feeding with utensils, hand washing, etc.).* To encourage dressing, try doing most of the dressing of your child yourself—but let him do the last step. Once a step is mastered, continue by leaving more of the responsibility to your child. He might also be more interested in attempting to put on dress up or play clothes than his own clothing.

  To encourage the use of utensils, try using a smaller and wider shaped one. This size utensil might be easier for a child to manipulate than regular adult flatware.

  Have your child wash his dolls or toys to encourage washing his hands.
- *He isn't imitating you.* Try to encourage your child to participate along with you as you perform daily tasks—make a game of it.
- *His speech isn't increasing exponentially.* Foster speech by beginning the sentence with your child, "Sam wants . . ." or "Sam says, 'I want . . .'" This should help jump-start an answer from him.
- *His ability level in gross and fine motor skills is not noticeably improving.* This is a warning sign that holds a lot of weight. If your child hits a plateau for an extended period of time, consult your pediatrician. Evaluation and therapeutic intervention might be warranted.

Common Concern

Why doesn't my child jump with two feet? She's almost three years old.

In order to jump, a child needs a certain amount of strength, balance, and bilateral motor coordination: She needs to be able to use the two sides of her body together (as in clapping, ball catching, and swinging a bat). Children who have difficulty with bilateral motor coordination tend to jump one foot at a time. It's important to find out if there are any underlying reasons why your child might be having this difficulty, and to intervene accordingly.

- *He doesn't understand commands.* Attempt to make eye contact with your child first. Speak slowly and try to use only three or four words at a time: "Henry, come here" or "pick up your toys" rather than "Henry, I would like you to walk over here to play, please, honey," or "I would like you to be able to pick up your toys and put them away in the next five minutes."

- *His movement is hesitant instead of being fluid and fun.* Try not to force activities that may be threatening to your child. Offer to help him, or to have him do the activity with you—for instance, have him sit on your lap as you attempt to string beads.

Common Concern

At preschool, my four-year-old son is always at the end of the line because he is slow going down the stairs. Why doesn't he go faster?

He may have balance or weight-shifting difficulties that could cause him to be afraid of falling or feel insecure on steps. At two and a half to three years of age, no specialist would see this sort of hesitancy as a problem, but the potential issues should be addressed. This kind of behavior usually belongs to the same child who, when a bit older, won't go on the monkey bars or down the slide. Proprioceptive and vestibular issues are then more likely to be a reality.

- *He doesn't like the playground, or is fearful of it. He doesn't want to climb on any equipment, swing, or use the slide.* Try taking walks to the playground at quiet times, when it is less crowded. Attempt to go on the equipment or down the slide with him. Be positive; try not to dwell on what your child can't do but rather on what he can do.
- *He falls frequently.* There could be many reasons why a child is falling or tripping a lot. It would be important to investigate further.
- *He runs awkwardly.* Many new and inexperienced toddlers have a funny running style. Running patterns often improve with maturation. By five, a child should have a coordinated running style.
- *He is easily overstimulated.* There are a number of ways to help calm your child. Try keeping his environment uncluttered, and lower the decibel level—don't have the TV blaring, have the computer on, and be trying to have a discussion simultaneously. Routines and structure, as discussed throughout the book, can also help organize a child who is easily overstimulated.
- *He tends to overreact to situations that don't generally bother other children—such as being bumped into or brushed up against.* Some children find it overwhelming to be in loud or crowded places—such as birthday parties or gyms. If your child has difficulty in similar situations, try to be supportive. Don't force a situation on him. See if he can gradually become accustomed to these kinds of circumstances by introducing them slowly, over time.
- *He avoids different textures—stuffed animals, various foods, messy art projects.* Again, try to slowly introduce new textures to your child to desensitize him. Show him that you can touch and feel these textures, as well.
- *He has not developed a hand dominance by five years of age.* There may be several reasons why a child has not developed

The Well-Balanced Checklist

What You Can Do: Three to Five Years
All of your child's basic developmental skills are now present. Your greatest contribution at this point is to take the time to enhance these skills with various activities.

- Continue to foster language development—read, read, read to your child.
- Discuss the book. Ask questions about it that are appropriate for your child's level of comprehension.
- Repeat and introduce new tactile experiences as well as manipulative/fine motor activities and gross motor activities (including outdoor play and basic sports games).
- Activities should be appropriate. Building with Legos is one thing. Building model boats is quite another.
- Encourage new experiences: museums, different parks, the aquarium, a beach, etc.
- Children like to feel responsible. Helping you around the house is a great way to foster appropriate responsibility.

hand dominance. An occupational therapist should be consulted.

- *He appears frequently inattentive, and his language skills are not improving.* If a nonfamily member has difficulty understanding your child or if he is unable to make his wants or needs known, then a hearing test and a speech consultation may be warranted.
- *He is not visually tracking or following objects. His eyes are not smoothly moving separately from his head movements.* Your child should be able to stabilize his head and use his eyes independently. One activity to promote this ability is to suspend a ball (ideally, at about chin level) and have him hit it. This also promotes hand-eye coordination. Another activity is to have your child follow a light (from a flashlight) on the wall without moving his head, just moving his eyes.
- *He is not able to place shapes into a shape sorter or form board.* By three years of age, a child should be able to fit shapes into a sorter without trial and error. Playing with puzzles and block building help develop the necessary visual-motor skills.
- *He can't rip paper.*
- *He drops things frequently.*
- *He hasn't progressed past scribbling and has difficulty using a mature grasp to hold a crayon or pencil.* Most children are able to rip paper by one year of age and can hold a pen using a mature grasp by age two. If your child has difficulty with any of these activities he might have an underlying weakness. A further evaluation might be needed. However, some hand-strengthening games—such as turning coins over, snapping lock bags using the thumb and index finger, playing with Silly Putty, and using tweezers to pick up objects—can be helpful. To

facilitate his grasp, place grippers on his pencil, or wind a rubber band around the bottom of the pencil. This gives him a better texture and a bigger grip to hold onto. The softness also allows his fingers to be more malleable.

Common Concern

The school called to discuss the possible need for occupational therapy for my son. They said he has difficulty holding a pencil and crayons. It is also hard for him to draw pictures. He's only four and a half years old—and I don't think this should be considered an issue. I just thought he had never been taught a proper grasp. Is there really a problem?

There could be some underlying issues. Most two-year-olds can pick up a pencil and automatically draw. Perhaps your child has low muscle tone or motor planning problems. There may be a lack of stability due to his inability to manipulate the pencil well. Did your child spend time creeping? Creeping helps with sequencing and upper body strengthening.

Warning Signs Specific to the Three- to Five-Year-Old

- *He avoids trying to accomplish more challenging gross motor milestones such as hopping or skipping.* Activities that improve balance may be helpful in encouraging your child to achieve these milestones. Such activities include swinging, using ride toys, sitting on a large ball with support, and bouncing on a smaller ball, to name a few. Your child might also need you to hold him in order to "practice" these activities. Try to incorporate them into games or songs, such as "Jack be nimble, Jack be quick, Jack *hopped* over the candlestick" or "Skip, skip, skip to my Lou."
- *He doesn't play by himself.* If this is the case, he may need an adult to help organize an activity or to help him get started—setting up or initiating the activity might be difficult for him. An adult can help him choose the activity to start and then say something like "I need to go to the kitchen for a minute—I'll be right back." Then you (or the responsible adult) can check in every few minutes, gradually decreasing the frequency of your visits.

And Always Remember . . .

- *Do not compare your child with someone else's—each child has his own unique personality and set of abilities. Focus on what your child can do, not what you would ideally like him to do.*
- *A well-rounded child is fundamental to the well-balanced child. Don't overload on sports or any one particular activity.*
- *Speak positively to your child and work with him to bolster his confidence.*

PART

4

Special Considerations

CHAPTER

There Is No Such Thing as a Lazy Child

How Low Muscle Tone Affects Development

In my practice, it's not uncommon to hear a parent say:

"My baby doesn't roll."

"My two and a half-year-old doesn't know how to jump."

"My three-year-old doesn't like to play on the playground."

"My child will only sit in the sandbox. She won't play on the playground."

"My son is a twin. His sister is creeping, pulling to stand, and beginning to walk, while he is still crawling on his belly. He loves to be upright but won't move on his own."

"My 10-month-old scoots on her bottom and doesn't creep."

All of these things can be related to low muscle tone.

Parents whose children exhibit any of these (or similar) behaviors often say that their babies are lazy. Children may *appear* lazy because they don't move around much, or don't want to be in certain positions. This isn't obstinacy or apathy on their parts—certain positions or movement patterns may be too challenging for them, especially if they have low muscle tone.

As we discussed in Chapter 1, muscle tone is the amount of resistance we have to passive movement. Without it, we would not be able to move in any normal way—if at all. Just ask any parent of a child who has abnormally high or low muscle tone, and he or she will tell you how much of our movements, posture, balance, and control rely on muscle tone—and how much we take these abilities for granted.

Muscle tone is different than strength. Tone is the state of the muscle at rest and is controlled by the brain, which automatically adjusts tone when it receives information from the muscles and the environment. Strength depends on the number of muscle fibers being called upon to work, and is voluntarily controlled. Increasing one's muscle strength won't change underlying muscle tone, but it can alter the effects of low muscle tone. For instance, a child with low muscle tone can improve joint stability by strengthening the muscles around those joints.

Low Muscle Tone

Abnormally low muscle tone is known as *hypotonia*. There are many conditions, disorders, diseases, and syndromes involving hypotonia. It can be caused by diminished (or a cessation of) fetal movement, trauma, prematurity, or prenatal postural infections, as well as metabolic or neuromuscular disorders among other things. On the other hand, infants and children with *low muscle tone*—as distinct from hypotonia—often have no known prenatal or neonatal issues. However, one or both parents may have had low muscle tone. Furthermore, a child with low muscle tone can have diminished resistance to a passive range of movement, and increased—or even an excessive—range of motion at the joints without being diagnosed with true hypotonia. Consequently, the children this book addresses are those with low muscle tone, not hypotonia. If true hypotonia is suspected, your pediatrician can refer you to a pediatric neurologist for a complete neuromuscular assessment.

An infant with low tone might move using certain compensatory patterns of movement that cause her to "cheat," that is, she might not use all the proper muscles to complete a movement or action. If she uses these patterns repeatedly, they will be reinforced. Consequently, her low muscle tone can have an impact on her development. For example, an infant with low muscle tone may roll from her back to her front by pushing into extension rather than using her flexor muscles to pull herself forward. Her poor abdominal use can cause an anterior pelvic tilt, affecting posture and stability. She might also elevate her shoulders to help with head control, which causes shoulder tightness. If there is weakness in the shoulder girdle, fine motor skills can be affected. Perceptual development can also be affected if an infant is not moving well.

The effects of low tone in toddlers show up in regular physical activities, and can hinder athletic ability. For instance, a child may trip because his ankle muscles are not working efficiently. Or, from Chapter 1, remember all the components needed just to catch a ball: a child needs isolated upper extremity control, must be able to react on time, and needs appropriate balance reactions. All of these requirements can be difficult to accomplish if a child has low muscle tone. Please keep in mind, though, that every child is not meant to be a superhero—we all have our strengths and weaknesses. That being said, when difficulties impede our ability to enjoy activities, it may be time to take a closer look.

Common Concern

My daughter's preschool teacher called to tell us that Sarah is disruptive to others during story time. I was very surprised, since she is generally the type of child that keeps to herself. The teacher told us that while the other children sit and listen during the story, Sarah lies down and bumps her body and legs into them. When she is asked to sit up like everyone else she says it's hard for her to do. What should I do?

Sarah could have low muscle tone. In general, children with low tone look for support surfaces to rest their bodies on. It's hard to maintain an upright posture for significant periods of time when gravity is constantly pulling you down and you don't have adequate control to resist it. Consequently, when a child like Sarah lies down during story time, people may think she has behavioral issues because she is not listening. Actually, she's doing what she needs to do in order to be able to listen effectively to the story. Educating her teachers about low muscle tone may help everyone come up with a solution. Perhaps Sarah could be near the back of the group so she can lie down without disrupting others, or perhaps there is a wall on which she could rest. Otherwise, it might help if all of the children could sit on their chairs. Then again, story time might be lasting for too long. A story time lasting for 35 minutes is too long for any three- or four-year-old to sit still through.

Often infants with low muscle tone prefer sitting and standing to rolling and creeping. This is because it's easier to lock up joints against gravity than it is to fight gravity and activate muscles near the ground. When on the floor, children with low tone tend to use the *W* sitting position rather than other mature sitting positions that require better trunk control, balance, and rotation to move. As we discussed in Chapter 4, the *W* sit position requires no rotation or abdominal use to get into, to get out of, or to maintain. It's also a safe position because it is hard to fall sideways or backward while in it. Other sitting positions are easier to fall over in because they require more mature balance reactions than a child with low tone tends to have.

By four or five, a child with low tone may have increased lumbar lordosis (a swayback due to weak abdominal muscles), scapula winging (the shoulder blades stick out), and rounded shoulders. In addition, her overall postural tone may need to be improved. It's difficult to have a good foundation for proper movement when postural tone is low. Think of a sunflower growing with its sturdy stem. As it grows it can remain upright and straight—in essence it has some postural control. Now think of an orchid. Its stem is long and very thin. It cannot stand tall without support or without a compensatory mechanism (such as a stick). The same is true with children (and adults) without proper postural control—they can't move without compensations, or stand tall with good posture.

It's worth noting that a "clumsy" child is not necessarily a child with low muscle tone. In fact, a clumsy child may not be weak. However, a weak child is often clumsy. Clumsiness is a term used for motor difficulties, while weakness is a symptom of not enough muscle fibers being recruited to perform a particular skill. A clumsy child might walk into furniture or drop things out of inattentiveness or for a number of other reasons—she's just clumsy. A weak child, however, might *appear* clumsy because her reaction time is delayed, causing her to trip more easily. Or, she might not be able to hold an object as tightly as she needs to.

Common Concern

My four-year-old is not as active as her friends, which I understand—but why is it hard for her to play a simple game of catch?

Remember, there is nothing "simple" about playing catch. If your child is exhibiting low muscle tone, she may have weakness proximally (at the trunk) and distally (at her hands) as well. This affects stability. If stability is affected, she'll have difficulty maintaining balance. Her posture will also be affected. Postural control needs to be activated while her center of gravity is shifted throughout the movement, or she'll fall off balance. It would certainly be hard for us to catch a ball if we had to constantly worry about our balance.

Activities to Enhance Muscle Activation

There are many activities that you as a parent can do to enhance your child's muscle activation. For the newborn and infant: you should pick up your newborn as described in Chapter 2 (by rolling your baby to the side first and not pulling straight up). When bottle-feeding your infant, remember to maintain her head in midline, with her ears in line with her shoulders. This promotes optimal oral-motor function. Use prone propping and pivoting of your infant, as described in Chapters 3 and 4. Encourage your baby to play with her feet in order to activate the abdominal muscles, as described in Chapter 3. Continue providing movement through space for proprioceptive and vestibular input.

For the older baby and child, continue using ride toys so that she pushes with her feet. This is a good activity for the 12- to 24-month-old. Activities in kneeling and half kneeling, as described in Chapter 4, are also helpful, as are the creeping and "bear walking" games. Try squatting games. Have her push "heavy" objects or a large ball (22- or

24-inch size) or carry "heavy" objects (a child's chair) with two hands.

Upper-extremity weight-bearing activities, such as hand and knee balancing games, work your child's arm muscles. Have your child play on her hands and knees, then lift one hand out in front of her along with the opposite leg, and try to balance. Play games involving trunk rotation, such as kneeling while reaching for a ball to each side. You can also try to knock your child off balance with gentle pushes and see if she can maintain the position. You can try to do the same in half kneeling. Similar activities are described in Chapter 4.

Use the manipulation activities as described in Chapters 4, 7, and 8—block stacking, drawing, cutting, pasting, beading, and so forth. Have her pull brussels sprouts off the shoots and scrub the carrots.

Have your child walk on uneven surfaces, such as large pillows from the sofa, to promote righting reactions. Have her walk on a balance beam, play tug-of-war, and practice leapfrog. Have your child use both hands to hold on to a rope or a hula hoop and then pull her as she sits on a scooter. If you have a dolly, or a scooter with a broad, flat surface, your child can sit or lie on her stomach, which is good for postural activation and bilateral arm use.

Work on balance activities by using a large ball. Have your child lie across the ball on her stomach. You hold her at the hips and slowly roll the ball from side to side. Notice how your child shifts her weight and balances. You can also move the ball forward and back and notice if your child has a protection response (putting her hands down on the ground when you move her forward). Have her sit and bounce on a ball. Her knees and hips should be at 90-degree angles, so use ball sizes that are appropriate for your child. Refer to activities described in Chapters 4, 7, and 8. Have her put one foot on a 12-inch ball and maintain her balance. See how long she can balance on one foot (she may need a chair for support at first).

Play kick ball and catch. Make an obstacle course (walking and climbing over, under, and through various household items such as chairs, tables, pillows, and cans) as described in Chapter 6. Encourage running, stair climbing, and playground activities as well as roller-skating or in-line skating. (It's sometimes helpful to practice these last two indoors on a carpet, first.)

Developmental Warning Signs for Low Muscle Tone

An infant or child with low muscle tone may have some of the following characteristics.

- An increase in joint range of motion.
- Reaching of motor milestones much later than other children.
- Skipping of certain motor skills like rolling or creeping.
- Prolonged scapular winging (past 15 to 18 months).
- Decreased hip extensor activation (may creep with knees under her hips rather than with a full extension of the leg).
- Weak abdominal muscles.
- Preference of scooting on her bottom rather than creeping on her hands and knees.
- Balance difficulties.
- *W* sitting.
- Difficulty stair climbing without the use of a handrail.

- Weak grasp.
- Poor coloring or writing skills.
- Difficulty using a straw.
- Use of an increased base of support (legs remain wide apart for balance and support).
- Decreased postural stability.
- Low endurance (some children have difficulty walking one city block at four years).
- Clumsy appearance (falling or tripping frequently).
- Difficulty maintaining lip closure.

In determining low muscle tone, it would be helpful if your pediatrician could quickly assess some higher-level balance skills, between the three- and four-year-range. At age two and a half your child should be able to jump. By three and a half to four years, she should be able to recite the ABC's. Heel-to-toe walking generally occurs by eighteen months to two years, and hopping by age four. At five your child should be able to walk a straight line and balance on one foot. If any of these skills are nonexistent or severely lacking, it might be time to see a physical or occupational therapist for an evaluation.

Low tone in the body often corresponds to low oral tone. The tongue may not be able to cup securely around a nipple. This affects sucking, and may affect articulation later on. Improving tone in the body may improve tone in the mouth as well.

And Always Remember . . .

- *Good postural control affects all of our activities—throughout our lives.*
- *You need good alignment for good muscle activation, and you need proximal stability to get distal mobility.*
- *A secure child is a happy child.*

CHAPTER

9

Appreciating Prematurity

The Premature Baby's Special Development

Having a baby is supposed to be a wonderful experience, one that parents envision many times in the months leading up to delivery. They have a set of expectations they hold on to amidst their nerves and excitement. Sometimes, however, babies for one reason or another are born prematurely and have to be sent to the neonatal intensive care unit. These babies are taken away from their parents and placed in an unnatural environment, deprived of a normal sensory and nurturing experience. For most parents, giving birth to a premature infant is an overwhelming experience.

Many articles have been written and much research conducted on premature infants. A premature baby is any infant with a gestational age of less than 37 weeks. There are generally two types of preemies in the neonatal intensive care unit. The stable premature baby is there for feeding and growing, and for monitoring and treatment of typical problems related to immaturity. Generally, these babies stay in the unit until they have reached their full-term age. The other premature baby is one with respiratory, cardiac, metabolic, neurological, or congenital difficulties, disorders, or infections. But even for very sick premature babies, there is a much greater chance of survival today. Steroids given to the mother prior to her baby's delivery, artificial surfactants, antibiotics, and improved technology are just a few of the reasons why these babies are more likely to survive than in years past.

If your baby was born prematurely, then he is not what you expected. He is tiny, his skin color is different, veins may be showing everywhere, he may have tubes and lines connected to him, and there is an air of illness about him. It's important that you remain hopeful and confident. Do not be afraid to ask lots of questions—even if you have asked them already. When information is first presented to you by specialists you may be overwhelmed with the situation and may not be able to absorb the information.

As you come to know your baby, you'll notice specific, unique aspects of his development that are different from the full-term baby's. The full-term baby is born with physiological flexion, as discussed in Chapter 2. This flexion creates a small surface area from which he can move. For example, when a newborn is placed on his stomach, his buttocks are in the air (the hips are flexed). When the buttocks move, the forces and pressure on the weight-bearing surface change. Remember, if the movement feels good, a baby will repeat it, and all babies learn from experience. However, the premature infant, because of his size, does not have this physiological flexion of the full-term baby—there was no "crowding" in the womb. When a preemie lies down he is flat, making it difficult for him to move. Even though he has more contact with the surface area, it tends to be passive contact with little activation. It is also hard for the premature baby to move or flex against gravity (which also has to do with the immature state of the nervous system).

The extensor (back) muscles tend to be stronger than the flexor (front) muscles in preemies. This extension is facilitated by the baby's having to be in the supine (back) position. When supine, the baby quickly learns to push away from the surface by forcefully using his extensor muscles, which makes it difficult to organize his body to move. Thus, in general, the movements of preemies tend to be more disorganized than those of full-term babies.

Without physiological flexion, not only is the premature baby more extended, but he also has low muscle tone. The combination of greater extensor tone and low muscle tone causes the preemie to stabilize his body by *fixing*. Fixing is a term used to describe an infant's ability to tighten up certain areas of the body in order to move other parts. This fixing leads to overuse of certain muscle groups while blocking the activity of others. A common example of a premature baby fixing is in the neck and shoulder area. The infant tends to keep his shoulders up and back (also known as shoulder elevation and retraction). This persistent pattern can eventually inhibit midline activities, hand-to-hand contact, hand-to-mouth play, righting reactions, and equilibrium reactions. Because of lower muscle tone, premature babies also need greater extremes of movement to feel the input. They tend to bypass midline quickly while looking for a support surface (turning the head to the side or back).

Interestingly, though, a preemie at 40 weeks tends to also have better visual acuity and better head-righting abilities than the full-term baby. This appears to be related to the increased length of time spent outside the womb.

Providing Developmental Care for Your Premature Infant

The key to providing developmental care for your premature baby is to create as normal an environment as possible, without increasing your baby's stress levels. This isn't easy to do in a neonatal unit, but there are things you can control that will greatly benefit your infant. Many studies have shown that early intervention in the neonatal unit has positive, lasting effects on preemies. Try to request a meeting with the physical or occupational or feeding specialist who covers the neonatal intensive care unit. There are many aspects to a developmental care plan, and the therapist can provide you with a specific program designed for your baby. In addition, the specialist's role is to promote normal tactile experiences for preemies in the unit, and to educate the staff and parents as to what they can do to normalize the baby's environment.

The application of a developmental approach, or *therapeutic intervention*, in the neonatal intensive care unit developed from two basic findings: premature babies were being deprived of sensory input and, at the same time, were being overstimulated. They were being deprived of experiences that the full-term baby has such as touch, movement, sound, and smells—and overstimulated with noxious agents such as bright lights, needles, noise, medications, and machines. Therapeutic intervention incorporates the dichotomy of overstimulation and deprivation in the neonatal unit and attempts to normalize the environment by providing the appropriate amount of input at the most appropriate time for the baby, as well as by decreasing stressful stimulation.

The various types of sensory input—as well as their frequency and duration—that therapeutic intervention introduces are obviously tailored to the individual child. However, certain types of movement, touch, or positioning might not be tolerated on a daily basis, depending on changing circumstances in the baby's environment and/or his condition. Some babies have setbacks. Consequently, it's important to accept the fact that progress may be slow. One day your baby could be thriving and the next you may find five people around him, placing more intravenous lines somewhere and running more tests. This is to be expected.

Any baby who spends an extensive length of time in the unit or who has at least one of several conditions could benefit from therapeutic intervention. These conditions include stiffness, low muscle tone, increased (or excessive) muscle tone, persistent fisting, a lack of spontaneous movement, poor feeding, hyperexcitability, easy startling, a dislike of the prone position, and limited mobility due to surgical intervention.

There are several signs your premature infant will give you to let you know he is ready for therapeutic intervention. Therapy should be scheduled for a time when he is in a quiet, alert state with decreased random movements. His eyes should be open and his hands (and limbs in general) relaxed. He may be able to bring his hands to his mouth or chest and may be able to suck on his fingers. His heart and respiratory rate should be stable, and he should be able to smile. Finally, though he may have a slow sucking pattern, he should be able to vocalize or coo.

Regardless of whether your child receives therapeutic intervention, it's important that you provide positioning, tactile, visual, auditory, vestibular and proprioceptive, olfactory, and oral-motor input for your baby—to the extent that he can tolerate it. All of this input will help him integrate himself and adjust to his sudden, new world. It can also help him catch up to full-term babies, developmentally, down the road. The activities listed in the remainder of this chapter are guidelines. Remember, not all babies react the same way to handling or input. You want to be careful not to overstimulate, or stress, your baby.

Positioning

It is important to place infants in "functional" positions to avoid abnormal postures. For instance, a muscle may become short and resistant to stretching if it has been kept in a shortened position. A period of just three weeks is long enough to create a modification of muscle length and elasticity. That being said, while developmental positioning may foster calm states as well as organization and stability, it can also be too much for some high-risk infants who are simply not ready for handling and positioning and who may react to them with stress. The adverse signs of stress can include an increase or decrease in heart rate, a decrease in oxygen saturation, and an increase in random unorganized movements. Remember to always use slow movements when repositioning your infant. Fast, abrupt movements will stress most preemies. Keep in mind that premature babies need to be monitored during position changes.

In general, we want to position a preemie in flexion. Flexion provides good body contact and a strong sense of security. It is also good for visual input and provides a foundation for weight-shifting abilities. Keep in mind that premature babies like boundaries. They tend to move near the walls of the isolette (incubator) to feel safe and warm. So think of providing a nest for your baby. If you place him in the middle of blankets and roll the sides under him, your baby will achieve a more flexed position—with his legs in a neutral position and his arms near midline. In supine, flexion can be facilitated with rolls that help maintain midline. The side-lying position also promotes flexion and movement to midline, as well as hands-to-mouth movement. Again, rolls can be used to maintain this position. Your baby can also hug a stuffed animal to help him maintain it. In side-lying, rolls are used between the legs and the back to keep the legs in a neutral position and to keep the baby from rolling back. The prone position also facilitates flexion, is calming, promotes hands-to-mouth movement, provides a tactile experience on the stomach, and provides sensory input to the face and oral area.

When a baby is on the warming table he tends to be the least stable. Babies are placed on warming tables immediately after birth and when medical intervention is required. Warming tables are also necessary for babies who require close supervision. But even when babies are on warming tables, they can be better positioned without interfering with medical intervention. For instance, limbs that are usually pinned away from the body (to prevent the baby from pulling lines out or moving unnecessarily) can be secured in a developmentally advantageous position. For example, using rubber bands, limbs can be secured near to, or across, the body to allow for spontaneous movement.

Intravenous (IV) lines may also be placed in better positions, as long as the placement is not during an emergency and is medically possible. While there may not be any long-term advantages to such placement of IV lines, it doesn't hurt to be considerate of a developmental approach when it is medically possible. For example, placing a line in the upper or lower arm (using a radial artery) may be better than placing it in the armpit (in the axilla). With an axillary line the baby's arm may have to be overhead, which is not a desirable developmental position. Furthermore, boards (known as IV boards) are used to help to keep the intravenous lines in place. However, they don't have to be extended over the entire arm. If a board is cut down, an infant can bend his arm at the elbow while the line is maintained. Also, the IV board does not have to extend over the tips of his fingers, preventing finger flexion (the natural position of the fingers is to flex or bend). Intravenous lines in the scalp tend to be the most worrisome for parents to see, yet placement here allows for freedom of all a baby's limbs.

As soon as your baby is medically stable and out of imminent danger, he is moved into an isolette for a quieter environment and temperature regulation. Premature babies have immature physiological systems and have difficulty regulating their body temperature. The incubator regulates an infant's temperature when he cannot do so on his own. Once your baby is able to regulate his own body temperature and remain stable, he will be put into an open crib for growing.

Common Concern

Why does my baby have a different shape to his head than his brother, who was born full-term?

Premature babies tend to have long faces with narrow foreheads and may have deep-set eyes. The narrow face is likely due to positioning while the baby was in the unit. Prior to using proper positioning techniques in the neonatal unit (which is now commonplace), more babies had heads that were pointy. The pointed head, along with low muscle tone, made it difficult for babies to maintain their heads in midline for purposes of feeding, visual input, or play. But we know now that early proper positioning can help to round the occipital area. For this reason, midline positioning with rolls and "nests" is very important—especially for those babies who will spend months in the unit. Saline bags can be used to help position the baby's head as well.

Once a preemie is medically stable enough, he might also be able to tolerate the semi-inclined position while in the isolette. I have fabricated many infant seats out of diaper boxes and toweling to be used in the isolettes. This allows the stable and alert baby to sit in a supported fashion and view the world from a different angle. For the very stable baby, hammocks (which provide midline positioning, flexion, and slight movement) can also be fabricated out of linens inside the isolette. Older infants may be stable enough to sit in an infant seat outside the isolette or open crib. Again, toweling is needed to maintain midline positioning.

How the Sensory System Is Affected in Premature Babies

As with full-term infants, the sensory system is highly important for preemies. The way that premature infants receive sensory input, though, is different from that of full-term babies and is perhaps even more critical to their healthy development. Let's review how each sense contributes to a preemie's development.

Tactile Input

A healthy newborn gets a lot of tactile input—hugs, kisses, feeding, bathing, skin-to-skin contact, and random movement on the surface. Premature babies do not get to experience all this normal sensory input. They have tubes, IV lines, ventilators, intravenous lines, and tape on their face and/or limbs, not to mention cumbersome urine collection bags. They may even have had to endure the necessity of surgical intervention. The premature infant also missed out on all the tactile experience of pushing against the uterine walls while in the womb. Instead, he has had no boundaries and thus tends to be fully extended, as we've noted. It's no surprise, then, that an infant may not be ready to be held for several weeks after birth. But by touching his limbs or body you can provide a pleasurable bonding experience for both of you that might also help remind him of his experience in the womb. As with full-term babies, a gentle firm touch feels better than a light touch. Resting your hand over your baby's arm, leg, or body generally feels calming. Light, tickling movements are generally not well received.

All the tactile hand-to-mouth, hand-to-hand, and foot-to-foot play, as well as general movements, are what allow a baby to learn about his body. The premature baby is missing out on all this tactile stimulation. In fact, premature babies often associate pain with tactile input. We want to change that. Rubbing cotton balls, silk, satin, and soft fabrics on exposed limbs and on his body may help stimulate peripheral nerve fibers in a pleasurable way. Sheepskin also generally appeals to an infant's tactile system, and is a soothing fabric to make a nest out of. It can also be used for the very sick infant, or the heavy infant who sinks into a nesting surface (such as a water bed). Babies generally seem to like being placed on water beds for movement, positioning, and warmth. Water beds also help alleviate and redistribute pressure areas for the fragile infant.

The more stable baby may also enjoy being swaddled. Swaddling encourages flexion and helps a baby organize and control his movements. It also calms him and may

Signs of Stress in the Premature Infant

Physiological Signs
- Decrease in oxygen saturation (desaturation).
- Increase in blood pressure.
- Irregular respiration.
- Apnea (lapses in breathing for longer than 15 seconds).
- Becomes acidotic (decrease in pH level).
- Decrease in heart rate (bradycardia).

Behavioral Signs
- Poor sleep patterns.
- Startles easily.
- Cries more.
- May eat less.
- Hiccups.
- Arches away.
- Looks away.
- Stiffens his body.
- His color changes.
- Gags.
- Splays his fingers.
- May have difficulty with handling and movement.

help him to better attend to visual and auditory input (refer to Chapter 2 on swaddling). Babies that are stable enough to come out of the isolette tend to enjoy skin-to-skin holding. Hold your baby upright against your body and wrap your clothing around him. This is an exciting moment—it may be the first time your baby can feel, smell, and hear you. You may need a heat lamp nearby to provide extra warmth. Make sure your baby's head is covered (most heat is lost through the head). Remember, temperature regulation is important.

During diaper changes, your baby might feel insecure. You can decrease the startle reaction just by preparing your baby first. Use your voice to let him know you are approaching him. Touch his arms, legs, or trunk first, with gentle pressure. Then proceed to change the diaper. In addition to its obvious advantages, tactile input can improve gastrointestinal function and enhance weight gain.

Visual Input

The very young premature baby may not be able to tolerate much visual input. That may include looking at you. Consequently, parents need to understand that their baby may not fixate on them. You need not worry that your baby doesn't like you—this is just a sign of prematurity. At 27 weeks, for instance, a premature baby has difficulty staying awake, let alone fixating on his parents. Just to open his eyes he may need to hear your voice, but once he does open them, other sensory input (such as your voice or your touch) may be too much to handle and he may quickly go into sensory overload, showing signs of stress.

Premature babies tend to visually fixate on the bright lights of the neonatal unit and may have a difficult time breaking away from them. That being said, these lights may bother your baby, so it's important that his eyes are shielded from them. Although the bright lights are on 24 hours a day (some neonatal units do lower the light level in the evening), it is important to simulate night and day by covering the isolette with a baby blanket or coverlet.

When placing photos or a mobile in the isolette, place them in your baby's visual field. Since your baby will be lying down most of the time, the photos (just one or two) need to be taped low on the walls of the isolette. Furthermore, mobiles need to be positioned in such a way that your infant does not have to hyperextend his head to see them. Babies prefer contrasting colors and patterns to plain ones and simple patterns to complex ones (a smiley face or a checkerboard). Consequently, the complexity of the pattern will affect the visual attention of the infant. It is also important to change the mobile and the pictures after a few weeks so the infant does not tire of them.

When working on visual input specifically, try swaddling your baby first to help his focus. Then try to get him to fixate on you. Once he is able to do this, you may want to try to slowly move from side to side and see if he can track you. If he is stable enough to be taken out of the isolette, do so. But always keep in mind that you don't want to overstimulate your baby.

A preemie at 28 to 30 weeks gestation may still show signs of stress when attempting to fixate on an object. By 30- to 32-weeks, he is able to visually fixate and track from the center to the side, while the 32- to 35-week baby can visually track from side to side (past midline) and is beginning to track vertically. Between 35 weeks and term, he can track in all planes (horizontal, vertical, and in a circle). Infants on long-term ventilation may have delays in visual tracking because head movement tends to be limited for fear of dislodging the ventilator.

One possible complication of prematurity is *retinopathy of prematurity,* or ROP. The retina is the light-sensitive portion of the eye, where visual images are received. The premature baby is born with an immature retina. The retinal blood supply is not complete, putting the retina at risk to develop abnormally, with associated scar tissue. This abnormal development causes ROP, also known as *retrolental fibroplasia,* or RLF. Babies at risk for ROP are generally born at a gestational age of less than 32 weeks and weigh less than 1,500 grams (3 lbs. 5 oz.). High oxygen levels in the blood, along with risk factors associated with extremely premature babies, increase the risk for ROP. (There are exceptions—some babies with very low birth weights can develop ROP even without being given oxygen.) There are varying stages to the disease. In most cases, the disease resolves spontaneously. However, it can progress, leaving a baby with crossed eyes, a lazy eye, near-sightedness, glaucoma, or blindness (though complete blindness from ROP is rare today). Any baby who has received oxygen therapy needs to be evaluated by an ophthalmologist.

Auditory Input

Being in the neonatal intensive care unit is intrusive to the auditory system and can be extremely stressful for a preemie. Twenty-four hours a day, a baby may hear the phones ringing, water running, people talking, doors slamming, and constant humming from the isolette. Garbage can lids bang, beepers and alarms go off, and radios play. We need to protect our babies from such noise pollution by decreasing decibel levels whenever possible. All staff and parents should be educated on noise control. Conversations can take place away from the baby's bedside, alarms can be silenced quickly, radios can be removed from the room, and trash cans can be padded. There is no reason to slam doors of isolettes or bang notepads on top of them. Pagers can be put on vibrate rather than beeper mode.

We want to generate sounds that will foster recognition, serenity, and attachment. Tape recorders can be placed in the isolette or crib to play parent and sibling voices. Soft classical music can be played. These two things—voices and music—can be alternated, which will stimulate the right and left sides of the brain. The sound of a heartbeat, which can also be placed in the isolette, tends to have a calming and soothing effect on babies. When you are visiting with your baby, coo, talk, and sing to him—whether you can hold him or not. He will be comforted by your voice.

Any baby in the neonatal unit needs to be evaluated by an audiologist prior to discharge and up to three months after.

Vestibular and Proprioceptive Input

The vestibular and proprioceptive systems and their effects on us have been discussed in Chapter 1. Among other things, the vestibular system regulates muscle tone and develops our sense of balance and equilibrium. Studies have shown that vestibular input for the premature baby promotes sleep and decreases bradycardia, apnea, and fussiness—as well as increases visual and auditory response levels.

The healthy newborn is driven to move and is frequently placed in many different positions, thus developing his vestibular and proprioceptive senses. The simple act of head lifting creates a vestibular response. But in the neonatal unit, most movement is not possible. Sometimes the only movement a baby may feel (until he is medically stable) is that of being transported in an isolette (which is a static movement in the horizontal plane). Think of a baby that has been lying still on a warming table, unable to move at all—even head movement may be extreme. Not surprisingly, sudden movements may stress your infant, so always prepare him first. Approach your baby using your voice, and then slowly place your hand on a limb or on your baby's trunk. Try to position him in a flexed or swaddled position before providing movement. Keep in mind that it's important to carefully monitor your baby, looking for signs of stress while you provide movement.

A slightly older and more stable baby may tolerate upright movement. For instance, try holding your baby over your shoulder while you move him up and down. Some babies need to start in a side-lying position first, and then work up to an upright position. If your baby is stable, rolling him over to change his diaper also provides vestibular input. Hammocks, water beds, and mechanical swings can be brought into the unit to be used by older and more stable babies. Water beds were initially designed as a way to provide an external flotation experience similar to what a baby would experience in the womb. Oscillating water beds, in particular, provide vestibular input.

Common Concern

My baby has been in the neonatal unit for two and a half months. He is medically stable now, with no complications, and is here to grow. Each time I go near his bedside and try to pick him up to hold him, he has a negative reaction. His heart rate and oxygen saturation drop. Then the nurses tell me I can't hold him. What am I doing wrong and what can I do to change this?

First of all, you are not doing something wrong. It is very common for premature babies to demonstrate signs of stress when they are moved rapidly. Moving in an upright position provides an extreme vestibular response and may be too much for your baby to handle—especially since he's not getting as much movement as a full-term baby. You may want to begin with rolling your baby into side-lying first, then slowly work your way into the upright or sitting positions.

Olfactory Input

The olfactory system helps us recognize and discover things. It can activate our digestive enzymes and can be used as a protective mechanism. The few studies that have been completed in this area indicate that newborns have olfactory discrimination, and may have preferences to certain odors. Unfortunately, babies in the neonatal unit tend to be exposed to medical smells from rubbing alcohol, betadine, tape, machines, and medications.

In contrast, sweet smells can be soothing. A small sachet filled with cinnamon or rose can be left in the isolette to help calm your baby. And, leaving an open bottle of breast milk in the isolette prior to feedings may actually help him feed better. However, you should remove the stimulus if your baby appears to have an avoidance response to it. For instance, avoidance reactions can occur when a strong perfume or cologne is introduced.

Oral-Motor Input

Feeding is important for growth as well as parent-infant bonding. For this reason, the team of professionals in the neonatal unit must help the infant and parent make feeding as pleasurable as possible. Babies that are fed through a nasal gastric tube (through the nose) or oral gastric tube (through the mouth) may need to be fed while they are in the isolette. If the baby is stable enough, he should be able to tolerate tube feedings while being held. However, if he can't be handled outside the isolette, then he should still be swaddled and flexed during the tube feedings.

During tube feedings, nonnutritive sucking should be promoted by using a pacifier or finger. This type of sucking helps stimulate a gustatory response and increases saliva production, which in turn can improve digestion, as well as help accelerate weight gain. Specific to a premature baby, many studies show that the benefits of nonnutritive sucking also include earlier bottle feedings, calming effects, the promotion of quiet sleep, enhanced development of the oral muscles,

Checklist for the Premature Baby in the Neonatal Intensive Care Unit

What You Can Do

- Provide as normal an environment as possible.
- Provide positions that facilitate flexion.
- Provide appropriate tactile input including hands to chest and mouth.
- Provide input during alert state.
- Provide visual input.
- Massage when possible.
- Provide movement in different planes.
- Decrease unnecessary noise and light and inappropriate tactile input.
- Swaddle when possible.
- Use linens and rolls to facilitate flexion and midline positions.
- Avoid quick movements.
- Provide rocking motions when appropriate.
- Shade eyes from bright lights.
- Pick up your baby using rotation—try not to lift him in straight planes.
- Have an individualized care plan.
- Initially approach the active alert baby with gentle pressure and the drowsy baby with auditory input.
- Visit frequently. Bring in audiotapes with both your voice and classical music. Hang homemade mobiles with pictures of yourself and family members. Bring in breast milk and sheepskin.

and enhanced weight gain. Sucking also helps a baby provide his own tactile input.

Prior to oral feedings, an assessment should be completed by the nurse, feeding specialist, or therapist in order to enhance your baby's success. Determine if your infant is ready to begin oral feedings. Is he in an alert state? Is he medically stable? Does he tolerate nonnutritive sucking? Is his overall muscle tone adequate? (Remember, if muscle tone is low, then oral motor tone may be low.) Will your infant have greater supplemental oxygen demands due to the increased energy expenditure needed to feed? Is he hungry? If your baby has been on continuous feedings he may feel satiated and may not want to feed. Since it's important that he takes an active interest in nipple feeding, is it possible to feed him based on his cues—and not on a schedule set up by the nursing staff?

You also need to determine the behavioral state that your infant is in. If he is disorganized, feeding will be difficult. Feeding is best accomplished in the alert or active state. Sucking, swallowing, and breathing all need to be coordinated. This can depend on positioning, type of nipple used, and readiness of the infant (infants younger than 34-week gestation may have greater difficulties in coordinating sucking, swallowing, and breathing).

Babies can fatigue easily, and there are those who gulp as well. Nipple firmness, size, and shape play a large part in both of these factors, and need to be continuously assessed. The nipple shape needs to fit with your infant's mouth and affects the way his lips can seal around the nipple. Its size will also determine how his mouth fits around the nipple, and its firmness will determine how hard he needs to suck to draw the liquid out of the bottle. The size of the hole in the nipple will also have an effect on the amount of liquid drawn into the mouth, as well as affecting how strong the suck needs to be to get the liquid out. The larger the hole is in the nipple, the greater the flow is, with less effort required from the infant.

Expectations regarding the amount of formula or breast milk that is to be consumed during each feed may need to be adjusted, contingent on your baby's ability to suck and swallow and his fatigue level. Furthermore, his jaw stability may need to be assessed. If your baby cannot maintain lip closure around the nipple, you (or the nurse or therapist) may need to apply jaw stability by supporting his chin with your fingers. If your baby is tense and clamps down on the nipple, relaxation techniques may be needed. Parental education by a therapist is important to learn these oral-motor techniques.

Once he is medically stable, it's beneficial to your baby to be held outside the isolette for feedings. Proper positions can include swaddling, placing your baby in the side-lying position on your lap, or cradling him in the flexed position on your legs. During feedings, it may be helpful to shade your infant's eyes from the bright lights and to find a quieter location to nurse.

Breast-feeding should be encouraged in the neonatal unit. It's important to provide privacy for the mother and infant, although this is not always possible in the unit. If feeding is difficult for you or your baby, a lactation specialist on staff at the hospital can be called in for a consultation. If difficulties persist with breast- or bottle-feedings, a consultation with an occupational, physical, or feeding therapist may be needed.

Common Concern

Feeding my baby in the neonatal unit is a stressful time for both of us. So how do I know if my baby is actually having a problem?

If the experience is stressful for you or your baby, something is not right. Common feeding problems with preemies include an uncoordinated sucking/swallowing/breathing pattern, formula leakage from the mouth, a poor sucking pattern, low muscle tone, and tongue thrusting (forward thrusting of the tongue). There are ways to make feeding times less stressful. You can try swaddling; feeding in a quiet place; and making sure your baby is alert, calm, stable, and positioned properly. You yourself should be comfortable and relaxed. If you and/or your baby continue to be stressed, and your baby continues to have difficulty eating, you might want to consult with a therapist.

Going Home

Upon your baby's discharge from the neonatal unit you will learn about standard baby care, as well as special considerations for your baby, such as assessing breathing and color changes. You will also learn how to use any medical equipment that he may need at home such as monitors, oxygen, or medications. It's important that you feel confident—

this is your baby! It's also important that you adjust your expectations about your baby's development. Milestones may be reached on a different timetable. Remember, your baby is different. He was born early and may have had some complications. When looking at developmental stages, you need to correct or adjust for your baby's age. For example, if your baby is now six months old but was born at a 28-week gestation, then he was born three months early and is corrected to three months of age. In general, corrected ages are used up to two years of age

You are now finally able to touch, kiss, hold, and play with your baby as much as you have dreamed about. However, many premature infants are sensitive to touch after a long hospitalization, and may reject certain types of touch. Don't be discouraged. Try to take note of what your baby likes and dislikes. Refer to Chapters 1 and 2 to see what you can do for your baby. And remember, it is with your loving touch that your baby will learn to associate sensory messages with pleasure, instead of with medical intervention.

Neonatal Follow-Up Programs

Neonatal follow-up care provides ongoing assessments by developmental specialists for the premature infant. The purpose of these assessments is to identify delays in development in infants at risk for neurodevelopmental problems. Referrals to appropriate early-intervention programs, specialists, and therapists might be recommended by the neonatal follow-up program. The primary care physician should be included in all recommendations. It's important to note, however, that not all babies are referred for intervention. Many changes occur within the first few months at home, and the nervous system needs time to mature. Furthermore, as therapists, we want parents to be very involved and to do as much as they can without our intervention.

Many parents are confused and afraid to participate in follow-up programs. They feel that their baby is alive and well, and that the follow-up visits will bring up bad feelings. They are not ready to have their infant "judged." To alleviate these concerns, parents need to understand the goals of the neonatal follow-up program prior to discharge. This is the responsibility of doctors and nurses in the neonatal unit. Once parents understand the role of the program, they generally feel intense relief, along with gratitude for a new avenue of dialogue. One couple said that during their first follow-up visit, they felt like they had just woken up from a coma: In the unit everyone dictated their every move. They had to function on a kind of autopilot. Now they could finally ask questions, and take charge of their—and their baby's—lives.

And Always Remember . . .

- *Remember, you don't want to overstimulate, and thus stress, a premature infant. These babies are used to minimal tactile input and too much visual and auditory input.*
- *Don't be afraid of neonatal follow-up programs. They exist to provide ongoing support, information, and dialogue about your baby.*

Sensory Disorders

Manifestations and Guidelines

The intent of this book is to enhance a child's developmental abilities, as well as to point out the small-scale signs of delayed development and/or subtle dysfunction in the sensory system. It is important, however, to have an overview of where such dysfunctions can lead if they are left undiagnosed and untreated. Here then, we will take a brief look at the symptoms and manifestations of full-blown disorders.

Vestibular and Proprioceptive Disorders

Children with vestibular and proprioceptive dysfunctions generally suffer from either over (hyper) or under (hypo) reactions to motion. Some children who are hypersensitive to movement suffer from terrible vertigo, others from nausea and/or disorientation when they move. They may have this feeling when their feet leave the ground or when their head position changes in relation to their body. Still others get very frightened or sick on carnival rides—as well as on swings, in cars, in elevators, or even in airplanes. Children who are hyposensitive to movement love—even crave—motion. It seems that their central nervous systems can't kick into gear unless they receive what, to most people, would be an overload of stimulation. We can think of these children as "crash-and-burn kids." They prefer running to walking because their balance reactions tend to be less developed. They will spin themselves around and around, never seeming to get dizzy. This being said, it's hard to distinguish between a normal, active child and one who is showing signs of this particular disorder. After all, healthy children do move around constantly. (Chances are your four-year-old won't sit through an entire religious service, either.)

Often, children with low muscle tone are also hyposensitive to movement. While some of these children move constantly to keep themselves stimulated (and then wilt when they sit still), many kids with this disorder prefer sedentary activities such as sitting because they feel somewhat defeated in their attempts to achieve action-oriented tasks. Sedentary activities require less effort from them and are thus less taxing emotionally. Imagine how frustrating it would be to need to move to feel stimulated and engaged—and yet find movement so strenuous.

Sometimes, parents of a child with a vestibular or proprioceptive disorder might think that she has a vision or hearing problem. Heather, a little girl I treated, would stop and stare down in fright at doorjambs. Crossing the threshold seemed insurmountable. When she did finally cross over one, she used giant steps as if she were crossing a canyon, or mincing steps as if she were sidestepping down a steep slope. This peculiar ritual made her parents concerned, particularly given that it was one of a number of strange, exaggerated reactions to simple activities. It seemed to Heather's parents that her sense of perception was off, and they took her to an ophthalmologist. Her vision was fine. They checked her hearing, which was also fine. Her pediatrician did notice that Heather had low muscle tone, and that's when she came to see me. I referred her to an occupational therapist in addition to my working with her. Once her parents learned the true nature of Heather's disorder and how it affected her motor abilities and her sense of well-being, they took all the right steps to help her. After two years of therapy with professionals, along with a home program, Heather is proud of her accomplishments, which include swimming, dancing, and climbing. She is still cautious about her movements, but she is no longer fearful of trying new activities. She's content with herself and she's happy despite her challenges.

Children with vestibular and proprioceptive disorders can suffer additionally from motor planning difficulties and bilateral integration difficulties, as well as gravitational insecurity and/or postural insecurity. Just like children with hyper- or hyposensitivity issues, these kids look awkward when they move. Their motions tend to be jerky, exaggerated, and unstable. Often, they seem to be looking for visual cues to help them navigate through invisible obstacles. Daily life can present huge hurdles for them, and they can be fearful and withdrawn. It takes time and patience to comprehend the issues that alienate them, since these same activities are second nature to us.

The importance of motor planning is easiest to comprehend when we see what happens if a child does not have it: Jenny is a three-year-old girl who, when she tries to climb onto a chair, either lands on the floor or ends up half on it and half off it. She can't figure out how to seat herself properly even when her parents show her repeatedly. She cannot crawl under or out from a table without bumping her head. Games like "duck, duck, goose" are hard for her because she can't follow the sequence of events. As a result of these hindrances, she might seem fearful of activities or withdrawn. An assessment would have to be completed in order to determine which sensory systems are deficient. Most likely she will need to be given a program of activities that enhance proprioceptive and tactile awareness, vestibular activation, and postural control.

Often, children with bilateral integration difficulties have impaired motor skills. Childhood pleasures like catching and throwing a ball are hard to achieve. Playground activities—skipping, hopscotch, jumping rope—can be beyond reach. Riding a bike can become a torture. Even smaller-scale fine motor tasks (e.g., putting a wooden puzzle together, using a shape sorter) can be agonizing if a child has trouble bringing her hands across her body or getting her eyesight to converge. One telling symptom of a child who suffers from a bilateral integration disorder is that she has not developed a dominant side—specifically, a strong hand preference. (Generally, hand preference is established by the time a child is two years of age and hand dominance by four or five years of age.) Earlier warning signs can include difficulty in rolling (for infants) and in jumping with two feet off the floor (for toddlers).

Children with gravitational insecurity feel irrationally threatened and completely disoriented in any position with the exception of being upright with both feet planted on the ground. They become frightened and startle excessively if they tip backward. They might become anxious leaning back in a bathtub or panic if they find themselves upside down. Somersaults are out of the question. Even walking down steps can be frightening (some children refuse to walk down, while others must hold on to a railing). Play activities such as swinging or getting on a seesaw might be impossible without a trusted adult standing close by (or even holding the child), because the fear of falling is overwhelming.

Parents of a child who suffers from one of these disorders might believe that he or she needs to outgrow "resistant" or "fearful" behavior. Recently, I noticed a family at the local carnival. The mother and father were watching many of the children enjoy a standard amusement activity that incorporated climbing and jumping through a series of inflated spaces, ending with a turn on a long, inflated slide. The mother took her son (who was about four years old) through the various sections of the climbing maze while the father waited at the bottom of the slide. The "tantrums" that the child was having told everyone that he was not enjoying himself. But the parents insisted he endure the activity—not once, but several times. Each time, the little boy screamed louder. When I asked the parents why they continued to push their son to participate, they told me, "The more he practices, the better he will feel." I couldn't disagree more. This couple was not listening to their child, who clearly demonstrated his anxiety. If his parents had made any sort of compromise—for instance, if his mother had held him while going down the slide—he might have felt more secure.

While I cannot definitively say that this boy had a clinically defined disorder (since I observed him for such a brief period), I could tell that at the very least, he had genuine fears of the activity pushed upon him. That's not an acceptable situation. As parents, we all want our children to experience everything we have experienced and more. But this knowledge should not come at our children's emotional or physical expense. No child needs to feel defeated or threatened as part of the process of feeling safe, secure, and happy.

Vestibular and Proprioceptive Warning Signs

The following "checklists" of warning signs of vestibular and proprioceptive dysfunctions are loosely ordered in the sequence in which the signs might appear on a developmental time line. (There will also be a checklist for tactile dysfunction.) Please keep in mind that there are no stringent criteria for these dysfunctions—there is no "DSM" (the diagnostic manual for standardized psychological disorders) equivalent that dictates quantity, timing of onset, or duration of symptoms to diagnose a disorder. Furthermore, there may be considerable overlap in symptoms, since the proprioceptive and vestibular senses share similar functions. Consequently, these signs are meant only as guidelines, not as a substitute for a true diagnosis. I urge parents who suspect that their children might have a sensory integration disorder to seek out the opinion of a qualified professional. The list of "Helpful Organizations" at the end of this book can help direct parents to the appropriate kind of therapist for evaluation and treatment.

Vestibular Warning Signs

- Avoids trying new positions (especially those involving the head)—e.g., rolling, somersaulting, turning upside down.
- Tires easily (but may appear lazy).
- Avoids playing with two hands.
- Has poor protective responses.
- Is slow or sluggish in response to movement demands.
- Avoids or fears movement (such as on swings and slides).
- Is very clumsy when the base of support is varied (e.g., an uneven path).
- Loses balance easily.
- Locks joint to stabilize movements.
- Falls often.
- Collapses onto the floor or furniture.
- Holds on to the walls or furniture for balance.
- Does not like to be upside down.
- Bumps into objects.
- Paces or rocks body.
- Turns whole body (instead of just head) to look at you.
- Becomes disoriented after bending over.
- Holds head upright, even when leaning over.
- Is a sensory seeker (spins a lot, jumps a lot, never gets dizzy on repeated carnival rides).

Proprioceptive Warning Signs

- Does not creep or crawl on hands and knees.
- Has a weak grasp.
- Has difficulty manipulating small objects.
- Has tense muscles.
- May walk on toes.
- Locks joints to stabilize movements.
- Has rigid, jerky, or ungraded movements (overshoots placement and reach).
- Is clumsy.
- Falls a lot.
- Lacks awareness of body position in space.
- Has low endurance.

- Is a sloppy eater.
- Can't lift heavy objects.
- Resists new activities or movement games.

Tactile Defensiveness

Some children cannot tolerate being hugged. Others won't put on an "itchy" pair of socks, go for a haircut, or walk barefoot on grass or sand. Still others won't have their hair combed or brush their teeth. Some cannot stand the consistency of certain foods. There are kids who flip out at getting their hands dirty or who can't stand to have a shirt label rub against their skin. These are a few of the symptoms of tactile defensiveness, a sensory disorder that manifests itself through aversiveness to various kinds of touch.

Just imagine how difficult it must be for parents to want to hug their baby, and provide love and reassurance, and have that baby become more upset or distant. I frequently see this kind of confusion and despair. Recently, a mother came to me with her 10-month-old daughter, Sarah. Upon first seeing her I realized she was tactile defensive. Sarah did not crawl, but scooted on her bottom instead. She was a very picky eater. She could not tolerate weight or touch on the soles of her feet. I also noticed that she would pick her toys up ever so gently using two fingers, look at them for a moment, and then drop them. There was no mouthing, holding, turning, or transferring from one hand to the other. Sarah's mother thought she was a "girly-girl" who was simply sensitive and shy. But after I pointed out several of Sarah's behaviors as being commonly associated with tactile defensiveness, Sarah's mother was more than happy to intervene to help Sarah become a more balanced, happier child.

There are many children like Sarah who are born full-term with no medical complications, yet who appear to have tactile defensiveness. But there are also many children who are hypersensitive to touch and who have proprioceptive problems because they received little physical contact during infancy. This early physical contact is necessary to help infants learn to modulate tactile input, which is important for organizing, calming, and self-regulating. This sad fact brings to mind some of the screenings I have done for children adopted when they were infants or toddlers. They are brought in by their confused, frustrated, and yet obviously caring parents. Some of these children just have subtle signs of hypersensivity to touch, while others have a true SI (sensory integration) disorder manifested by tactile defensiveness. Their early environment in an orphanage has left these children sensory deprived. They did not have someone holding, moving, or playing with them all day. They had no variety of toys to mouth or manipulate. They did not have songs sung to them or swings to swing on. They had no wardrobe of clothes from which to experience different textures, no menu of various foods to explore. They did not have the luxury of a playful bath time. So when these children do come in I give a home program to their families and explain the importance of massage, touch, gentle pressure, movement, and other tactile experiences. Following is a list of warning signs for tactile defensiveness.

Tactile Warning Signs

- Becomes excessively fussy during changing time.

- Avoids tasks that are wet or messy, such as finger painting.
- Has an aversion to stepping on sand, mud, grass, or even carpeting.
- Is very fussy about clothing choices (textures).
- Continues to take clothes off or, conversely, needs to wear long-sleeved shirts and pants (to protect body from touch).
- Pulls down sleeves constantly (sometimes pulls them up as well).
- Is a sloppy eater (doesn't notice food on face).
- Spits out foods.
- Is a picky eater, particularly regarding food consistency.
- Does not want to be barefoot or insists on being barefoot.
- Does not like to have hair combed, to have teeth brushed, or to be bathed.
- Needs a large amount of space for herself.
- Becomes fearful or aggressive if someone approaches (especially if unexpected).
- Fears being touched or held; conversely, doesn't seem to notice when she is being touched.
- May need to touch everything or everyone.
- Hides under furniture or in a corner.
- Hits people who get too close.

And Always Remember . . .

- *You are your child's best advocate. If you see any of these warning signs in your baby or child, don't hesitate to mention them to your pediatrician. Early intervention can prevent small dysfunctions from turning into full-blown disorders.*

CHAPTER

11

The Most Commonly Seen Orthopedic Conditions in Pediatrics

It's possible that as many as 50 percent of children have some form of the following orthopedic conditions. It is important to distinguish between a condition that can self-correct and a real pathology that can lead to further problems. For example, an unstable hip (hip laxity) may be a predisposed condition, but if the hip dislocates, the laxity can lead to severe problems. Some of these conditions may appear alarming to a parent, although in actuality they are more benign than they look. If your infant or child shows signs of any of these orthopedic conditions he should be seen by a pediatric orthopedist. The orthopedist will conduct a complete examination including a family history, and at times an X ray, to rule out associated conditions or deformities, as well as to provide you with the proper course of treatment. Treatments can range from observation to stretching, bracing, or surgical intervention.

Congenital Dislocation of the Hip (Hip Dysplasia)

There are a number of variations to hip disorders that, as a group, are referred to as congenital dislocation, or dysplasia. *Instability* of the hip occurs when the head of the femur (the thigh bone) moves into and out of the acetabulum (the area of the pelvis that the femur belongs in). *Subluxation* of the hip occurs when part of the femoral head is positioned out of the acetabulum but contact is still made. *Dislocation* of the hip occurs when the femoral head and the acetabulum have no contact. *Dysplasia* of the hip occurs when the acetabulum is more shallow than it should be. This condition increases the incidence of subluxation.

There may be several causes for congenital dislocation of the hip including fetal positioning, laxity of the ligaments, and genetic factors. One out of 60 births falls into one of these categories and about one out of one thousand has a true dislocation of the hip (with a slightly higher incidence in girls). About 60 percent of unstable (increased laxity) newborn hips spontaneously correct within the first two to four weeks after birth.

In terms of diagnosis, X rays before an infant is six to eight weeks of age may be unreliable because bony changes have not yet occurred. However, regularly scheduled newborn checkups have helped with early identification. While treatments vary depending on severity, the goals are the same—to restore proper alignment between the acetabulum and the head of the femur. The treatment ranges from observation for subluxation to using a harness in order to maintain alignment in dislocated hips. For babies over six months of age who have a dislocation, traction may be needed to bring the femoral head down into the acetabulum. If the dislocated hip is left untreated, then cartilaginous, muscular, and bony changes will occur, causing malformation at the hip joint, gait deviation, pain, and possible spinal misalignment. But even with nonsurgical treatment, efficacy drops once a child is greater than two because of the pathological (abnormal) changes that could occur in the bones, joints, soft tissues, and muscles. At this point, surgical correction becomes more of a likely option. Surgery can tighten the ligaments of the hip joint as well as the muscles around it. It might also involve an osteotomy (a bone revision).

Knocked Knees (Genu Valgum) and Bowlegs (Genu Varum)

While bowlegs are very common in newborns and toddlers, knocked knees appear to be more common during the preschool years and in children six to ten years of age. Both knocked knees and bowlegs depend on the degree of angulation of the hip-knee-ankle alignment. Generally, both conditions resolve themselves as the child grows—although a minimum amount of excess rotation may remain if tibial torsion is a component. In some cases, depending on the underlying cause, surgical correction is needed at puberty. If this is the case, X rays and diagnostic workups related to other neuromuscular disorders (such as rickets, osteogenesis imperfecta, dwarfism, or Blount's disease) will need to be separately addressed.

Pigeon Toes (Internal Tibial Torsion) and Inward Turning of Entire Leg (Femoral Anteversion)

In utero, a fetus's legs are positioned inward. Therefore, internal torsion is normal prenatally. However, during the latter part of the neonatal and postnatal periods, and to a lesser extent throughout childhood, the upper leg (the femur) and the lower leg bones (the tibia and fibula) should begin to rotate outward. This is an actual twisting of the bones—not the joints. Both weight bearing and growth will cause the "derotation" of the limbs in due course. This normal derotation is important for proper lower extremity alignment. However, when this derotation of the leg is excessively delayed or inadequate, it presents itself as toeing in—whether as internal tibial torsion or femoral anteversion. With either of these conditions, it's important to note that the femur and/or the tibia and fibula are turned in—not the foot. (However, foot conditions and/or deformities still need to be ruled out as well.)

In diagnosing femoral anteversion, hip dysplasia needs to be ruled out, since both variations share some of the same symptoms. Femoral anteversion is typically seen bilaterally and is often detected when it's clear that a child's preferred sitting position is the "W" position. Due to limitations in lateral hip rotation, sitting cross-legged is uncomfortable. This condition tends to have a higher incidence in girls than boys.

Overall, 99 percent of children with torsional abnormalities self-correct by puberty, and 95 percent of children with femoral anteversion resolve spontaneously as well. Consequently, the most common course of action is close observation. Bracing has not been proved to be effective in correcting the rotation, although some doctors continue to recommend early splinting (between three and six months of age). Their philosophy is that bracing won't hurt a child and might help. Furthermore, many parents feel better knowing that they are doing *something* for their child. (In many cases, doctors admit that they are treating the parents and not the child.) Surgery is only warranted in the most severe cases, and it is not recommended before a child is five to six years of age for tibial torsion and eight to twelve years of age for femoral anteversion. By performing surgery too early, there is a chance of missing those patients who may spontaneously correct.

Metatarsus Adductus

Metatarsus adductus is a condition most often due to fetal positioning in the womb. It usually presents itself at about two months of age and might not be obvious at birth. The forefoot, or metatarsal, deviates inward. About five of every thousand babies are born with this condition. There doesn't seem to be a genetic component, since only about one in 20 siblings have the deformity. Treatment varies depending on the severity of the condition. If the foot can passively be brought back to midline (or neural position), treatment may be a daily home stretching program. If the foot is not passively correctable to a neutral position, then casting may be indicated. If casting does not work, then an X ray may be needed to rule out something more severe (such as a skew foot). Most cases have very good corrective results by one and half years of age.

Flatfoot, or Foot Pronation (Flexible Pez Planus)

Flatfoot is a condition in which the longitudinal arch of the foot is flat, which causes the forefoot to abduct (turn out) and the heel to collapse inward. When the child is sitting with the foot unsupported, an arch is present. But when the foot is on the ground bearing weight, the arch is lost. This is a benign condition, the cause of which is mostly related to the internal bony alignment of the foot and somewhat related to muscular activity. Because of the foot's position, heel cord tightening can result. It's important to remember that all children will appear to have flatfeet until four to six years of age. However, there does appear to be a high incidence of children with hypotonia who also have flatfeet. The condition is usually asymptomatic, and there is generally no treatment indicated. However, if a child with flatfeet complains of foot fatigue or pain and/or leg pain, a custom orthotic device that fits into his or her shoe is recommended. The orthotic will help place the foot in proper alignment so that it doesn't collapse in the shoe. Often parents think that wearing a sturdy, nonflexible shoe (in lieu of an orthotic) will help correct the foot's positioning. This isn't true: the foot will continue to collapse inside the shoe.

When a foot is out of alignment it can adversely affect both knee and hip alignment and mechanics (although this is not a common occurrence). As a child gets older, foot and knee pain may increase during sports due to uneven stresses placed on the joints. A painful foot can cause fatigue as well as gait deviations. If it hasn't been recommended previously, an orthotic may be recommended for use during such times. While there is no evidence to indicate that an orthotic device will "cure" or "fix" a flatfoot, the orthotic will help maintain proper alignment of the foot, can assist in correcting biomechanical function of the muscles, and will also relieve symptoms.

Conditions that can imitate flexible pez planus (such as rigid pez planus, partial colitions, and neuromuscular deformities) should also be ruled out.

Congenital Muscular Torticollis

Torticollis is a shortening of a neck muscle called the sternocleidomastoid muscle, which helps to tilt and rotate the head. Its shortening results in the tilting of the head toward the affected side and rotation of the face toward the opposite side. For example, with a right torticollis, the head tilts toward the right side (the right ear goes toward the right shoulder) and the chin is deviated toward the left ear. This condition is known to affect about 2 percent of all newborns. In up to 80 percent of all cases, a mass of fibrous tissue can be felt in the affected muscle. One possible cause of this fibrotic mass is blood restriction to the area, which would result in fibrotic changes in the muscle. But the most common causes are intrauterine positioning and birth trauma, or both. Since there does appear to be a correlation between torticollis and hip dysplasia (10 to 20 percent of those affected have both torticollis and hip dysplasia), congenital hip dysplasia needs to be ruled out. X rays are recommended to rule out a tumor or cervical spine abnormalities.

Torticollis is usually detected by the time a newborn is four to eight weeks old. If left untreated, the affected muscle will continue to become tighter, decreasing the range of motion in the neck along with causing a corresponding tightness throughout the affected side—including the trunk and the hip (remember, everything is connected). Compensatory scoliosis may develop as well. The cervical fascia (the lining around the muscle) may also thicken and tighten, affecting blood flow. Facial asymmetry is often associated with torticollis due to uneven pressure on the affected side.

Conservative treatment should begin as early as possible. This includes stretching the muscles on the affected side as well as strengthening muscles on the opposite side. A home program can be provided if the torticollis is mild. In moderate cases, the infant should be seen on a regular basis for intervention by a physical therapist or a doctor of osteopathic medicine who specializes in pediatric cranial osteopathy. If the condition is left untreated, or in severe cases, surgical intervention may be needed to release or lengthen the affected muscle. However, surgery is generally not considered until after one year of age for a muscle release. X rays may also be needed to rule out cervical scoliosis.

Idiopathic Scoliosis

Scoliosis is a structural deformity involving rotation of the spine and ribs. Idiopathic scoliosis accounts for up to 80 percent of all scoliosis. The remaining 20 percent is associated with many other diagnoses (tumors, infections, connective tissue diseases, trauma, bony abnormalities, and various syndromes). But there is a strong genetic component to idiopathic scoliosis. About 90 percent of children who suffer from it have a familial recurrence, and girls are nine times more likely to develop idiopathic scoliosis than boys. Screening (by a pediatrician or a school nurse) is the best detection for early diagnosis and treatment. Depending on the age of onset, idiopathic scoliosis can be divided into infantile (before age three), juvenile (ages three to ten), and adolescent (ages 10 to skeletal maturation). Usually, the earlier the curve develops, the worse it tends to be.

One goal of treatment is to maintain a curve of under 30 degrees until adulthood. The rate of progression can be between one and two degrees per year. Consequently, a 30-degree curve can become as much as 40 to 50 degrees in 10 years. Generally, when a curve is between 20 and 25 degrees, close observation is needed. A 30-degree curve requires bracing. A stretching and strengthening program can help with mild pain. In severe adolescent cases, meaning that a curve has become greater than 50 degrees, surgery is often necessary. In general, children should be referred to centers specializing in scoliosis where a team of experts will review all possible interventions. In some cases, surgical intervention is actually a more conservative treatment than bracing, since bracing may be needed throughout a child's developing years.

Congenital Clubfoot (Talipes Equinovarus)

Clubfoot is considered a pathology (abnormality) rather than a variation. Here not only is the forefoot adducted (in) as in being pigeon-toed, but the heel or hind foot is adducted as well. The ankle is also in plantar flexion (the toes point downward—known as the equines position) and the heel cord is shortened. The incidence is about one per one thousand births. While the cause of clubfoot is unknown, it can be diagnosed prenatally by ultrasound. There also appears to be an underlying genetic predisposition, since it does tend to run in families. It may also be related to an arrest in development. Ranges of the deformity run from mild to severe. A mild case may be correctable by casting, whereas severe cases frequently require a surgical procedure involving muscular releases of the foot and heel cord as well as bony realignments of the forefoot. Surgical intervention is generally recommended from three months of age to one year, depending on the efficacy of the nonsurgical treatment and the development of the infant. Older children and young adults who did not have the benefit of early treatment can still benefit from surgical intervention.

Other foot deformities related to neurological and muscular disorders (such as cerebral palsy, muscular dystrophy, or spina bifida) should be carefully ruled out when diagnosing clubfoot.

And Always Remember . . .

- *Many of the conditions noted here are correctable or are conditions that children typically outgrow. However, we should be diligent in monitoring our children and intervening when necessary. Please consult and keep an open dialogue with your pediatrician and/or pediatric orthopedist.*

Source Materials

Much of the material used in this book has been obtained from the following sources. Each, in its own way, makes a significant contribution to the discussion of this subject.

Chapters 1 and 10

Anzalone, Marie E. "Sensory Contributions to Action: A Sensory Integrative Approach." *Zero to Three* (October/November): 17–20.

Ayres, A. Jean. 1978. "Learning Disabilities and the Vestibular System." *Journal of Learning Disabilities* 12: 18–29.

Ayres, A. Jean. 1979. *Sensory Integration and the Child.* California: Western Psychological Services.

Ayres, A. Jean. 1980. *Southern California Sensory Integration Tests Manual: Revised.* Los Angeles: Western Psychological Services.

Clark, D. L., et al. 1977. "Vestibular Stimulation Influence on Motor Development in Infants." *Science* 196: 1228–1229.

Fisher, Anne G., et al. 1983. "Tactile Defensiveness: Historical Perspectives, New Research—A Theory Grows." *Sensory Integration Special Interest Section Newsletter* 6, no. 2: 1–2.

Fisher, Anne G., et al. 1991. *Sensory Integration Theory and Practice.* Philadelphia: F. A. Davis Co.

Forsyth Blacha, Sarah. 1983. "Concepts in Early Sensory Development." *South African Journal of Physiotherapy* 39, no. 1.

Greenspan, Stanley I. 1993. "The Emotional Development of Infants and Young Children." *Pediatric Basics* 63: 9–16.

Greenspan, Stanley I., and Nancy T. Greenspan. 1985. *First Feelings: Milestones in the Emotional Development of Your Baby and Child from Birth to Age Four.* New York: Viking Penguin.

Haith, Marshall M. 1986. "Sensory and Perceptual Processes in Early Infancy." *Journal of Pediatrics* 109, no. 1 (July): 158–171.

Lewerenz, Tara L., et al. 1996. "Sensory Processing in At-Risk Infants." *Sensory Integration Special Interest Section Newsletter* 19, no.1: 1–4.

Martin Stern, Francine. 1971. "The Reflex Development of the Infant." *The American Journal of Occupational Therapy* 25, no. 3 (April): 155–158.

McGrew, Laura, et al. 1985. "The Landau Reaction in Full-Term and Preterm Infants at Four Months of Age." *Developmental Medicine and Child Neurology* 27: 161–169.

Reisman, Judith E., et al. 1992. *Sensory Integration Inventory Revised for Individuals with Developmental Disabilities.* Hugo, Minnesota: PDP Press.

Stock Kranowitz, Carol. 1998. *The Out-of-Sync Child.* New York: The Berkley Publishing Group.

Wilbarger, Patricia. 1984. "Planning an Adequate Sensory Diet—Application of Sensory Processing Theory During the First Year of Life." *Zero to Three* (September): 7–12.

Woollacott, Marjorie, et al. 1987. "Neuromuscular Control of Posture in the Infant and Child: Is Vision Dominant?" *Journal of Motor Behavior* 19, no. 2: 167–186.

Chapters 2, 3, 4, 6, and 7

Barnes, Marylou R., et al. 1982. *The Neurophysiological Basis of Patient Treatment, Vol. 2. Reflexes in Motor Development.* Georgia: Stokesville Publishing Company.

Bayley, Nancy. 1969. *Bayley Scales of Infant Development.* Princeton, New Jersey: Princeton Educational Testing Service.

Bly, Louis. 1983. *The Components of Normal Movement During the First Year of Life and Abnormal Motor Development.* Oak Park, Illinois: The Neuro-Developmental Treatment Association.

Brown, Sara L., et al. 1981. *Developmental Programming for Infants and Young Children.* University of Michigan Press.

Caplan, Frank. 1971. *The First Twelve Months of Life.* New York: Grosset and Dunlap.

Case-Smith, Jane, et al. 1996. *Occupational Therapy for Children.* St. Louis, Missouri: C. V. Mosby.

Connecticut Infant-Toddler Developmental Assessment Program. 1986. New Haven, Connecticut: Yale University Press.

Crook, C. 1981. "Functional Aspects of the Chemical Senses in Newborn Period." *Developmental Medicine and Child Neurology* 23: 247–259.

Crouchman, Marion. 1986. "The Effects of Baby Walkers on Early Locomotor Development." *Developmental Medicine and Child Neurology* 28: 757–761.

Davis, B. E., et al. 1998. "Effects of Sleep Position on Infant Motor Development." *Pediatrics* 102, no. 5 (November): 1135–1140.

Denver II screening test. 1990. W. K. Frankenburg and J. B. Dodds.

Dubowitz, Lilly, and Victor Dubowitz. 1981. *The Neurological Assessment of the Preterm and Full-Term Newborn Infant.* Philadelphia: J. B. Lippincott Co.

Forsyth, Sarah C. 1989. "Hand Facilitation in Children with Neuromotor Dysfunction." NDTA Conference, San Diego, California.

Furuno, Setsu, et al. 1984. *Hawaii Early Learning Profile Checklist: Ages Birth to Three Years.* VORT Corporation, Palo Alto, California.

Gould III, James A., et al. 1985. *Orthopedic and Sports Physical Therapy, Vol. 2.* St. Louis, Missouri: C. V. Mosby.

Hoppenfeld, Stanley. 1976. *Physical Examination of the Spine and Extremities.* Norwalk, Connecticut: Appleton-Century-Crofts.

Illingsworth, Ronald S. 1987. *The Development of the Infant and Young Child.* London: Churchill Livingstone.

Jantz, J. W., et al. 1997. "A Motor Milestone Change Noted with a Change in Sleep Position." *Archives of Pediatrics and Adolescent Medicine* 151, no. 6 (June): 565–568.

Kauffman, Ira B., et al. 1977. "Influence of an Infant Walker on Onset and Quality of Walking Pattern of Locomotion: An Electromyographic Investigation." *Perceptual and Motor Skills* 45: 1323–1329.

Kavanagh, Carol A., et al. 1982. "The Infant Walker: A Previously Unrecognized Health Hazard." *Am. J. Dis. Child* 136: 205–206.

Ludington-Hoe, Susan M. 1983. "What Can Newborns Really See?" *American Journal of Nursing* (September): 1286–1289.

Morris, Suzanne E., et al. 1987. *Pre-Feeding Skills.* Tucson, Arizona: Therapy Skill Builders.

Perry, Jacquelin. 1967. "The Mechanics of Walking." *Physical Therapy* 47, no. 9: 778–801.

Rieder, M. J., et al. 1986. "Patterns of Walker Use and Walker Injury." *Pediatrics* 78, no. 3 (September): 488–493.

Scheerer, Carol R. 1992. "Perspectives on an Oral Motor Activity: The Use of Rubber Tubing as a Chewy." *American Journal of Occupational Therapy* 46, no. 4 (April): 344–352.

Shulman, Lisa H., et al. 1997. "Developmental Implications of Idiopathic Toe Walking." *Journal of Pediatrics* 130, no. 4 (April): 541–546.

Siegel, Andrea C., et al. 1999. "Effects of Baby Walkers on Motor and Mental Development in Human Infants." *Developmental and Behavioral Pediatrics* 20, no. 5: 355–361.

Simpkiss, M. J., and A. S. Raikes. 1972. "Problems Resulting from the Excessive Use of Baby Walkers and Baby Bouncers." *Lancet,* 1: 747.

Trembath, Jack. 1977. *The Milani-Comparetti Motor Development Screening Test.* Lincoln, Nebraska: Meyer Children's Rehabilitation Institute, University of Nebraska Medical Center.

Chapters 5 and 7

Arvedson, Joan C., et al. 1993. *Pediatric Swallowing and Feeding.* San Diego, California: Singular Publishing Group, Inc.

Cermak, Sharon A., et al. 1986. "The Relationship Between Articulation Disorders and Motor Coordination in Children." *American Journal of Occupational Therapy* 40, no. 8 (August): 546–550.

Morris, Suzanne, et al. 1987. *Pre-Feeding Skills.* Tucson, Arizona: Therapy Skill Builders.

Paul, Rhea. 1995. *Language Disorders from Infancy Through Adolescence.* St. Louis, Missouri: C. V. Mosby.

Weber, Friederike, et al. 1986. "An Ultrasonographic Study of the Organization of Sucking and Swallowing by Newborn Infants." *Developmental Medicine and Child Neurology* 28: 19–24.

Wolf, Lynn S., et al. 1992. *Feeding and Swallowing Disorders in Infancy.* Tucson, Arizona: Therapy Skill Builders.

Chapter 8

Dubowitz, Victor. 1985. "Evaluation and Differential Diagnosis of the Hypotonic Infant." *Pediatrics in Review* 6, no. 8: 237–243.

Fremion, Amy S. 1986. "Evaluation of the Floppy Infant, or Congenital Hypotonia." *Indian Medicine* (August): 680–681.

Jacobson, Richard D. 1998. "Approach to the Child with Weakness or Clumsiness." *Pediatric Clinics of North America* 45, no. 1 (February): 145–168.

Zalneraitis, Edwin L. 1989. "The Pathophysiology of the Floppy Infant." *Rhode Island Medical Journal* 72 (October): 351–354.

Chapter 9

Allen, Marilee C., et al. 1990. "Gross Motor Milestones in Preterm Infants: Correction for Degree of Prematurity." *Journal of Pediatrics* 116, no. 6: 955–959.

Als, Heidelise, et al. 1981. "A New Model of Assessing Behavioral Organization in Preterm and Full-Term Infants." *Journal of the American Academy of Child Psychiatry* 20: 239–263.

Als, Heidelise, et al. 1994. "Individualized Developmental Care for the Very Low-Birth-Weight Preterm Infant: Medical and Neurofunctional Effects." *Journal of the American Medical Association* 272: 853–858.

Bauchner, Howard, et al. 1988. "Premature Graduates of the Newborn Intensive Care Unit: A Guide to Follow-Up." *Pediatric Clinics of North America* 35, no. 6 (December): 1207–1226.

Bernbaum, Judy C., et al. 1983. "Nonnutritive Sucking During Gavage Feeding Enhances Growth and Maturation in Premature Infants." *Pediatrics* 71, no. 1 (January): 41–45.

Brazelton, T. B. 1984. *Neonatal Behavioral Assessment Scale.* Philadelphia: J. B. Lippincott Co.

Connolly, Barbara H. 1985. "Neonatal Assessment: An Overview." *Physical Therapy* 65, no. 10: 1505–1513.

Dietrich Comrie, Joan, et al. 1997. "Common Feeding Problems in the Intensive Care Nursery: Maturation, Organization, Evaluation, and Management Strategies." *Seminars in Speech and Language* 18, no. 3: 239–259.

Ellison, Patricia H. 1984. "Neurologic Development of the High-Risk Infant." *Clinics in Perinatology* 11, no. 1 (February): 41–57.

Fay, Mary J. 1988. "The Positive Effects of Positioning." *Neonatal Network* (April): 23–28.

Field, Tiffany, et al. 1982. "Nonnutritive Sucking During Tube Feedings: Effects on Preterm Neonates in an Intensive Care Unit." *Pediatrics* 70, no. 3 (September): 381–384.

Field, Tiffany, et al. 1987. "Massage of Preterm Newborns to Improve Growth and Development." *Pediatric Nursing* 13, no. 6 (November-December): 385–387.

Harris, Mary Beth, et al. 1990. "Joint Range of Motion Development in Premature Infants." *Pediatric Physical Therapy* 2, no. 4 (winter): 185–191.

Harrison, Helen, et al. 1983. *The Premature Baby Book.* New York: St. Martin's Press.

"The High-Risk Neonate: Developmental Therapy Perspectives." 1986. *Physical and Occupational Therapy in Pediatrics* 6, no. 3/4 (fall/winter).

Katz, Kathy S., et al. 1989. *Chronically Ill and At-Risk Infants.* Palo Alto, California: VORT Corporation.

Korner, Anneliese F., et al. 1972. "The Relative Efficacy of Contact and Vestibular-Propioceptive Stimulation in Soothing Neonates." *Child Development* 43: 443–453.

Korner, Anneliese F., et al. 1978. "Reduction of Sleep Apnea and Bradycardia in Preterm Infants on Oscillating Water Beds: A Controlled Polygraphic Study." *Pediatrics* 61, no. 4 (April): 528–533.

Kramer, Lloyd I., et al. 1976. "Rocking Water Beds and Auditory Stimuli to Enhance Growth of Preterm Infants." *Journal of Pediatrics* 88, no. 2 (February): 297–299.

Ludington, Susan M. 1984. "A Comprehensive Course of Study in Infant Growth and Development." Sponsored by Symposia Medicus.

Meyer Palmer, Marjorie, et al. 1993. "Neonatal Oral-Motor Assessment Scale: A Reliability Study." *Journal of Perinatology* 13, no.1: 28–35.

Mouradian, Laurie E., et al. 1994. "The Influence of Neonatal Intensive Care Unit Caregiving Practices on Motor Functioning of Preterm Infants." *The American Journal of Occupational Therapy* 48, no. 6 (June): 527–533.

Pearl, Lynda F. 1990. "Transition from Neonatal Intensive Care Unit: Putting It All Together in the Community." *Infants and Young Children* 3, no. 1 (July): 41–30.

Rapport, Mary Jane K. 1992. "A Descriptive Analysis of the Role of Physical and Occupational Therapists in the Neonatal Intensive Care Unit." *Pediatric Physical Therapy* 4, no. 4 (winter): 172–178.

Schaefer, Margret, et al. 1980. "Prematurity and Infant Stimulation: A Review of Research." *Child Psychiatry and Human Development* 10, no. 4 (summer): 199–212.

"The Spectrum of Developmental Disabilities XII: Prematurity: Neurodevelopmental Assessment and Intervention Issues." 1990. Baltimore, Maryland: The Johns Hopkins Medical Institutions (March).

Staff of the Children's Hospital, Denver, Colorado. 1989. *Developmental Interventions for Preterm and High-Risk Infants.* Tucson, Arizona: Therapy Skill Builders.

VandenBerg, Kathleen A. 1990. "Nippling Management of the Sick Neonate in the NICU: The Disorganized Feeder." *Neonatal Network* 9, no. 1 (August): 9–15.

White Jerry L., et al. 1976. "The Effects of Tactile and Kinesthetic Stimulation on Neonatal Development in the Premature Infant." *Developmental Psychobiology* 9, no. 6: 569–577.

Chapter 11

The Foot and Ankle—A Selection of Papers from the American Orthopaedic Foot Society Meetings. 1980. New York: Brian C. Decker.

Hoffinger, Scott, A. 1996. "Evaluation and Management of Pediatric Foot Deformities." *Pediatric Clinics of North America* 43, no. 5: 1091–1111.

Lovell, Wood W., and Robert B. Winters. 1990. *Pediatric Orthopaedics.* Pennsylvania: J. B. Lippincott Co.

MacEwen, G. D., et al. 1990. "Congenital Dislocation of the Hip." *Pediatrics in Review* 11, no. 8 (February): 250–252.

Oski, Frank A., et al. 1994. *Principles and Practice of Pediatrics.* Philadelphia, Pennsylvania: J. B. Lippincott Co.

Pediatric Clinics of North America. 1996. Vol. 43, no. 4. Philadelphia: W. B. Saunders Co.

Sherk, Henry H., et al. 1981. "Congenital Dislocation of the Hip." *Clinical Pediatrics* 20, no. 8 (August): 513–520.

Additional Readings

Of General Interest

American Academy of Child and Adolescent Psychiatry. 1998. *Your Child.* New York: HarperCollins.

American Academy of Pediatrics. 1991. *Caring for Your Baby and Child.* New York: Bantam.

Brazelton, T. Berry. 2002. *Touchpoints: Both Volumes of the Nation's Most Trusted Guide to the First Six Years of Life.* New York: Perseus.

Brooks, Robert, Ph.D., and Sam Goldstein, Ph.D. 2001. *Raising Resilient Children.* Chicago: Contemporary Books.

Campbell, Don. 2000. *The Mozart Effect for Children: Awakening Your Child's Mind, Health, and Creativity with Music.* New York: William Morrow.

Caplan, Frank. 1971. *The First Twelve Months of Life.* New York: Grosset and Dunlap.

The Editors of *Parents* Magazine. 1998. *The Parents Answer Book.* New York: Golden Books.

Fraiberg, Selma. 1996. *The Magic Years.* New York: Fireside.

Greenspan, Stanley I., and Nancy T. Greenspan. 1985. *First Feelings: Milestones in the Emotional Development of Your Baby and Child from Birth to Age Four.* New York: Viking Penguin.

Illingsworth, Ronald S. 1987. *The Development of the Infant and Young Child.* London: Churchill Livingstone.

Leach, Penelope. 1977. *Your Baby and Child.* New York: Knopf.

Levine, Mel. 2002. *A Mind at a Time.* New York: Simon & Schuster.

Levine, Mel. 2003. *The Myth of Laziness.* New York: Simon & Schuster.

Sears, William, M.D., and Martha Sears, R.N. 2002. *The Successful Child.* Boston: Little, Brown.

Seligman, Martin P., M.D. 1995. *The Optimistic Child.* New York: Perennial.

Shapiro, Lawrence, M.D. 2003. *The Secret Language of Children.* Naperville, Illinois: SourceBooks.

Stock Kranowitz, Carol. 1998. *The Out-of-Sync Child: Recognizing and Coping with Sensory Integration Dysfunction.* New York: The Berkley Publishing Group.

On Premature Babies

Harrison, Helen, et al. 1983. *The Premature Baby Book: A Parent's Guide to Coping and Caring in the First Years.* New York: St. Martin's Press.

Madden, Susan L., M.S. 2000. *The Premie Parent's Companion.* Boston: Harvard Common Press.

Mehren, Elizabeth. 1991. *Born Too Soon.* New York: Kensington.

Techniques of Touch

McClure, Vimala Schneider. 2000. *Infant Massage: A Handbook for Loving Parents.* New York: Bantam Doubleday Dell.

Walker, Peter. 2001. *The Practical Art of Baby Massage: A Step-by-Step Guide to Massage Routines and Flexibility Exercises for Babies up to Three Years Old.* New York: Perseus.

Suggested Books for Infants and Toddlers

Arma, T. 1994. *Dress-Up Time.* New York: Grosset and Dunlap.

Asch, F. 1984. *Moongame.* New York: Simon & Schuster. (We recommend the entire *Moongame* series.)

Barton, B. All books.

Bonforte, L. 1981. *Illustrated Farm Animals.* New York: Random House.

Carle, E. 1994. *The Very Hungry Caterpillar.* New York: Philomer Books. (We recommend all of Eric Carle's books.)

Carter D. 1998. *Bed Bugs.* New York: Little Simon.

Freeman, Don. 1968. *Corduroy.* New York: Viking.

Hill, E. 1995. *Spot's Baby Sister.* New York: Penguin Books. (We recommend all of the *Spot* books.)

Hoban, T. 1994. *What Is That?* Scranton, Pennsylvania: HarperCollins.

Kunhardt, D. 1962. *Pat the Bunny.* New York: Golden Press/Western Publishing.

Leaf, Monro. 1936. *The Story of Ferdinand.* New York: Viking.

Lobel, Arnold. 1971. *Frog and Toad Together.* New York: HarperCollins.

Martin, B., et al. 1989. *Chicka Chicka Boom Boom.* New York: Simon & Schuster.

McBratney, Sam. 1994. *Guess How Much I Love You?* Cambridge: Candlewick Press.

Merberg, J., and S. Bober. 2002. *A Magical Day with Matisse.* San Francisco: Chronicle Books.

Merberg, J., and S. Bober. 2002. *In the Garden with Van Gogh.* San Francisco: Chronicle Books.

Waddell, M. 1992. *Owl Babies.* Cambridge: Candlewick Press.

Wells, R. 1998. *Max's Bath.* New Jersey: Dial Books. (We recommend all of the *Max* books.)

Wilson-Max, K. 1996. *Little Red Plane.* New York: Scholastic.

Wise Brown, M. 1947, 1977. *Good Night Moon.* New York: Harper and Row.

Suggested Books for Toddlers to Five and Up

Aardema, V. 1975. *Why Mosquitoes Buzz in People's Ears.* New York: Dial Books for Young Readers.

Alborough, J. 1992. *Where's My Teddy?* Cambridge: Candlewick Press.

Bemelmans, Ludwig. 1956. *Madeline.* New York: Viking. (We recommend all of the *Madeline* books.)

Berger, Barbara H. 1996. *Grandfather Twilight.* New York: Putnam and Grosser Geap.

Cannon, J. 1997. *Stella Luna.* San Diego: Harcourt Brace and Company.

Cronin, D. 2000. *Click, Clack, Moo—Cows That Type.* New York: Simon & Schuster Books for Young Readers.

De Brunhoff, J. 1931. *The Story of Babar the Little Elephant.* New York: Random House. (We recommend all of the *Babar* books.)

Ehlert, L. 1989. *Eating the Alphabet–Fruits and Vegetables from A to Z.* San Diego: Harcourt Brace Jovanovich.

Falconer, I. 2000. *Olivia.* New York: Atheneum Books for Young Readers.

Geisel, Theodor Seuss. 1960, 1968. *Green Eggs and Ham.* New York: Random House. (We recommend all of *Dr. Seuss's* books.)

Giganti, P. 1988. *How Many Snails?* New York: Mulberry Books.

Guaring, D. 1989. *Is Your Mama a Llama?* New York: Scholastic.

Hague, K. 1984. *Alphabears.* New York: Henry Holt and Company.

Hague, K. 1997. *Calendarbears.* New York: Henry Holt and Company.

Hall, D. 1979. *Ox-Cart Man.* New York: Puffin Books.

Hayles, K., and C. Fuge. 1992. *Whale Is Stuck.* New York: Simon & Schuster.

Heine, H. 1991. *Mollywoop.* New York: Farrar, Straus and Giroux.

Henkes, K. 1990. *Julius—The Baby of the World.* New York: Mulberry Books.

Henkes, K. 1996. *Lilly's Purple Plastic Purse.* New York: Greenwillow Books.

Hissey, Jane. 1986. *Old Bear.* New York: Philomel Books.

Johnson, C. 1955. *Harold and the Purple Crayon.* New York: HarperCollins.

Joosse, B. 1996. *I Love You the Purplest.* San Francisco: Chronicle Books.

Kalan, R. 1981. *Jump, Frog, Jump.* New York: Mulberry Books.

Kimmel, E. 2000. *The Runaway Tortilla.* Delray Beach, Florida: Winslow Press.

Kirk, D. 1995. *Miss Spider's Wedding.* New York: Scholastic.

Leaf, M. 1936. *The Story of Ferdinand.* New York: Viking.

Luciani, B. 2000. *How Will We Get to the Beach?* New York: North-South Books.

McCloskey, R. 1941, 1969. *Make Way for Ducklings.* New York: Macmillan.

Micklethwait, L. 1994. *I Spy a Lion—Animals in Art.* New York: Greenwillow Books.

Numeroff, L. 1985. *If You Give a Mouse a Cookie.* New York: HarperCollins.

Paraskevas, B. 1999. *Hoppy and Joe.* New York: Simon & Schuster.

Rathmann, P. 1994. *Good Night Gorilla.* New York: G. P. Putnam and Sons.

Rey, M. 1941. *Curious George.* Boston: Houghton Mifflin Company. (We recommend all of the *Curious George* books.)

Sendak, M. 1963. *Where the Wild Things Are.* New York: HarperCollins.

Silverstein, S. 1976. *The Missing Piece.* New York: HarperCollins.

Slobodkina, Esphyr. 1987. *Caps for Sale.* New York: HarperCollins.

Taback, S. 1997. *There Was an Old Lady Who Swallowed a Fly.* New York: Viking.

Taback, S. 1999. *Joseph Had a Little Overcoat.* New York: Viking.

Thurber, J. 1943. *Many Moons.* Orlando: Harcourt Brace.

Viorst, J. 1972. *Alexander and the Terrible, Horrible, No Good, Very Bad Day.* New York: Atheneum.

Waber, B. 1965. *Lyle, Lyle Crocodile.* Boston: Houghton Mifflin. (We recommend all of the *Lyle* books.)

Wells, R. 1998. *Yoko.* New York: Hyperion Books for Children.

Wick, W. 1994. *I Spy Fantasy.* New York: Scholastic. (We recommend the entire *I Spy* series.)

Williams, M. 1958. *The Velveteen Rabbit.* New York: Doubleday.

Wise Brown, M. 1942. *The Runaway Bunny.* New York: HarperCollins.

Helpful Organizations

The following organizations can help if you feel your child is in need.

American Occupational Therapy Association, Inc.
P.O. Box 31220
Bethesda, MD 20824
(301) 652-AOTA or (800) 668-8255
Fax: (301) 652-7711
www.aota.org

American Physical Therapy Association
1111 N. Fairfax Street
Alexandria, VA 22314
(703) 684-2782 or (800) 999-2782
www.apta.org

American Speech-Language-Hearing Association
10801 Rockville Pike
Rockville, MD 20852
(301) 897-5700 or (800) 638-TALK
Fax: (301) 571-0457
www.asha.org

Council for Exceptional Children
1920 Association Drive
Reston, VA 22091
(703) 620-3660

National Information Center for Children and Youth with Disabilities
P.O. Box 1492
Washington, DC 20013
(800) 695-0285
Fax: (202) 884-8441
www.nichcy.org

Sensory Integration International (SII)-The Ayres Clinic
P.O. Box 5339
Torrance, CA 90501
(310) 787-8805
www.sensoryint.com

Index

A

Activities. *See also* Exercises, play; Play/skills
- to enhance muscle activation, 156–57
- to enhance sound production, 94–95
- imaginative and symbolic play, 125
- language play, 125–26
- manipulative play, 121–24, 141
- physical play, 115–20, 136–41
- with water, 124–25

Art projects, 122–23
Asymmetrical tonic neck reflex, 9
Auditory system, developing
- imaginative and symbolic play for, 125
- language play for, 125–26
- for newborns, 34–36
- for one- to six-month-olds, 57
- premature infants and, 166–67
- for seven- to twelve-month-olds, 87

Automatic movements, 8–11. *See also* Movement; Voluntary (volitional) movements
- postural reactions, 10–11
- postural regressions, 11
- primitive reflexes, 8–9
- reflex progression for, 9–10

Automatic walking reflex, 23
Awareness. *See* Sensory awareness

B

Babies. *See* Newborns; Premature infants; specific age groups
Baby bouncers, 25
Baby proofing, 76
Back sleeping, 50
Back (supine) play/skills, 54
- for four- to six-month-olds, 46–48
- for one- to three-month-olds, 43
- for seven- to nine-month-olds, 64

Backpacks, carrying, 140–41
Ball playing, 118, 138
Base of support, 14
Bassinets, 24–25
Bath-bottle-book-bed routine, 40, 41
Baths
- for newborns, 32–33
- routines for, 40
- as sensory activities, 53

Bear walking, 66
Bedtimes, routines for, 41–43
Behavior changes, transitions and, 134
Belly (prone) play, 13, 54
- for four- to six-month-olds, 48
- for one- to three-month-olds, 43–44
- for seven- to nine-month-olds, 64

Bench sitting. *See also* Sitting
- for one- to three-year-olds, 118–20
- for ten- to twelve-month-olds, 82

Benchmarks. *See* Developmental benchmarks
Bicycles, 138
Bilateral integration
  disorders, 175
  for voluntary movements, 15
Block building, 123
Body position, sense of, 4
Body-on-body righting reactions, 10–11
Bowlegs (genu varum), 180
Bubble blowing, 124

C

Car seats, positioning newborns in, 25
Carrying positions, for newborns, 25–27
Central nervous system, movement and, 15–17
Checklists
  for feeding skills, 103
  for language skills, 96
  for newborns, 35
  for one- to six-month-olds, 58
  for one- to three-year-olds, 129
  for premature infants, 169
  for seven- to twelve-month-olds, 89
Cheerios, as food, 104
Climbing, 80
Clothespins, for manipulative play, 124
Clubfoot, 184
Cognitive abilities, developing
  imaginative and symbolic play for, 125
  language play for, 125–26
  for one- to three-month-olds, 59
  for seven- to twelve-month-olds, 85–86
Comfort levels of babies, understanding, 6
Compensatory movements, 14–15
Congenital clubfoot (talipes equinovarus), 184
Congenital dislocation of the hip (hip dysplasia), 180
Congenital muscular torticollis, 182–83
Crawling games, 117
Creeping, 71–73
  for ten- to twelve-month-olds, 80
Cruising, 76–77
Cup drinking, 105–7

D

Developmental benchmarks
  for feeding first-year babies, 99
  for feeding one- to three-year-olds, 127
  for four- to six-month-olds, 52
  for language skills, 95
  for newborns, 34
  for one- to three-month-olds, 45
  for one- to three-year-olds, 116
  for seven- to nine-month-olds, 72
  for ten- to twelve-month-olds, 82
  for three- to five-year-olds, 137
Developmental sequence
  importance of completing, 41
  overview of, 39–40
Dexterity, hand and finger, 62–63
Discriminatory system, of tactile system, 17
Disorders
  proprioceptive, 173–76
  vestibular, 173–76
Door jumpers, 85
Drawing, 122–23
Drinking. *See* Cup drinking; Feeding skills
Drooling, 105

E

Eating. *See* Feeding skills
Effort, voluntary movements and, 15

Exercises, play. *See also* Activities
for seven- to nine-month-olds, 77–79
walking, for three- to five-year-olds, 138
Exersaucers, 52–53, 83–85
Expressive language, 91

F

Feeding schedules, 40–41
Feeding skills
checklist for, 103
communication and, 99
developmental benchmarks for first-year babies, 99
environment and, 99–100, 108
introduction of cup drinking and, 105–7
introduction of semisolid foods and, 100
introduction of solid foods and, 100–105
for newborns, 27, 33–34
for one- to three-year-olds, 126–27
overview of, 97–98
premature infants and, 168–70
sensory system and, 107–8
Femoral anteversion (inward turning of entire leg), 181
Fencing reflex, 9
Finger dexterity, 62–63
Finger painting, 123
Fitballs, 138–39
Flashlight games, 137
Flatfoot, 182
Flexed position, 22–23
ways to encourage, 23–26
Flexible pez planus (foot pronation), 182
Flexion, 22–23
prone, 24
side-lying, 24
supine, 23
Floor play, 13, 29
for seven- to nine-month-olds, 63–67
Foot deformities, 184
Foot development
for one- to three-year-olds, 113–14
for seven- to twelve-month-olds, 88–89
Foot play, four- to six-month-olds and, 51
Foot pronation (flexible pez planus), 182
Four- to six-month-olds
back play/skills for, 46–48
belly play/skills for, 48–49
developmental benchmarks for, 52
foot play and, 51
side-lying and rolling for, 49–51
standing and, 52
toys for, 47

G

Games. *See* Activities; Exercises, play; Play/skills
Genu valgum (knocked knees), 180
Gingerbread play-dough, recipe for, 122
Glue projects, 123
Gravitational insecurity, children with, 175
Gustatory (taste) senses, developing
for one- to six-month-olds, 58–69
for seven- to twelve-month-olds, 87–88

H

Hands
development of, 45–46
dexterity and, 62–63
Head control, 44
Heartbeat devices, 29
High chairs, 103–4
Hip dysplasia (congenital dislocation of the hip), 180

Hypersensitivity, 173–76
  warning signs for, 108
Hyposensitivity, 173–76
Hypotonia. *See* Low muscle tone (hypotonia)

I

Idiopathic scoliosis, 183–184
Infant seats, positioning newborns in, 25
Infants. *See* Newborns; Premature infants; specific age groups
In-line skating, 138
Integration, sensory, 4–5
Internal tibial torsion (pigeon toes), 181
Inward turning of entire leg (femoral anteversion), 181

J

Joint stability, for voluntary movements, 14
Jumpers, door, 85
Jumping, 140

K

Kaufman, Ira B., 83
Kneeling, 79
  for ten- to twelve-month-olds, 80, 81
Knocked knees (genu valgum), 180

L

Labyrinth righting reactions, 10
Landau reactions, 10
Language play
  for one- to three-year-olds, 125–26
  for three- to five-year-olds, 143
Language skills
  activities to enhance, 94–97
  development benchmarks for, for three- to five-year-olds, 145
  development of, 91–94
  development of, for one- to three-year-olds, 128–29
  development of, for three- to five-year-olds, 143
  warning signs for impediments to developing, 129–31
Lap sitting, 78
Lateral protection response, 67–68
Lifting, proper techniques for, 139–40
Log rolling motion, 23
Long sitting, 68, 78
Low muscle tone (hypotonia), 154–56. *See also* Muscle tone
  developmental warning signs for, 157–58

M

Manipulative play. *See also* Activities; Physical play
  for one- to three-year-olds, 121–24
  for three- to five-year-olds, 141
Massages, for newborns, 32
Meals. *See* Feeding skills
Metatarsus Adductus, 181–82
Midline, 22
Mirror play, 54–55
Mobiles, for newborns, 30
Modeling clay, 123–24
  recipes for, 122
Moro (startle) reflex, 8–9
Motor planning (praxis), 16
Motor skills, play and, 115–20
Movement. *See also* Automatic movements; Voluntary (volitional) movements

baby's sensory system and, 6–7
central nervous system and, 15–17
newborn's patterns of, 22–23
sense of, 4
Muscle strength, voluntary movements and, 12–14
Muscle tone, 12, 13, 154. *See also* Low muscle tone (hypotonia)
activities to enhance activation of, 156–57
sitting and, 68
Musical instruments, for manipulative play, 124

N

Naps, routines for, 40
Neck development, 44
Neck righting reactions, 10
Neonatal follow-up programs, for premature infants, 171
Nervous system. *See* Sensory (nervous) system
Newborns. *See also* Premature infants; specific age groups
activities to enhance sound production for, 94
auditory system and, 34–36
bassinets for, 24–25
baths and, 32–33
calming, 28–29
carrying, 25–26
developing sense of awareness and, 5–6
developmental benchmarks for, 34
engaging, 29–30
feeding, 27
feeding skills and, 33–34
massages for, 32
movement patterns of, 22–23
olfactory sense and, 36
picking up, 31–32
positioning, in infant or car seats, 25
swaddling, 27–28
tactile input for, 32–33
toys for, 33
visual development for, 30–32
Nonnutritive sucking, 23
NUK nursers, 27

O

Olfactory (smell) sense
developing baby's, 68
feeding skills and, 107
newborns and, 36
for one- to twelve month-olds, 58
premature infants and, 168
for seven- to twelve-month-olds, 87–88
One- to six-month-olds
auditory input for, 57
back play for, 54
bath time activities for, 53
belly play for, 54
checklist for, 58
cognitive input for, 59
gustatory (taste) input for, 58–59
mirror play for, 54–55
olfactory input for, 58
proprioceptive input for, 56
tactile input for, 56–57
vestibular input for, 55–56
visual input for, 53–65
One- to three-month-olds
activities to enhance sound production for, 94–95

One- to three-month-olds, *continued*
developmental benchmarks for, 45
hand development for, 45–46
prone play/skills for, 43–44
prone propping for, 44–45
recommended toys for, 42
supine play/skills for, 43
One- to three-year-olds
developmental benchmarks for, 116
feeding benchmarks for, 127
feeding skills for, 126–27
foot development and, 113–14
imaginative and symbolic play for, 125
language development benchmarks for, 129
language play for, 125–26
manipulative play for, 121–24
overview of, 111–13
physical play for, 115–21
toys for, 119
water play for, 124–25
Oral defensiveness, warning signs for, 108
Oral-motor tone, premature infants and, 168–70
Outdoor play, 118–20

P

Painting, 122–23
Palmar reflex, 9
Pelvic play, 44–45
Physical play. *See also* Activities; Exercises, play; Manipulative play
one- to three-year-olds, 115–20
for three- to five-year-olds, 136–41
Physiological flexion, 22
Picking up newborns, 31–32
Pigeon toes (internal tibial torsion), 181
Play-dough, recipe for, 122
Playground safety, 121
Playgroups, 125
Playpens, 51
Play/skills. *See also* Activities; Exercises, play
back
for four- to six-month-olds, 46–48
for one- to three-month-olds, 43
belly
for four- to six-month-olds, 48–49
for one- to three-month-olds, 43–44
floor, 13, 29, 63–67
Playtex nursers, 27
Postural reactions
progression of, 11
types of, 10–11
Praxis (motor planning), 16
Premature infants
checklists for, in neonatal intensive care units, 169
going home and, 170–71
neonatal follow-up programs for, 171
overview of, 159–61
positioning of, 162–64
providing developmental care for, 161–62
sensory system and, 164–70
signs of stress in, 165
Primitive reflexes, 8–9
Pronation, 43
Prone (belly) play/skills, 13, 54
for four- to six-month-olds, 48–49
for one- to three-month-olds, 43–44
for seven- to nine-month-olds, 64
Prone flexion, 24
Prone propping, for one- to three-month-olds, 44–45

Proprioceptive disorders, 173–76
  warning signs for, 176–77
Proprioceptive input, 4, 16
  for newborns, 31
  for one- to six-month-olds, 56
  for premature infants, 167
  for seven- to twelve-month-olds, 86
Protective system, of tactile system, 16–17
Pulling up to stand, 74–75
Push and pull games, 139
Push toys, 83
Puzzles, 123

Q

Quadruped position, 65–66

R

Reactions
  body-on-body, 10–11
  labyrinth righting, 10
  Landau, 10
  neck righting, 10
  postural, 10–11
Reading to children, 126
Receptive language, 91
Reciprocal creeping, 72–73
Reflexes
  postural reaction, 10–11
  primitive, 8–9
  progression of, 9–10
Repetition, 59
Retinopathy of prematurity (ROP), 166
Ribbon dancing, 139
R.I.C.E (Rest, Ice, Compression, Elevation) Rule, 121
Ridnour, Marcella, 83
Ring position, for sitting, 68
Rolling, for four- to six-month olds, 49–51
Rooting Reflex, 8
ROP (retinopathy of prematurity), 166
Routines
  for bedtimes, 41–43
  importance of, 40–43
  for naps, 40
  for play, 115
Running games, 137

S

Sand play, 124
Scapular winging, 45
Scoliosis, 183–84
Scooters, 138
Self-calming skills, 54
Self-entertainment, 54
Semisolid foods, introduction of, 100
Sensory activities
  for one- to six-month-olds, 53–59
  for seven- to twelve-month-olds, 85–90
Sensory awareness
  activating, 5
  learning, 5
Sensory disorder, 135
Sensory integration, 4–5, 17
  warning signs for, 89–90
Sensory integration disorders, 17–18
Sensory (nervous) system
  importance of, 3–4
  integration of, 4–5
  movement and, 6–7
  premature infants and, 164–70
Sensory overload, 135

Seven- to nine-month-olds
bear walking and, 66
creeping and, 71–73
cruising and, 76–77
developmental benchmarks for, 72
floor play/skills for, 63–67
hand and finger dexterity for, 62–63
kneeling and, 73–74
pelvic mobility and, 66–67
play exercises for, 77–79
pulling up to stand and, 74–75
quadruped position and, 65–66
side propping for, 65
sitting and, 67–71
Seven- to twelve-month-olds
auditory input for, 87
checklist for, 89
cognitive development for, 85–86
proprioceptive input for, 86
tactile input for, 86–87
toys for, 88
vestibular input for, 86
visual development for, 85–86
Shoes, selecting, 114
Shoulder development, 44
Shoulder strength, 12–13
Side propping, 65
Side-lying, for four- to six-month-olds, 49–51
Side-lying flexion, 24
SIDS (sudden infant death syndrome), 50
Sitting. *See also* Bench sitting
common problems with, 69–71
for four- to six-month-olds, 51–53
ring position for, 67–68
for seven- to nine-month-olds, 67–71
for ten- to twelve-month-olds, 81
for three- to five-year-olds, 140
Smell, sense of. *See* Olfactory (smell sense), developing
Sock puppets, for manipulative play, 124
Solid foods, introduction of, 100–105
Speaking. *See* Language skills
Speech. *See* Language skills
Speed, voluntary movements and, 14–15
Sports, three- to five-year-olds and, 135–36
Squatting position, for ten- to twelve-month olds, 81
Stair climbing, 137
Standing, 140
for four- to six-month-olds, 52
Startle (moro) reflex, 8–9
Strength. *See* Muscle strength
Stress signs, in premature infants, 165
Sucking, 23
Supination, 43
Supine (back) play/skills, 54
for four- to six-month-olds, 46–48
for one- to three-month-olds, 43
for seven- to nine-month-olds, 64
Supine flexion, 23
Swaddling, 27–28
Swings, 25

T

Tactile defensiveness, 177
warning signs for, 177–78
Tactile system, 16–17
developing
for one- to six-month-olds, 56–57
for seven- to twelve-month-olds, 86–87
discriminatory system of, 17
feeding skills and, 107–8

for newborns, 32–34
premature infants and, 164–65
protective system of, 16–17
Talipes equinovarus (congenital clubfoot), 184
Talking. *See* Language skills
Taste, developing sense of
for one- to six-month-olds, 58–59
for seven- to twelve-month-olds, 87–88
Temperament, knowing baby's, 6
Ten- to twelve-month-olds
ball play and, 82–83
ball sitting and, 83
bench sitting and, 82
developmental benchmarks for, 82
kneeling and, 81
overview of development for, 79–81
sitting and, 81
toys for, 83
Therapeutic interventions, 161–62
Three- to five-year-olds
developmental benchmarks for, 137
developmental continuum for, 134–36
language development benchmarks for, 145
language development for, 143–45
language play for, 143
manipulative play for, 141
overview of, 133–34
physical play for, 136–41
sports for, 135–36
toys for, 142, 143
warning signs and solutions for, 145–50
Tone. *See* Muscle tone
Torticollis, 182–83
Touch, sense of, 4. *See also* Tactile system
newborns and, 32
Toys
for four- to six-month-olds, 47
for newborns, 33
for one- to three-month-olds, 42
for one- to three-year-olds, 119
push, 83
for seven- to twelve month-olds, 88
for ten- to twelve-month-olds, 83
for three- to five-year-olds, 142, 144
Transitions, behavior changes and, 134
Tricycles, 138
Trunk control, development of, 12–14, 64
for ten- to twelve-month-olds, 79
Trunk rotation, 67, 68

U

Unilateral creeping, 73

V

Vestibular disorders, 173–76
warning signs for, 176
Vestibular input, 4, 16
feeding skills and, 107
for newborns, 30–31
for one- to six-month-olds, 55–56
for premature infants, 167
for seven- to twelve-month-olds, 86
Visual development
feeding skills and, 107
for newborns, 30–32
for one- to six-month-olds, 53–54
for premature infants, 165–66
for seven- to twelve-month-olds, 85–86
Volitional movements. *See* Voluntary (volitional) movements

Voluntary (volitional) movements, 11–15. *See also* Automatic movements; Movement
amount of effort and, 15
base of support for, 14
bilateral integration for, 15
compensatory movements and, 14–15
joint stability for, 14
muscle strength and, 12–14
muscle tone and, 12
speed and, 14–15

W

W sit position, 69
Walkers, 83–85
Walking, 113
bear, 66
exercises for three- to five-year-olds for, 138
games for, 117
Water play, 124–25